James Henthorn Todd

The Books of the Vaudois

The Waldensian manuscripts

James Henthorn Todd

The Books of the Vaudois
The Waldensian manuscripts

ISBN/EAN: 9783741175688

Manufactured in Europe, USA, Canada, Australia, Japa

Cover: Foto ©Andreas Hilbeck / pixelio.de

Manufactured and distributed by brebook publishing software
(www.brebook.com)

James Henthorn Todd

The Books of the Vaudois

THE BOOKS OF THE VAUDOIS.

THE BOOKS OF THE VAUDOIS.

THE

WALDENSIAN MANUSCRIPTS

PRESERVED IN THE

LIBRARY OF TRINITY COLLEGE, DUBLIN.

WITH AN APPENDIX,

CONTAINING

A CORRESPONDENCE (REPRINTED FROM THE BRITISH MAGAZINE) ON THE
POEMS OF THE POOR OF LYONS, THE ANTIQUITY AND GENUINENESS
OF THE WALDENSIAN LITERATURE, AND THE SUPPOSED
LOSS OF THE MORLAND MSS. AT CAMBRIDGE.
WITH MR. BRADSHAW'S PAPER ON HIS
RECENT DISCOVERY OF THEM.

BY

JAMES HENTHORN TODD, D.D., M.R.I.A., F.S.A.,

SENIOR FELLOW OF TRINITY COLLEGE,
REGIUS PROFESSOR OF HEBREW IN THE UNIVERSITY,
AND PRÆCENTOR OF ST. PATRICK'S CATHEDRAL, DUBLIN.

London and Cambridge:
MACMILLAN AND CO.
HODGES, SMITH, & CO., DUBLIN.
1865.

DUBLIN:

𝔓𝔯𝔦𝔫𝔱𝔢𝔡 𝔞𝔱 𝔱𝔥𝔢 𝔘𝔫𝔦𝔳𝔢𝔯𝔰𝔦𝔱𝔶 𝔓𝔯𝔢𝔰𝔰,

BY M. H. GILL.

PREFACE.

A VERY short statement will suffice to explain to the reader the circumstances which gave birth to the papers and correspondence re-printed in the following pages.

In a work* now almost five and twenty years before the public, I had occasion to examine at some length the opinion of the learned Joseph Mede, that the "time of the end," that is to say (as he assumed), the end of the prophetic periods of 1290 and 1335 days, was to be characterized by a new light communicated to the Church, as to the interpretation of prophecy, in accordance with the prediction (Dan. xii. 4), " Many shall go to and fro, and knowledge" [of prophecy, as Mede interprets] "shall be increased." He maintained that this increase of knowledge had been manifested at the beginning of the twelfth century by the discovery of a new, and up to that

---

* " Discourses on the Prophecies relating to Antichrist in the Writings of Daniel and St. Paul." Dublin: 1840. Page 398, *sq*.

time unheard of, principle of interpreting the prophecies relating to Antichrist. The Antichrist
(" κυρίως dictus") had been previously looked for
in the person of an individual man, who should
obtain supreme power upon earth, teaching the
doctrines of Atheism and infidelity, setting himself up as an object of Divine worship, and seek-
ing by the most violent and bloody means to ex-
terminate Christianity. But now, in the twelfth
century, it was discovered that the Antichrist of
prophecy was not to be an individual, but a succession of individuals, namely, the series of Roman
Pontiffs, or the Papacy ; that a deep and subtle
corruption, which still retained the name of Christianity, not Atheism or avowed infidelity, was to
be the character of this Antichristian power; that
it was already come, and had silently taken the
name of the Catholic Church, before any one suspected its existence ; and that no other Antichrist
was to be looked for.

In proof of all this, Mede relied upon a treatise, which he assumed had been put forth by the
Waldenses,* and which had been dated 1120.

---

* That the Waldenses were not the originators of this new
interpretation of prophecy, as Mede supposed, has been shown.
" Discourses on the Prophecies relating to Antichrist," &c.,
p. 27, *sq.*

This tract, entitled *Qual cosa sia l'Antichrist*, set forth very distinctly the new doctrine; Antichrist was discovered to be a " *cosa*," and not a person.   The obvious inference was, that, if the Papal power was the Antichrist, it was the duty of all Christians to come out from the communion of the Roman Church.

Mede seems to have been under the erroneous impression that the date 1120 was an integral part of this treatise, and that its author or authors claimed to have written in that year.   It had been circulated or made public, as he maintained, be-· tween the years 1120 and 1125, and therefore he concluded that this period of five or six years must be the " time of the end," when the 1290 and 1335 days of Daniel were to be accomplished.   But it turned out that the date, 1120, was no part of the treatise itself.   This was a mistake arising from a typographical error in Perrin's history; and the tract *Qual cosa* was independently proved, by irresistible internal evidence, to belong to the age of the Reformation.   It had been endorsed with the early date, not without grave suspicion of fraud, by Perrin, and after him by Leger, the Protestant historians of the Vaudois. Even Mr. Faber himself, with all his zeal for Waldensian antiquity, had been forced to abandon the date of 1120, and to admit that " it must be viewed as purely arbitrary, and as altogether unauthoritative,"*—a decision which includes also several other tracts to which the same date had been assigned by the same historians.

A new question was now suggested, which had no reference to the interpretation of prophecy: Where was this Treatise on Antichrist? Was the MS. which Perrin asserted to be " en datte 1120," still extant? and was it possible to have it examined by competent scholars with a view to ascertain its real character and pretensions?

Mr. Faber and Mr. (afterwards Dr.) Gilly had distinctly stated that it was one of the MSS. which had been deposited by Sir Samuel Morland in the public library of Cambridge; and Mr. Gilly, in the first edition of his Excursion to Piémont, had spoken of it as being still there. This error, however, he corrected in subsequent editions of his work, having in the mean time discovered that the MS. was no longer at Cambridge. But he adhered to the opinion that it was one of the Morland MSS.; although Morland, in the Catalogue of his MSS., published in his " History of the Churches of Piedmont," made no mention of it, and had actually published the *Qual cosa sia l'An-*

---

* " Inquiry into the History, &c., of the Vallenses and Albigenses," p. 370. See also p. 94, *sq.*, of the present volume.

tichrist, adopting its early date, on the authority
of Mr. Paul Perrin, without saying that he himself had ever seen a copy of it in MS., or had ever
had one in his own possession.

It was now ascertained by inquiries at Cambridge, not only that the Treatise on Antichrist
had never been there, but that several of the
Morland MSS. had unaccountably disappeared.†
I was at first under the impression, from the information I had received, that they had *all* disappeared, and that there was no evidence of their
ever having been in the Cambridge library, except
the Catalogue of them printed by Morland, and
his distinct assertion that he had deposited them
there. The question was raised, were these MSS.
ever at Cambridge ? Did Morland ever fulfil his
promise, or had he been induced by the troubles
and corrupt influences of the times in which he
lived, to alter his intentions, and send them to some
other depository? No Cambridge catalogue or
inventory, as I was at that time led to believe,
made any mention of the Morland MSS., nor was
there the smallest evidence that they had ever
been in the public library of that University.‡

* " History of the Churches of Piedmont," p. 142.
† "Discourses on the Prophecies relating to Antichrist," p. 402.
‡ See p. 103 of the present volume.

At this stage of my information on the subject
I entered into a correspondence with the late
Hon. Algernon Herbert, and was much gratified
at finding that one so deeply learned in mediæval
history had arrived at the same conclusions as
myself with regard to the authenticity of the books
attributed to the Vaudois. He agreed with me
in distinguishing the ancient and undoubtedly genuine remains of the original Waldenses from the
treatises of the modern Vaudois, which internal
evidence demonstrated to have been composed at
the beginning of the sixteenth century, or translated from documents emanating from some
Hussite sect, or from the German and Swiss Reformers. To mark this distinction, Mr. Herbert
gives the Waldenses, properly so called, their old
name of *Pauperes* de Lugduno*, or Poor of Lyons,
in the papers which will be found in the Appendix
to this volume ; leaving to the modern sect the
appellation of Vaudois, although that name also is
ancient, and was borne by the original Waldenses.

Mr. Herbert, having been educated at Cambridge, had opportunities which I did not possess
for investigating the real history of the Morland
MSS. I was under the impression, as I have already said, and I believe so was he,† at the time

---

* See Appendix to this volume, p. 100, 101.   † See p. 103, *infra*.

when our correspondence began, that *all* the Morland MSS. had disappeared. This mistake led me
into an error, for which I must apologize. Having
observed that several documents now in Dublin,
and bearing undoubted marks of being originals,
agreed exactly with Morland's description of the
contents of his MSS. marked G and H, I too hastily
concluded that some of the actual papers once
contained in those volumes had found their way in
some unaccountable manner to Dublin. This suspicion I communicated to Mr. Herbert, and more
than one allusion to it will be found in his papers,
*On the Poems of the Poor of Lyons.**

Subsequently, however, we ascertained that
these volumes were never missing, and that the
MSS. supposed to have been abstracted from the
Library were the six volumes marked A, B, C,
D, E, F, which were in many respects the most
important in the collection; for they contained the
celebrated poem called " The Noble Lesson," and
other genuine remains of the ancient Waldenses.

Mr. Herbert continued to the end of his life
under the impression that these six volumes had
been in some mysterious way " spirited away," as
he expressed it, from the Cambridge Library ; and

* See p. 21, of the present volume ; and Appendix, p. 104,
143, 198.

he had also adopted the opinion that this abstraction was the result of a connivance between Morland and Leger, having for its object a dishonest purpose. He maintained also that the MS. now at Geneva, containing the " Noble Lesson," was the identical Morland volume B, which had been removed from Cambridge.

These accusations drew from Dr. Gilly the valuable letter which has been reprinted, p. 151, *sq.*, of the present volume. This letter contains a suggestion,* which, with the encouragement given by the editor of the " British Magazine," led to the publication, in the pages of that valuable miscellany, of the Catalogue of Waldensian MSS. preserved in the Library of Trinity College, Dublin. This Catalogue I have now been induced to present to the public, in, it is hoped, a more convenient form, with a few necessary corrections.

Dr. Gilly concludes his last letter on the subject of these MSS. by the remark : " We are advancing towards the truth, notwithstanding our present disagreement."

After the lapse of almost four-and-twenty years, I find myself (with the exception of the then Editor of the " British Magazine") the only survivor of those who were engaged in this discussion. And I

* See p. 163 of this volume.

can say for my most valued friends and correspondents, as well as for myself, that never were men more honestly in search of truth, or more ready to embrace what they discovered of it, in defiance of all consequences. But who could have foretold the result which our " advance towards the truth," after the lapse of so long a time, has produced ? Mr. Bradshaw's discovery* has now shown that the missing MSS., and all the MSS. deposited by Morland in the Public Library of Cambridge, have been all along where they ought to have been; that they had never been " spirited away;" and, moreover, that they had never, since Morland's time, been catalogued, never disturbed, not even by librarian curiosity. Whilst we were discussing, a quarter of a century ago, the circumstantial evidence which seemed to establish so strongly the dishonesty of Leger and the fraudulent connivance of Morland, the supposed missing volumes were lying unknown, and buried in their dust, untouched for upwards of 200 years, on the very shelf where Morland had placed them.

The other remarkable revelations of Mr. Bradshaw's paper open up new questions and new researches.

* See p. 210 of the present volume.

The celebrated line from which the date of 1100 has been claimed for the "Noble Lesson," must now be regarded as, to say the least, suspected. The long lost Codex B is not identical with that of Geneva ; but it is proved beyond all reasonable doubt to have been tampered with; and another MS., hitherto unknown, plainly reads, in the important passage alluded to, 1400 instead of 1100 years. The explanation of this remarkable reading is a new subject of inquiry, upon which I shall not now venture to pronounce.

For the evidence and details of this discovery the reader is referred to Mr. Bradshaw's paper, which, with the Author's kind permission, has been reprinted as a fitting and very instructive finale to the present volume.

CONTENTS.

—————

xvi   CONTENTS.

WALDENSIAN MANUSCRIPTS

IN THE

LIBRARY OF TRINITY COLLEGE, DUBLIN.

———◆———

No. I.

THE NEW TESTAMENT, WITH THE BOOKS OF PROVERBS, ECCLESI-
ASTES, CANTICA, WISDOM, AND ECCLESIASTICUS, IN THE ROMANCE
OR WALDENSIAN DIALECT. (Class A. Tab. 4, No. 13. *Ex Bi-*
blioth. Usser.)

THIS is a quarto volume, on parchment (size 8 inches by
6), in remarkably good preservation, and in a very legible
hand. On the back of the first leaf, which was originally
left blank, some early possessor of the volume has written,
in a hand of the sixteenth century, some texts of Scripture, and references, in the Romance language. The
initial letters are illuminated in red, blue, and green; and
the titles of the different books, chapters, &c., are inserted
in rubric. Marginal references are added throughout the
volume in pale red ink, and apparently by a more recent
hand than that of the text. Pointers 👉 and other marks,
made by some reader to draw attention to particular passages, are to be found on almost every page, and seem,
from the ink, to have been added, for the most part, by

the same hand as the marginal references. In the latter
part of the volume, which contains certain books of the
Old Testament, the marginal references and pointers are
much less frequent than in the New Testament.

It is necessary to state, that in the Catalogue of the
MSS. of Trinity College, Dublin, published in the " Catalogi librorum Manuscriptorum Angliæ et Hiberniæ in
unum collecti" (Fol. Oxon. 1697), this volume is described as an *Italian* version (" Cod. Dubl. 609, Hiberniæ 749") ; and this error is copied by Le Long, " Biblioth. Sacr." tom. i. p. 354. (Folio edit., Paris, 1723).

The contents of the volume are as follows :—

1. The Gospel of St. Matthew ; with the prologue of
St. Jerome, beginning, *Cum mathio agues premiera[i]. pre-
dica lauangeli en ieudea, &c.* As a specimen of the language and version, it may be well to quote the Lord's
Prayer, Matt. vi. : " D. uos orare enay[i]. O tu lo nostre
payre, loqual sies en li cel, lo teo nom sia sanctifica. Lo
teo regna uegna. La toa volunta sia fayta enay[a]. ilh es
fayta alcel sia fayta en la terra. Dona anos enquoy lo
nostre pan quottidian, e pardona anos li nre debit enay[a].
nos pardonen a li nostre debitor. Enon nos menar en-
tentation. M. desliora nos de mal. Amen."

2. The Gospel of St. Mark ; with a few sentences only
of the prologue, beginning, *Marc euuangelista apostol de
dio, e filh desant peyre al batisme.*

3. The Gospel of St. Luke ; without any portion of St.
Jerome's prologue ; but the first four verses of the first

chapter are separated from the Gospel, and prefixed as a preface, and after them is the rubric, "Incipit euangelium secundum lucam capitulo primo." The first chapter is represented as beginning thus : " Mas un preire per nom czacharia del lignage de abia fo en lidia de herode lo rey." This separation of the first four verses from the rest of the Gospel is common in manuscripts and early printed editions of the Vulgate. I have now before me a small and very beautifully printed Latin Bible, " impressa per magistrum Jacobum Sachon, anno Domini quingentesimo vndecimo supra millesimum, die xiii. Januarii," in which the same separation is to be found. It is almost universal in the English versions attributed to the Lollards, some of which have omitted the first four verses altogether.

4. The Gospel of St. John,* with the prologue, *A quest es ioan euuangelista vn d'li desciple del segnor.* The first verse of the Gospel is thus translated :—" Lo filh era al comencza'. e lo filh era enapres dio, e dio era lo filh." At the end of this Gospel the scribe has written " Deo gratias, Amen."

5. The Epistles of St. Paul, in the usual order. The general preface of St. Jerome is omitted, but the *prologus specialis*, the *argumentum* to the Epistle to the Ro-

---

* Since the foregoing account of this MS. was written, the late Dr. Gilly, of Durham, has published the Gospel of St. John, under the title, " The Romaunt Version of the Gospel according to St. John, from MSS. preserved in Trinity College, Dublin, and in the Bibliothèque du Roi, Paris " London (Murray), 1848.

mans, and the short *argumenta* to the other Epistles are prefixed in their proper places.

6. The Acts of the Apostles; with the prologue beginning, *Luc authiogient de la nacion de siri.*

7. The Canonical Epistles, in the usual order. The ", Prologus epistolarum canonicarum" is prefixed to the Epistle of St. James; and there are also arguments prefixed to the other Epistles, which, however, differ from those found in the common editions of the Vulgate. That prefixed to the Second Epistle of St. John, as it is short, may be selected for a specimen—" Joan scri a vna femia de babiloia laqual era appella per propi nom electa. E monestant lei mesey*. eli na de ley quilh non se pertan del prepausament d'la fe per li herege." The disputed passage, 1 John, v. 7, is thus rendered : " C.* trei son liqual donan testimoni al cel, lo paire elo filh, elo sanct sperit, e aquisti trei son vn. E tres son liqual donan testimoni en terra, sperit aigua e sang, e aquisti trei son vn."

8. The Apocalypse, without any preface or prologue. At the end is written, in rubric, by the original scribe, " Deo gratia. 1522 ;" a memorandum which enables us to fix the date of this manuscript.

9. Then follow, on the same page and column, and in the same handwriting as the rest of the volume, the five books following, viz. :—

* The abreviation C. is for *Car.*

(1.) The Book of Proverbs, with the prologue beginning, *Lentrepetratio deli* 3 *libre de salmon, masloth alqual
liabrio diczo parabola.*

(2.) The Book of Ecclesiastes, "*Aici comencza clesiates*
A questas son las parollas declesiastes filh de dauid rei
d'hierlm." No prologue.

(3.) The Cantica Canticorum. This book is broken
into portions, distinguishing in rubric those parts which
are supposed to be spoken by the Church to Christ, those
which Christ is supposed to speak to the Church, and
those which are supposed to be spoken by an angel. As
a specimen, it may, perhaps, be worth while to transcribe
a portion of the first chapter.

" *La uoucz de la gleisa desira lauenament de xpt.* El
baise mi del baisa¹. de la soa boca. C. las toas pupas son
melhor de vin, plus odorant deli noble vnguent. Lo teo
nom es oli spars, emperczo, las iouentelas ameron tu. *La
uoucz de la gleisa a xpt.* Tirame enapres tu, e couren en
lodor deliteo vnguent. *La uoucz d'la gleisa alegrant edic-
zent.* Lo rei dintre mene mi en liseo celier, nos nos ex-
autaren, e nos alegraren entu recordador delas toas pupas
li dreiturier aman tu sobre vm. *La uoucz de la gleisa d'li
seo apprenn¹.* O filhas d'hierlm yo soi mera, &c. . . . . .
La uoucz de la sinagoga. Li filh d'la mia maire, &c. . . . .
La uoucz de la gleisa a xpt. Demonstra ami aqual, &c.
. . . . . *Lo uoucz de x¹. a la gleisa.* O bella entre las
femias, &c. . . . . ." And so on throughout the whole
book.

(4.) The Book of Wisdom ; with the short prologue beginning, *Lo libre de sapientia non setroba en alcun luoc.*

(5.) The Book of Ecclesiasticus ; with the prologue beginning, *De motas cosas e de grant son mostras anos.* Of this book the first twenty-three chapters only have been written. The MS. ends with the twenty-third chapter, in the middle of the first column of the first page of a leaf, without any imperfection, and apparently as if the scribe had never completed his work ; the rest of the page, together with three other blank pages which follow, is ruled as if for a continuation ; and there is no mark of conclusion, or anything to indicate that the work was regarded as finished.

From Le Long's list of Bibles " in Lingua Romanensi," it would seem that the foregoing five books were very popular with the people for whose use such MSS. were written ; and if they were written for the Vaudois, as it is very probable the MS. before us was, this circumstance must be regarded as an additional presumption against the authenticity of those confessions of faith and other documents, in which the Vaudois are represented as distinguishing between the books of the Apochrypha and the rest of holy Scripture, in language exactly similar to that of the Reformation. No intimation of the apocryphal or uncanonical character of the books of Wisdom and Ecclesiasticus occurs in the MS. we are describing. Le Long, however, appears to have had no suspicions of the honesty of Perrin and Leger, whose authority he cites for almost all the MSS. he notices; he speaks of Morland's volumes E and F (the former of which he erroneously calls D), as if they had been in his time in Cambridge, but obviously without pretending to any other knowledge of the fact than what he inferred from Leger, whose words he quotes.*

It may be well to remark, that there is nothing peculiar to the MS. we have been describing, in the order in which it gives the books of the New Testament. The same order is to be found in many MSS. and early printed copies of the Vulgate; and, for example, in the edition of 1511, to which I have already alluded, now before me.

It is also important to observe, that the MS. before us has been in the library of Trinity College, Dublin, since the Restoration, and that before that period it was in the possession of Archbishop Ussher. The purport of this remark will appear as we proceed.

* Le Long, "Bib. Sac.," vol. i. p. 368, 369. Yet in another place (p. 351) he speaks in general terms of having seen at Cambridge the French version of the New Testament of 1534, with certain MSS. of the Vaudois. "Hujus quoque editionis exemplum ecclesiæ Valdensis monumentis mss. aliquot voluminibus comprehensis adjectum, Cantabrigiæ in Bibliotheca publica, me evolvisse recordor.'

No. II.

A COLLECTION OF LETTERS AND OTHER DOCUMENTS RELATING TO
THE MISSION OF GEORGE MAUREL AND PIERRE MASSON TO BUCER
AND OECOLAMPADIUS, IN 1530. (Class C. Tab. 5, No. 18. *Ex
Biblioth. Usser.*)

THIS is a small paper volume (6 inches by 4¼) written
about the middle of the sixteenth century. I have very
little doubt that it is the identical volume described by
Perrin in the following words :*—" Item, le livre de
George Morel auquel sont contenues toutes les demandes
que firent George Morel et Pierre Masson a Oecolampade
et Bucer, touchant la Religion, et les responses des dits
personnages."

Afterwards, in his list of Vaudois pastors (chap. ix.),
Perrin again notices the mission of these individuals,
whose names he spells somewhat differently. He says,
" Les derniers Barbes qu'ils ont eu furent George Maurel
et Pierre Masçon, qui en l'année mille cinq cens trente
furent envoyés en Alemagne, communiquer de la Religion avec Oecolampade, Bucer et autres. Pierre Masçon
fust pris prisonnier a Dijon."†

Leger gives us the additional information that the precise object of their mission was " pour conferer avec les
principaux ministres d'Allemagne, assavoir *Luther, Oeco-
lompade, Melancthon,* &c., touchant quelques points et ce-

---

* " Hist. des Vaudois," p. 59.　　† Ibid. p. 67.

remonies, dont ils estoient en doute :"[*] he tells us also that Pierre Masson, whom he calls *Pietro Massone*, was of Bourgogne, and George Morel (or, as he calls him, *Georgio Morello*) of Fraissinieres.[†] In another place[‡] he enumerates Bucer, Capito, and Haller, along with Oecolompadius, as the divines to whom this deputation was sent.

I proceed now to describe the contents of the MS. before us.

The leaves or *folios* were at first marked on the upper margin of the face of each leaf; but a more modern hand has erased these numbers, and substituted for them, on both sides of each leaf, the numbers of the *pages*. In an index of the contents of the volume, which occurs at the end, and of which I shall have occasion to speak hereafter, the *folia*, not the pages, are referred to; and it would seem that the *foliation* (if I may use the word) was made by the same hand that wrote the index. In the following list of the contents of the volume it will be more convenient to refer to the *pages*.

I. p. 1. "*Epistola ad Oecolampadium;*" beginning "Saluemi dm. benedicte Oecolampadii. Car moti racontant

---

[*] Livre i. p. 203.   [†] Ibid.

[‡] Ibid. p. 162. In Blair's "Hist. of the Waldenses," vol. ii. pp. 217, 218, is a fuller account of the mission of Maurel and Masson, to which latter personage is given the *alias* of *Latom*. See Abr. Scultet's "Annal. Evangelii renovati" (*Heidelb.* 1620), who calls him Petrus Latomus, and gives a Latin version of the correspondence contained in the volume before us (pp. 294–316).

asona en nostras aurelhas," &c. The extract which Leger
has given from this letter* is something less than the
latter half of it, with the omission of the following words,
which immediately follow those quoted by Leger, and
with which the letter apparently concludes—" pero aczo
que tu donnes conselh anos econfer⁰ˢ nos freuols. [Anne
lo rict eord⁰. lo qual es entre d'nos ministres.]" The
words enclosed within brackets are so marked in the
MS. by a more recent hand, and are omitted by Perrin,
who gives the rest of the letter, "Hist. des Vaud." p. 211.

II. *Ibid. Oecolompadius's Answer;* beginning, " Oecolampadii desira gracia de dio lo payr per lo nostre Segnor. yᵘ. xᵗ. al. s. spit ali amas fr. en. xᵗ. li qual appellan
vaudes. Amen. Nos hauen receopu non sencza grant
deleyt en xᵗ. d'georgi mourel, curador fidelissime d'la
vostra salu," &c. This letter occupies upwards of three
pages, and ends p. 5. Perrin has given it in a French
translation, "Hist. des Vaudois," p. 46, and Leger, liv. i.
p. 105. A long letter, beginning in the same way, is
published in Latin among the " Epistolæ virorum doctorum," edited by Bibliander (fol. Basil. 1548), p. 2.
This letter is headed, " Dilectis in Christi fratribus NN.
Io. Oecolampadius," and begins " Gratiam in Deo Patre,
per Dominum Jesum Christum, in Spiritu Sancto. Amen.
Non sine magna in Christum voluptate accepimus a G. M.
fidelissimæ vestræ salutis curatore," &c., where G. M.
are evidently the initials of George Maurel.

* Livre i. p. 162.

III. p. 5. "*Epistola ad bucerum;*" beginning, "Dñs tecum optime ac per doctrine in Christo bussere, Nos non poen far," &c.

IV. p. 6. *Bucer's Answer;* beginning, "Martin bussero prega que gracia sia multiplica, per lo nostro segnor, y^u. x^t. ali seo charissime frayres li qual son appella Vaudes. Lo segnor dio sia beneit," &c. This is the letter quoted by Perrin, p. 47, and by Leger, liv. i. p. 105.

V. p. 7. " *Georgi morel e peyre maczon peticion.* De ministrorum ritibus. Primerament tuit aquilh li qual di non eser receopu," &c. On p. 8 some passages of this letter have been erased by a more recent hand; the first of these erasures is of three lines; then one line is erased, and the words, " per tres ou quatre" substituted in a small French hand; lastly, a passage of five lines is blotted out, and the words " de Salomon, de David, et des prophetes" substituted. In the margin, in another modern hand (apparently the same as that in which the index already alluded to has been written), are two notes, marking the subjects spoken of in the text. One of these is not easy to read, and appears to relate to one of the erased passages; the other is " Imposition des mains."

Perrin has given an extract from the commencement of this document (" Hist. des Vaudois," p. 70), but with some omissions and variations. The words and sentences erased in the MS. are omitted by Perrin, and the alterations made by the more recent hand are uniformly adopted wherever they occur in this extract. He has also introduced the same passage (with some slight alterations) into the second chapter of the treatise which he has published in his "Hist. des Albigeois," livre ii. p. 225.

The answers of Oecolampadius and Bucer are inserted in the body of this Petition after the several articles to which they refer, and are marked thus : " R. Ocolampadii"—" R. busseri." The several articles of the petition are numbered thus: " Peticion 1."—" Peticion 2," &c.

On p. 10, a passage (not quite a line) is erased ; and in the margin adjacent to it, the same French hand already spoken of has written, " Le receu au ministere ne faut rien sans la licence de ceux qui l'ont devancé." Other similar marginal notes occur in the same hand throughout the volume, but it would swell these pages to an unnecessary length if I were to make particular mention of them all. There are also many erasures and corrections of the text, in a modern hand, different from that of the marginal notes, and in a blacker ink. Most of these erased passages are rendered illegible, but some of them might, with a little trouble, be recovered ; for example, " Peticion 10. Item, alcun d'nos ministres d'leuagli [*ni alcuna de las nos nostras fennas*] non se maridan." The words enclosed within brackets are erased, but are still visible ; and the same hand, in which the notes already alluded to are written, has added in the margin here, " Cest article na esté inseré dautant qu'il conste par les memoires du sieur de Vignaux que plusieurs Barbes se sont mariés." This and several other of these notes appear to intimate that this document was revised and prepared either for the press or to be copied for some other purpose. Thus, for example, in Bucer's answer to the 11th petition (which relates to the punishment of ministers who fall into sin), the following passage is underlined :—" Nos aprovarian que aquilh li qual tomban en fornicacion, fossan sconiga e degita si nos no neguessa lo remedi necessari a alcun;" and there is the following note in the margin:—" Cette response icy est aussi inserée, de peur que ladversaire veut estimer que Bucer extenue trop la paillardise."— p. 21.

The 12th petition (p. 21) is a confession of faith, and presents, in several places, a remarkable verbal agreement with that which Leger has published (livre i. p. 92), and which he tells us is dated A. D. 1120.   It may, perhaps be worth while to compare the first article in each:—

DUBLIN MS.	LEGER.
" Nos predit ministres cresen e fermament tenen, e iosta nostra poysacza en segnen lo nostre poble, tot quant se conten en li 12 article del cinbollo lo qual es dit d'li apostol, tenent e ensegnant esser heresia tota cosa la qual se d'scorda, e non es covenient a li doize dit article."	" Nos crescèn, e fermament tenèn tot quant se contèn en li doze Articles del *Symbolo* lo qual ès dict *de gli Apostol*, tenènt esser heresia tota cosa laqual se discorda, e non ès convenènt à li doze articles."

I shall venture to quote also the article on the sacraments :—

DUBLIN MS. (p. 24.)

"Item nos cresen que li sacrament son [*here a word is erased*] seignal de cosa sancta, ho forma vesibla d'gracia non vesibla, tenent esser bon et profotivol que li fidel usan alcuna vecz daquisti d^t. segnal, o forma vesibla, si la se po far. M. emperczo nos cresen e tenen, que li predit fidel pon esser fait salf, non recebent li predit signal, quant non han lo luoc ni lo modo de poer usar li predit segnal e forma."

LEGER (p. 95.)

" Nos cresen que li sacrament son signal de la cosa sancta, o forma vesibla,* tenent esser bon que li fidel uzan alcune vees daquisti dict signal, o forma vesibla, si la se po far. Ma emperço nos cresen, e tenen que li predict fidel pon esser fait salfs, non recebent li predict signal, quand non hanlo luoc ni lo modo de poer usar de li predict signal."

Then follows (p. 25) a paragraph which was originally headed, "R. busseri de baptismo" [meaning "Responsio Buceri de baptismo"] ; but these words are now erased, although they are still legible. It begins, " Nos amouestan le scriptura parlar enay¹. d'li sacrament enay¹. que regardon ala cosa d'l sacrament e non al sacrament." And the author of the marginal notes already noticed, probably on the authority of the above-mentioned title,

---

* The words " de gratia non vesibla" here omitted by Leger are retained by Perrin, " Hist. de Vaud.," p. 36, who has published the same Confession of Faith, and from whom indeed Leger seems to have copied.

appears to have considered Bucer the author of this part of the document, for he writes, " Bucer monstre quelle estoit la doctrine des Anabaptistes afin que les Vaudois se gardent de leur adherer." This note is appended to the words, " Alcuna disputacion encerque lo baptisme es en las nostras gleysas," and appears to have been intended to guard the reader against supposing that the Vaudois were infected with the Anabaptist errors. This part of the volume ends p. 31.

Page 32 is blank ; but on the next page the discussion of infant baptism is continued, and goes on to p. 46. This has been noted in one of the modern marginal notes in the margin of p. 25, which is as follows :—" Dispute contre les Anabaptistes iusquau feuil 23. b. ;" and in p. 46, which, by the old notation, was the back of fol. 23, the same hand has written, " fin de la dispute."

Then begins, on the same page, " peticion 7," as it is numbered, although a larger number of " peticions" had been noted in the preceding part of the volume. It is on the subject of auricular confession, and speaks of it as a practice that may be useful, if not abused :—" Item nos tenen la confession auricular esser profcytivol, &c." Then follows " R. 7. busseri," and " peticion 8," and on the next page, "R. busseri,"xi." What the numeral " xi." refers to I am unable to explain.

On p. 48 begins a paragraph entitled, " De nostro populum docendi modo ut et doctrine. Peticion . . . ." the original number is erased, and "16" added by a later hand in the margin. This article begins, " Nos amou-

esten ed'fenden al nostre poble, &c." Then follow several other petitions, with Bucer's answers, the original
numbers of which have been in like manner altered.
There are also several marginal notes in French appended
to this part of the document which would be worth transcribing, if space permitted. They would probably throw
some light on the use that has heen made of the volume
before us by Waldensian historians.

On p. 54 is an article entitled, " Qualis plebs sit nostra, Peticion . . . ." (the number erased.) This is the
place referred to by Perrin ("Hist. de Vaud." p. 106), in
which George Morel states that the number of persons
then belonging to the sect of the Vaudois was 800,000,
" car de lestremita de una fin alautra hya plus d' oyt cent
milh ;" a fact which Perrin speaks of as " une merveille
de Dieu non petite."

On p. 55 is a paragraph headed, "Que subduntur nobis
sunt ambigua atque acerta," the subject of which is thus
summed up by the same French annotator who has been
already mentioned :—" Si degres de dignites doivent
estre observés entre les Pasteurs." This is followed by
" R. Oecolampadii" and " R. busseri," in which both give
their judgment against there being any difference of degree or dignity amongst ministers.

The next petition, p. 56, is marked " peticion 2," and
is as follows :—" Item qual cosa se deo entendre per las
clavs dona a sanct peyre." The answer of Oecolampadius to this inquiry is identical with the paragraph, *De
clavibus ecclesiæ,* which occurs in the letter addressed,

"Joannes Oecolampadius dilectis in Christo fratribus N.," which is printed by Bullinger in his " Epistolæ doctorum virorum," p. 4. There is also an answer of Bucer's to this question ; and then follow several other "petitions" with answers from Bucer only. The 6th and 7th are remarkable, and may be quoted. They are :—

" Peticion 6.   Item si es licit que li ministre de la parolla amenon vita en vergeneta.   Peticion 7.   Item si li dit ministre poun licitament amenar fennas las volhon viore en vergenta." To these questions there is an answer, attributed to Bucer, the purport of which may easily be anticipated.

" Peticion 9" (p. 62) deserves to be noticed from the answer which Oecolampadius has given to it. The question was, " Item quals libres uos regua en la sancta scriptura por canonicos, equals non canonicos." To this Oecolampadius replies by enumerating the books of the Old and New Testament, distinguishing the apocryphal books of the Old Testament in the usual manner, as deserving of respect, although not canonical; but he adds, with respect to the books of the New Testament, " ben que nos non acomparen pas lapocalis en la epistola d'Jaco, e de Juda, e la 2ª. d'peyre, e la 2 derieras d'Johan cum li autres predit libre;" and this clause is also to be found in the Letter of Oecolampadius, published in Latin by Bullinger,*—" tametsi Apocalypsim, cum epistola Ja-

---

* " Epist. doctorum virorum," fol. 3, C.

cobi et Juda, et ultima Petri, ac duabus posterioribus
Joannis non cum cæteris conferamus."

"Peticion 23" (p. 76) savours of the ancient Waldensian doctrine :—" Item si tot iurament es deffendu sot
pena de pecca mortal, diczent xpt non volha iurar al
postol."

Many of the answers of Oecolampadius given in this
part of the volume are to be found in the letter published by Bullinger, which has just been quoted. On
p. 116 there is a letter of Oecolampadius, beginning,
" Donca o frayres karissimes," and apparently given as
a separate letter, which is no more than the conclusion
of the long letter printed by Bullinger,* from the words
" Igitur, Fratres mei," to the end.

Then follows (p. 117) a letter by Bucer, beginning,
" O frayres charissimes nos hauen respondu a questas
cosas breouiment," and ending, " In hoc valete. Anno
salutis nostre 1530. Christo Gracias."

VI. The next document in the volume (p. 118) is *An
Account of a Conference held at Angroma in* 1532, beginning, " Le propositione ch' sono state disputat, en angroma lanno d'l segnor 1532, et a di 12 d'septembro.
En presentia di tuti li ministri et eciam dio d'l populo.
El primo di fo disputato se hora licito al Xiano d'iurar
in alcun modo," &c. This account of the conference continues to the end of the volume, but the last three pages

---

* " Epist. doctorum virorum," fol. 3, D.

(pp. 123–5) are written in a running hand, although probably by the same scribe; the former part of the volume having been written in text hand.

VII. On the back of p. 125 begins *an index* to the principal subjects discussed in the volume, written in a small French hand, and in the French language. The author of this index was evidently the writer of the marginal notes to which allusion has already been frequently made.

In conclusion, the perusal of this MS. has convinced me that a careful comparison of it with the documents published by Perrin, Morland, Leger, &c., would throw much light on the manner in which those documents were compiled ; and, in particular, I think this volume will furnish evidence of the following statements :—

First. That at the period when the two barbes, Maurel and Masson, were sent to the German Reformers, much of the ancient doctrine of Waldism, as distinguished from Protestantism, still remained among the Vaudois; in particular, they seem to have approved of religious celibacy, auricular confession, and vows of poverty, and to have retained the ancient Waldensian objection to every species of oath.

Secondly. That the object of the mission of the two barbes appears to have been, to bring their people nearer in doctrine and discipline than they had hitherto been to the Reformed Churches of Germany and Switzerland.

Thirdly. That in the erasures made in the MS. by some early possessor of it, the object apparently was to omit everything, properly speaking, Waldensian; and if these erasures were made with a view to the publication of the document, I have no hesitation in saying that they were made with the dishonest intention of concealing the original difference in doctrine and discipline between the Vaudois and the Reformed, and of representing the ancient state of the former as identical with that to which the Reformers of Germany, at the beginning of the sixteenth century, were anxious to reduce the Church.

One remark more may be necessary in support of the opinion I have expressed that the MS. before us is the identical volume formerly in Perrin's possession, and cited by him under the titles of " Livre des Barbes George Maurel et Pierre Masçon" (pp. 46 and 70) ; and " Memoires de George Morel" (pp. 106 and 157). In the first place, the volume is obviously an original, written soon after the year in which Morel and Masson were sent on their expedition. And, secondly, what is still more conclusive, the pages of the MS. cited by Perrin, which he happens to have mentioned in three places—viz., p. 70, p. 106, and p. 157, of his "Hist. des Vaudois," coincide exactly with the pages of the Dublin MS.

———

I may take this opportunity of acknowledging a wrong done to the late Dr. Gilly in my "Discourses on the Pro-

phecies relating to Antichrist."*   The fact is, that I had
before me the first edition only of Dr. Gilly's first work,
the "Excursion to the Mountains of Piedmont;" and it
did not occur to me to refer to the subsequent editions of
that work, or to the author's other publications; thus I
was inadvertently guilty of attributing to Dr. Gilly an
error respecting the MSS. said to have been deposited by
Morland in the University Library of Cambridge, which
Dr. Gilly had himself corrected in his later publications.
As I have been thus led to mention the Morland MSS., I
may as well announce here that portions of the volumes
marked by him G and H are (if I am not mistaken) to be
found in the library of this University.† How they came
here I have been unable as yet to ascertain; but they
have certainly been in their present place for upwards of
a century.   I hope, however, to have another opportunity of speaking more fully upon this subject.

* Page 403. See Introductory Remarks, prefixed to this volume,
and Appendix, p. 162.

† This, as we shall see presently, was a mistake; the Morland
MSS. are safe, where they ought to be, in Cambridge, although
copies, or perhaps the originals, of some documents contained in
vols. G and H, are now in Dublin.   But I have allowed the above
passage to stand without alteration, because it may be necessary to
refer to it in connexion with the correspondence which afterwards
took place on this subject.

*

No. III.

A MISCELLANEOUS COLLECTION OF PROSE TRACTS IN THE ROMANCE OR WALDENSIAN PATOIS. (Class C. Tab. 5, No. 22. *Ex Biblioth. Usser.*)

A PAPER volume, 3⅞ inches by 5⅞, containing 389 numbered leaves; together with eight leaves at the beginning not numbered, on which is written the Calendar of the Church; and one leaf at the end, on which the contents of the work have been given in a modern French hand. This volume formed a part of Archbishop Ussher's collection. Its contents are as follows:—

I. *The Calendar of the Church :* occupying, as has been already said, eight leaves. The first leaf, the inside page of which contains the month of January, is a duplicate, and appears to have belonged to some other MS. The golden numbers, and days of the month (which are given by the old method of kalends, nones, and ides), as also the principal festivals, are in red; the Sunday letters (except A) are in black. The festivals of January may be given as a specimen—the red festivals are here distinguished by italics:—"*Circumcisio Domini. Octava sčti Stephani. Octava sčti iohis. Octava innocencium. Epiphanie Domini. Pauli primi heremite. Octava hepiphanie.* Marcelli papa [sic] et mrˢ. *Antoni abb.* Fabian et Sebastian mrᵐ. Agnetis vˢ. et mrˢ. Vincentii mrˢ. *Conversatio* [sic] *sčti Pauli.* Constanti epi et mrˢ."

I know not whether it may tend to fix the *locale* of this
MS. to note that the last-named saint, whose feast is put
upon the 29th of January, and whose name does not
occur in the Roman calendar, was especially honoured
at Perugia in Italy. In like manner we find, on the 16th
of February, " Juliane v*. et mr*;" and on the 23rd of
the same month, instead of the 26th of January, " Poli-
carpi epi et confessor."   On the first of March we have
" Ercuculian epi et mr*." another day proper to Perugia;
on the 10th, " Alexandre et Gari mr^m." where " Gari"
must be a mistake for *Caii;* on the 13th is " Eusubie v*."
a name which is unnoticed by Baronius, unless it be a
mistake for *Euphrasia;* and on the 24th, " Isidori epi et
mr*." On the 11th are the words *"Claves pasce;"* and on
the 29th, in rubric, " *Rexuressio domini.*"*   In April we
have, on the 1st, " Teodori mr*.," a mistake, probably,
for *Theodora;* on the 3rd (instead of the 6th), " Sisti
papa;" on the 4th, " Ambrosius epi [*sic*] et mr*. confessor;" on the 20th, " Victorius papa et mr*.," a mistake, for *Victor,* who, by the way, was not *Pope* Victor.
By another mistake, also, we read in rubric, on the 23rd,
" *Gregorius mr.*," evidently for *Georgius.*

* These words, *Rexuressio Domini*, ought probably to have been
on the 27th, as is usual in old Calendars, in accordance with the
tradition that our Lord was crucified on the anniversary of the An-
nunciation, and therefore that his Resurrection took place on the
27th of March. See *S. August. De Trinitate*, lib. iv. c. 5. For
the use of the *claves*, see Du Cange, in voc. *Annus.*

It seems hardly necessary to continue this list of the peculiarities of the calendar, as the foregoing examples afford sufficient ground for the inference that the MS. must have been written ,in Italy, or copied from an Italian MS., and that as an authority it can be of no value.

On the face of the last leaf is a table for finding Easter, by means of the golden number and the *claves*. It is dated at the top 1524, with a pointer indicating the Sunday letter B ; and the same date occurs again at the bottom, in the following note :—" Daquesta taula pascal las lettras meras seruo ha abril.   Mas las rosas a marcz 1524, per lettra dominical b., d'luna 8."*   And, accordingly, the days of April are written in black ink, those of March in red.

II. Fol. 1. a. *Liber Vertutum ;* beginning, " *Po es iusta cosa efort. consoniuol enclinar las aurelhas per las iustas preyreas alaraczon.*"   The initial letter P is ornamented very neatly and beautifully in red and black.   This tract enumerates thirty virtues, or graces, as they are afterwards called, which it goes on to discuss in separate chapters.   The work ends on the back of folio 78.

III. Fol. 78. b. *De lensegnament de li filh ;* beginning, " *Li filh liquol naison alipayrons carnals.*"   A portion of

---

* This, however, seems a mistake of the transcriber; for although B was the Sunday letter of the year, from the intercalary day, yet 5, and not 8, was the Golden Number.

this tract has been published by Perrin ("Hist. des Albigeois," livre ii., p. 230), as chap. iii. of the treatise "De la Discipline des Vaudois," &c., but with very great omissions: thus, for example, between the first paragraph and the second (p. 231), beginning "*Enseigna lo teo filli,*" almost half a page of the MS. is left out. The "&c." at the end of the next paragraph covers an omission of upwards of five pages; and the same contraction at the end of the chapter (p. 232) indicates a similar omission of six pages.

On fol. 83 of the MS. the running title on the upper margin of the pages alters into "De lensegnament de las filhas," that part of the treatise relating to the education of daughters. On fol. 84 the title is, "De la diligent garda d'las filhas." This tract ends fol. 85.

IV. Fol. 85 a. "*Ayci vollen parlar del Matrimonj a comfort deli bon;*" beginning, "*Yo entendo de dire qual cosa sia matrimoni e per que el sia ista ordena de dio.*" Perrin refers to this tract, and quotes it, most probably, from this very copy, or at least from a copy in which the *Liber virtutum* was also contained, for he cites it thus:—"Au liu. des Vaudois intitulé des vertus, au chapitre du marriage."* The extracts he gives from the tract are very much garbled.

V. Fol. 91. a. "*De li soyme;*" beginning, "*Salamon di che li soyme ensegon motas curas.*" The allusion is to

---

* Perrin, "Vaudois," pp. 16, 17

Eccles. v. 3. In this tract is discussed the question of the origin of dreams, and how far they proceed from the influence of evil spirits.

VI. Fol. 94. b. "*Ayci volen parlar de li pecca de la lenga, aczo quilh sian fugi e abandona;*" beginning, "*Motas cosas son que deorian moure lome ala diligent garda de la lenga.*" Twenty sins of the tongue are enumerated in this tract, and discussed in separate chapters; after which follows a chapter on the remedies of sins of the tongue— " Lo remedi contra lo pecca de la lenga."

VII. Fol. 118. a. " Lo pecca d'la superbia." This seems to be the first chapter of a treatise on the seven deadly sins. It begins—" Soperbia es reyna d'tuit li pecca. De laqual di lescriptura, Superbia es comencza-ment d'tot pecca. Sept principal pecca nayson en aquilla. Ço es a saber, Vanagloria, Enuidia, Ira, Tristicia, Ava-ricia, Golicia, Luxuria." On the back of fol. 120 is a chapter entitled in rubric, " *la cubiticia,*" beginning, " Autre pecca eys de superbia loqual non es deli sept pecca mortal. Enayma dis Ambroys, Cubiticia non se po partir d' superbia." The rubrical titles of the remaining chapters are as follow :—

Vana gloria; fol. 120. b.	*Lo pecca del iurament;* fol. 135. a.
Enuidia; fol. 126. b.	
Pecca dira; fol. 127. b.	*Del pecca de la retracion;* fol. 137. a.
Auaricia; fol. 130. a.	
Meczonia; fol. 133. b.	*Luxuria;* fol. 138. a.

The running titles on the top of the page are sometimes the particular headings of the chapters, in one or two instances the initial words of the chapter, but generally the subject of the treatise, " *Pecca mortal.*"

I have been thus particular in noticing the subdivisions of this treatise, in the hope that some reader may be enabled to identify it with something which already exists in Latin. It would be extremely important, in connexion with the question of the antiquity of these treatises, if it should turn out that they are translations from Latin tracts by the ecclesiastical writers of the middle ages. A great deal of the matter will be found in Wicliffe's "Trialogus," lib. iii.; but I cannot so far identify it with that treatise as to feel quite certain that Wicliffe was the only authority used in the compilation of the work before us.

VIII. Fol. 139. b. *La parolla di Dio;* beginning, " *Sobre aq̄lla parolla Mt.* 13. *Deuos aqual que semena illic semenar loseo semencz.*"

IX. Fol. 143. b. *De li perilh;* beginning, " *Nos vesen esser na* 3 *greos perilh en a quisti temp, per li qual la uia del regno deli cel es mot empacha.*"

X. Fol. 145. a. A short treatise on Jam. i. 17, entitled in rubric, *Tot don noble;* and beginning, " *Tot don noble et tot don perfeyt es desus deysendent del payre deli lume, second que nos ensegna la sancta scriptura.*"

XI. Fol. 146. b. *De la iusticia;* beginning, " *A quilh que fameian e seteian iusticia.*" On the upper margin of the following pages this tract is entitled *Sermon* in rubric.

XII. Fol. 150. a. *Sermon d' erodiana;* beginning,
" *En a quel temp herode fey pilhar eligar e encarcerrar ioh.
baptista.*"

XIII. Fol. 155. a. *Sermon d'las parollas auciosas;* beginning, " *Mas yo dic a nos que de tota parolla auciosa la
qual home parlaren redren raczon de ley aldia del Judici.*"

XIV. Fol. 158. a. *Li parler del phillosophe;* beginning, " *Enayma la uocz trapassa e de falh uiaczament.*"

It may be worth while to quote from this tract the following passage, as it will give the reader an idea of its
character, and perhaps may lead to its identification:—
" Dont cum un rey feyczes motas demandas a vn philosophe per nom Segond, Qual cosa era vista alui encerque
la uita de lome. E premierament en demande, Qual cosa
es lome. Loqual philosophe responde e dis. Lome es
familh de la mort, e es hoste, e es caminador trapassant.
Car enayma lo familh en la fin del terme recep lo pagament."

The "Dictes of the Philosophers" were printed in English by Caxton, and are said to have been translated from
the French, and that from the Latin. Perhaps this tract
may be an extract from some version of them. But it
does not seem to be so, if I may speak from a hasty comparison of it with the English, printed by Caxton in 1477.

XV. Fol. 160. a. A " *Sermon,*" as it is entitled in rubric on the upper margin of the page; beginning, " *Ue
uos vn mort unial filh de la soa meyre era apresenta. Luc.*7."

XVI. Fol. 163. a. " *Sermon de las noczas,*" begin-

ning, " *Yhū fu apella a las noczas eli deciple de luy.
Joh. 2 ca.*"

XVII. Fol. 167. b. "*De la vbriota;*" beginning, " *Ubri-
ota segond che di Augustinus es uil sepulchre de la raczon
e es furor de pensa.*"

XVIII. Ibid. " *Luxuria;*" beginning, " *Luxuria desira de complir la uolunta de la carnalita.*" In this tract,
which ends on the next page, Bernard, Gregory, Jerome,
and the Decretum, are quoted.

XIX. Fol. 168. a. "*De la familiarita;*" beginning, "*La
familiarita de las fenas e la lor cumpagnia des esser greo
a tuit, e specialment a aquilh que prometon de scervar con-
tenencza, e a aquilh que desiran montar en lautecza de la
contemplacion. Jerome di, A quel non po contemplar cum
tota la pensa loqual souendria con las fenas.*" I have
quoted so much of this passage because of the express
recognition it contains of vows of chastity. This tract is
very short, and quotes Basil, Hugo, Jerome, and the Decretum. The following passage may be transcribed as
tending to throw light on the " Sayings of the Philosophers" (No. XIV.) :—" Ma vn philosophe per nom Segond fo demanda qual cosa fossa la fena, e el dis ; La
fena es confusion de lome, bestia non sacziuol, cura quo-
todiana," &c. Something very like this, though not ver-
batim the same, is attributed to Socrates, in Caxton's
" Dictes of the Philosophers."

XX. Fol. 169. a. " *De la honesta;*" beginnning, " *La
honesta es considera en la conuersacion.*"

XXI. Fol. 169. b. " *De la sapientia de Dio ;*" beginning, " *La sapientia di Dio es non saber solament li parlament d'dio.*"

XXII. Fol. 170. a. "*Angel Second;*" beginning, "*Angel second che di Aug*. es sostancia spirital, e non corporal, o entelectual.*" The title " Angel Second," seems to be merely the initial words of the tract : " An angel *according* to what Augustine saith."

XXIII. Fol. 170. b. " *La consideracion dela breveta de la uita ;*" beginning, " *La consideracion dela breveta de la uita es a gradiuol ufferta a dio.*"

XXIV. Fol. 171. b. " *De li parler dalcuns doctors ;*" beginning, " *Car coma di Seneca qui non pensa alcun cosa de lauenir.*" The doctors quoted are, Seneca, Jerome, Augustinus, Gregory, Basil, and the Decretum.

XXV. Fol. 172. b. A tract beginning, " *A lenfern es mancament de tot ben, e habundancia de tot mal.*"

XXVI. Fol. 173. b. " *De li ben del paradis ;*" beginning, " *Tota humana eloquencia non es sufficient a recointar de la lausor,*" &c.

XXVII. Fol. 175. a. " *De la x*ianita ;*" beginning, " *Aquel es uerament christian lo qual fay misericordia a tuit.*" At the end of this tract (fol. 176. a.) the scribe has written, " *Deo Gracias. Amen.*"

XXVIII. Fol. 176. a. A very short paragraph on prayers for the dead, without title; beginning, "*Lo es dubita si las animas de li mort pon esser aiudas*" [i. e. adjutas] "*per li aiutori de li uio. E es iust che non per doas raczons.*"

XXIX. Fol. 176. b. "*Áyci comencza Lo prolic del libro apella tresor e lume defe;*" beginning, "*A tuit li fidel e carissimas x^i ans sia salu en y^u. x^t. lo nre redemptor e sauador.*"

This is the tract which Perrin has cited, under the title of "Lumiere et thresor de la foy," ("Hist. des Vaud." pp. 24 and 25; "Albigeois," p. 201); and this must be the very copy of it which he used, because the passage which he cites (p. 24) from "fol. 214" of the "Lumiere et thresor de la foy" occurs on fol. 214 of the MS. before us. In other places, however (ibid., pp. 16 and 17; and "Albigeois," p. 182), he has referred to this volume under the title of "Livre des Vertus," from the first tract which it contains.*

---

* It is instructive to observe how Leger has dealt with the extracts from the volume before us, supplied by Perrin. His "Echantillon 9" professes to be an extract, "fidelement traduit de l'original, intitulé 'Almanac Spirituel'" (liv. i. ch. xii. p. 64). But the first passage given is a garbled translation of the commencement of the tract on the Seven Sacraments, which occurs, fol. 182. b., of the MS. before us. The second, of which he gives the original, and which, he says, "se trouve encore au traité de l'Antichrist," exists, fol. 184 of the same tract on the Sacraments. The other extracts are also to be found in their proper places in the same tract, although Leger speaks of some of them as taken from the "Treatise on Antichrist," and some from the "Almanac Spirituel." Can it be that, in their ignorance, these writers have given the name of "Almanac Spirituel" to the volume before us, from the Calendar of the Church, which is to be found at the commencement?

The book called "Tresor e lume de fe," here transcribed into this collection, is divided into several chapters, or short treatises, on the Articles of the Creed, the Seven Sacraments, Commandments, Lord's Prayer, &c., of which the heads shall be here given; and it will be seen that this is the work from which Perrin, Morland, and Leger, have taken many of the Waldensian treatises they have published.

The work begins with two prologues, of which the commencement of the first has been given above; the second, entitled in rubric, "*prolic*" [fol. 177], meaning "Prologue," begins, "Donca uos preguen humil'. e devotament che la magnificiencia de leternal dio," &c. It is a general treatise on faith, and is entitled in rubric, on the upper margin of folio 179, "Del modo d'creyre en Dio." Then follow—

1. *Lo symbolo d'anastais* [sic], fol. 179. a. This has been printed by Perrin, "Hist. des Vaud.," p. 91.

2. *De li articles d'la fe*, fol. 180. a. The articles of the faith here given are divided into seven heads, and seem drawn up with very distinct reference to the Manichean doctrines, maintained by the Albigensian and Paulician heretical sects. The first is an exposition of the doctrine of the Trinity; the second asserts that this Holy Trinity has created all things visible and invisible, and is Lord of all things celestial and terrestrial; the third asserts that God gave the law to Moses, and that the Old as well as the New Testament is given by the Holy Ghost;

the fourth asserts the Catholic doctrine of the Incarnation; the fifth is a paraphrase upon St. Paul's words that God has chosen a glorious Church, not having spot or wrinkle, or any such thing; the sixth asserts the doctrine of the general resurrection; and the seventh, the last judgment.

3. *Li sept sacrament*, fol. 182. b.; beginning, "*Ara es adire d'li sept sacrament de la sancta gleysa.*" It may help, perhaps, to fix the date of this work to remark that in fol. 185. b. *Johannes de Dio (flor.* 1247) is quoted.* The seven sacraments are enumerated in the usual manner; and the treatise, although evidently belonging to a party not in connexion with the Roman Church, exhibits no trace of anything like Genevan doctrine. Extracts from it have been given by Perrin ("Albigeois," livre iii. p. 342, *et seq.*), and are represented by him as a distinct treatise. It is worthy of notice that the extracts given by him are almost all marked in the margin of this MS. by a line, and the substance of them is occasionally noted in a modern French hand. Perrin omits all mention of the number *seven,* as the number of the sacraments recognised in this treatise, and has otherwise taken such liberties with

---

* Since writing the above, I perceive that the passage in which Johannes de Dio is quoted, and indeed the greater part of the chapter on Penance, in which it occurs, is no more than a translation of chap. xxiii. lib. iv. of Wickliffe's "Trialogus." This brings the date of the treatise much lower, and furnishes us with a clue to the real origin of these works, that would, probably, throw much light on Læger's "dattée en an 1120," if that fable needed further refutation.

D

the tract as very much to alter its real character. The
limits of this work prevent my going into a detail of
all these changes ; for, to estimate them fully, it would
be necessary to quote a considerable portion of the tract.

I may just mention, however, as a specimen, that
the words printed by Perrin (*ubi supr.* p. 326), "per-
tinent a la Sancta Cena," are in the original "perte-
nent simplament requist a la messa." The chapter
on extreme unction also (p. 330) furnishes so good
an example of the general character of the alterations
made in the original, that I am tempted to give a somewhat fuller account of it. It begins in the original thus:—
" Lo septen sacrament es lognament de loli de li enferm. Enayma se legis en Sant Marc. E issent hog-
nian moti enferm e eran sana. E sant Iaco di, Si alcun
de nos es enferm amenon li preyre de la gleisa e oron
sobre lui ognent lui doli al nom del Segnor," &c.
The writer goes on, for about a page, to speak of this
passage of St. James, and other testimonies of holy Scripture, to the miraculous powers of the Church in raising
the sick; and then proceeds in the passage which Perrin
has given, and which shall be here quoted in juxtaposi-
tion with the original :—

Dublin MS. (fol. 192. b.-195).	Perrin, " Albigeois," p. 330.
M. loncion de lenferm en las part determinas cum oli dolivas premierament consacra del vesco	Lo septen Sacrament de la Gleisa Romana es l'extrema Onction de li enferm, la qual

e retengu sovent entro a la cor-
rupcion ministra del preyre per
parolla conlentencion del' me-
sey⁰. per ferent iosta la forma e
husancza de la gleisa romana
que communament apellan sacrament de lextrema honcion,
perforezan se fondar lui al dit de
Sant Jaco apostol non es vist
esser ordona de xᵗ. ni de li apostol de lui.　Aici lo doctor evangelic al seo trialogo parlant da
quest sacrament de loncion dis,
M. a questa fundacion, &c. . . .
Car si aquesta honcion corporal
fossa sacrament eneyma sen feng,
xpt e li autre apostol non taisi-
rian la debita promulgacion e
exequicion de ley, *hæc ille.* Nota
a quest doctor lo qual entre li
autre attendia maximament la
forma de la ley, &c. Li
pensant ben aquestas cosas sobre
dictas non devon ausar tenir ni
cunfessar enayma article d'fe
aquest sacrament essar ordena
de xᵗ. ni deli apostol.　Jasia czo
que ala fin e enterpcion apostolica husa etengua tot fidel la
deo tenir e confessar esser util e
perfeitivol.

perforean se fondar lei al dit de
Sanct Jaco apostol.　Non es
vist esser ordenna de Christ ni
de li Apostol de luy.　Car si
aquesta onction corporal fossa
sacrament, en aizi coma se feing;
Christ o li apostols non taisiria
la debita manifestation de lexe-
cution de lei.　Li pensant ben
aquestas cosas non deven ausar,
tenir, ni confessar en aizi coma
article de Fe, a quest Sacrament
esser ordenna de Christ e de li
apostel.

For the sake of brevity I have omitted two passages in the foregoing extract, as they have nothing corresponding in Perrin's text. The first consists of eleven lines, and is the continuation of the quotation from the "Trialogus"* of Wickliffe, who is called "lo doctor evangelic,"; the other occupies two pages of the MS., although Perrin passes it over without any intimation of the omission. In it are quoted Jacobus de Missa, and the Summa of St. Thomas Aquinas. It will be seen that Perrin's extract gives an erroneous impression of the real doctrine of the treatise on the subject of unction of the sick, as he has quoted those portions only where the Romish abuses of the practice are condemned.

4. *Ayci commenczan li commandment di dio*, fol. 197. a. Perrin has given an extract from this tract (" Vaudois," p. 29), and an abridged translation of the whole (" Albigeois," p. 182). See also Leger, livre i. p. 51. It should be observed, however, that Perrin has taken the liberty of altering the disposition of the commandments so as to bring it into conformity with the Protestant catechisms, whereas, in the original, the division is according to that still common amongst Roman Catholics ; the first and second of the Protestant arrangement being taken as one. The second commandment in the MS. is thus introduced (fol. 206. b.).—"Lo segond comandament es aquest. Non

---

* The passage of the "Trialogus" quoted is lib. iv. cap. xxv. fol. cxlii. of the edition printed in 1525.

recembres lo nom del teo segnor dio en van, czo es non
Jurares;" whereas Perrin has given the second commandment thus : *Tu ne te feras image taillée*, &c., although the
original made this the second part of the first commandment (fol. 200) :—" La secunda part daquest commanda-
ment es non fares a tu entalhament czo es ymagenas
entalhas en peyras, o en leng, o en autra cosa bont sepo-
issa en talhar."

At the end there is a concluding chapter, treating of
the general obligation to keep the commandments; one
portion of which is headed in rubic on the margin, "*Ma-
ledicions a li desubidient*," and on the next leaf (fol. 229),
" *De li x Lebrous*," in which the ten lepers are explained
as figuring those who transgress the ten commandments.

5. "*Tracta de loracion*," fol. 230. a.; beginning, "*Euan-
geli second Sant M{.} e Luc. lo qual tracta*," &c. This is
the exposition of the Lord's Prayer, of which Perrin has
given an abridged translation, " Albigeois," livre i. c. v.
p. 201; and he considers it as forming a part of the
" Thresor et Lumiere de la Foy," which probably ends
with it; although there is nothing in the Dublin MS.
distinctly pointing out where that work concludes.

This tract is entitled in rubic on the upper margins of
fol. 231 and 232, " *Exposicion del pr. nr.* ;" and from fol.
233 to fol. 242, " *Glosa pr. nr.*" It is not the same as that
published by Leger under this latter title, livre i. ch. vii.
p. 40.

XXX. Fol. 242. b. " *Ayci parla d'la penitencia ;*" be-

ginning, " *Nos deuen saber que lo baptisme de penitencia
es conceopu de la temor d' dio.*" The rubrics on the upper
margins of the leaves point out the topics discusssed in
this treatise : they are from fol. 243 to 246, incl., *Baptisme de penitencia;* on fol. 247, *Falsa penitencia ;* fol. 248,
Penitencia; fol. 249 to 251, incl. *Falsa penitencia;* fol.252,
La penitencia de li dampna ; fol. 254, *Penitencia vera ;*
and the rest *Penitencia,* or *De la penitencia.*

XXXI. Fol. 262. a.   Another short tract on the
Lord's Prayer ; beginnning, " *Mas lo es d'nota, que lorac-
zon dominical,*" &c.

XXXII. Fol. 264. a.   On fasting ; " *Del deiuni ;*" beginning "*Ara sen sec del deiuni,*" &c.   Perrin has printed
a portion of this tract in his usual unsatisfactory manner,
"Albigeois," livre iii. p. 331.

XXXIII. Fol. 268. b. On almsgiving; "*De lalmona ;*"
beginning, " *M. aquillas cosas que non se pon esmendar,*"
&c.

XXXIV. Fol. 271. a.   On the tribulations of the last
days ; " *Ayci commenczan las tribulacions ;*" beginning,
" *Grant tribulacions sere d'uant lo dia del Judicii la qual
non fo del comenczament del mont,*" &c. A portion of this
tract has been printed in a very garbled and imperfect
manner by Leger, livre i. ch. vi. p. 35. The part so
published begins on fol. 278 of the manuscript.

XXXV. Fol. 284. b.   A catechism ; " *Las Enterro-
gacions menors ;*" beginning, " *Si tu fossas demanda qui
es tu, Respont, Yo soy creatura de dio racional e mortal.*"

This is given by Perrin ("Albigeois," p. 157) as a catechism, between a *barbe* and a *child;* but the words *barbe*
and *l'enfant* are of his own insertion, and are not in the
MS.; and there are also several omissions and other mistakes, most of them perhaps originating in ignorance.

XXXVI. Fol. 292. a.   Against balls; " *De li Bal;*"
beginning, " *Ayci volen parlar delibal demonstrant premierament per testimonis descripturas, daquienant per
motas raczons quant mala cosa sia ballar.*" An extract
from this tract, although apparently from another copy
of it, has been printed by Perrin, " Albigeois," p. 240.

XXXVII. Fol. 297. b.   Against taverns ; " *De la taverna;*" beginning, " *La taverna es fontana de pecca e le
scola del diavol.*" This is published by Perrin, *ubi supr.*
p. 238.

XXXVIII. Fol. 298. a.   " *Lo credo in unum deum.*"
The Nicene Creed as used in the Western Church in
Latin.

XXXIX. Fol. 298. b. " *Alcuns testimonis de la poc-
calis ;*" beginning, " *A quel es benayra loqual legis,*" &c.

XL. Fol. 300. a.   " *Deli 8 pensier;*" beginning, " *Oyt
cosas son que nos deven pensar per cascun dia.*"

XLI. Fol. 301. a.   " *De las 4 cosas che son avenir ;*"
beginning, " *Lo es dentendre au cascun che 4 cosas son
avenir.*"

XLII. Fol. 334. a.   " *De la legrecza deli salua;*" beginning, " *Lo es de saber que enapres la general resure-
cion li eyleyt auran gloria,*" &c.

XLIII. Fol. 337. a. " *Del pecca dela desubediencza ;*" beginning, " *Del pecca dela desubidiencza. Ascumini-qament del qual po primerament valer,*" &c.

XLIV. Fol. 341. " *De la veniancza ;*" beginning, " *Alcuns son liqual sapersumisson de far veniancza.*"

XLV. Fol. 343. b. " *De la desperacion ;*" beginning, " *Lo es de saber che 4 son las caysons per lasquals lome se sol desperar,*" &c.

XLVI. Fol. 346. b. " *Lo fellon abandone ;*" beginning, " *Lo fellon abandone la soa via e lo baron,*" &c.

XLVII. Fol. 348. b. " *Mesquins ;*" beginning, " *Donca nos mesquins per que tarczen deben far, e per que volen mal obrar.*"

XLVIII. Fol. 352. a. Sermon on the Nativity ; beginning, " *En a quellas contras debellam eran pastors gardant las vigillias de la noyt sobre lo lor grecz.*"

XLIX. Fol. 353. b. " *Sermon de la nativita ;*" beginning, " *Ecu y^u fossa na embellem d'iuda en li dia de herode lo rey.*"

L. Fol. 357. a. " *Autre Sermon ;*" beginning, " *Jhesu dis a li seo deciples, li olh son benayra li qual veon czo que vos vee.*"

LI. Fol. 360. a. " *Sermon ;*" beginning, " *Johan diczia al poble lo cal annava a luy,*" &c.

LII. Fol. 365. b. " *Sermon ;*" beginning, " *Yhu montant en la naveta,*" &c.

LIII. Fol. 367. a. " *Sermon ;*" beginning, " *Yhus iste al mey de li seo deciples, e dis a lor pacz sia a vos.*"

NO. III.]   PROSE TRACTS.   **41**

LIV. Fol. 368. a. " *Lo fantin y*. renias en ierlm,*"
&c.   This is entitled in rubric on the upper margin,
" *Sermon del fantin yhu.*"

LV. Fol. 373. a. " *Del purgatori soyma.*"   This is
printed by Perrin as a part of the treatise on Antichrist.
" Albigeois," p. 295.

LVI. Fol. 379. b. " *De la envocacion de li sant ;*" beginning, " *Donca nos seu a parlar da questa envocacion de
li sant.*"   This is also given by Perrin, *ibid.* p. 310.

LVII. Fol. 383. a.   " *Absolucion ;*" beginning, " *Absolucion czo es remission o indulgencia,*" &c.

LVIII. Fol. 385. b.   " *Sermon ;*" beginning, " *O Fra-
res sabent a quest temp, car hora es ia a nos levar del sopn.*"
This is the last tract in the volume, and ends on the back
of fol. 389.

It is probable that a little research would enable us to
show that many of these sermons are no more than
translations from writers of the thirteenth, fourteenth, or
fifteenth centuries.

At the end, on what was originally a blank leaf inserted by the binder, there is now written, in a small
hand of the seventeenth century, a very imperfect list of
the contents of the volume, with references to the pages,
or rather to the leaves.

One or two remarks will suffice to conclude our
notice of this curious collection of tracts :—First, we
have seen reason to believe that this identical volume
was in Perrin's possession, not only because he describes

it and its contents in his " Hist. des Vaudois," pp. 57,
58, but also because he refers to its pages or leaves,
which references exactly agree with our manuscript.
I am inclined to think, however, that he had other copies
of some of the tracts contained in it, especially of the
" *Thresor et lumière de la foy*" (which he mentions, *ibid.*
p. 59), and of the tract on *balls* or *dancing*, of which I
hope to have another opportunity of speaking. Secondly,
we have also seen that Wickliffe's "Trialogus" is actually
quoted and translated in some of these tracts; and it
may perhaps be worth noticing, that the "Trialogus"
was printed in 4to, in the year 1525, which, from its
near coincidence with the date of this manuscript, seems
remarkable.   The edition of the " Trialogus" alluded to
has no printer's name or place, but Panzer* conjectures
that it was printed at Basil.   There are two copies of it,
both of them in remarkably fine preservation, in the library of Trinity College, Dublin.

* " Annal. Typogr." vol. ix. 142, 343.

No. IV.

WALDENSIAN POEMS, AND OTHER TRACTS.

A SMALL paper volume, 5⅞ inches by 3⅝, written at the
same time, and, from the similarity of the handwriting,
most probably by the same scribe, as that last described.
The volume contains 184 leaves ; the initial letters are
illuminated in red and green ; and the book is in remarkably good preservation. This volume was also in
Archbishop Ussher's collection, and is now marked Class.
C. Tab. 5. No. 21. Its contents are as follow :—

I. Fol. 1. a. *Novel Confort ;* beginning,

> " A quest novel confort de vertuos lavor
> Mando vos scrivent en carita e amor."

II. Fol. 7. b. "*Aici commença levangeli deli* 4. semencz." This poem begins thus :—

> " Ara parlen d'lavangeli deli quatre semencz
> Que Xᵗ. parlava al segle present."

III. Fol. 13. b. *Barca ;* beginning,

> " La sancta trinita nos done parlar
> Cosa que sia donor ede gloria."

IV. Fol. 20. b. *Payre eternal ;* beginning,

> " Dio paire eternal poysant confortaen
> Enayma lo teo filh karissime governaen,
> Enayma degnament retornant atu recepen."

In this poem the lines which rhyme are in triplets

V. Fol. 23. b. A poem without rubrical title, beginning,

> " O Carissimes mete ayci la vestra cura
> Car lo es dit per la divina scriptura."

VI. Fol. 25. a. *Nobla Leyczon*; beginning,

> " O Frayres entenda vna nobla leyczon
> Souent d'orian uelhar e istar en oraczon."

This is the well-known poem upon which so much has already been written. It differs in many of its readings from all the printed copies.

VII. Fol. 35. a. Another poem entitled, in rubric, *Nobla Leyczon*, and beginning,

> " O li meo frayres karissimes entende lo meo parlar.
> Prego uos non teg. envan ço que yo uolh recontar."

I am not aware that this poem has been noticed by any of the writers on Waldensian subjects. It is about the same length as the former and more celebrated Noble Lesson, which Morland has published. It concludes (fol. 44. a.) with the following prayer, or benediction:—

> " La poisancza del payre, é la sapiencia del filh,
> E la bonita del sanct sperit,
> Nos garde tuit denfern, e nos dona paradis. Amen."

VIII. Fol. 44. a. On mendicancy; *Del mesquin*, a prose tract; beginning, " Donca nos mesquin perque tarçen de ben far," &c. On the upper margins of the following pages it is entitled " *Sermon*," and " *Sermon del mesquin*."

There is a copy of this tract in the volume which has been last described, fol. 348. b.   The two copies differ, however, both in spelling and in several various readings, and are evidently independent copies of the work.

IX. Fol. 47. a.   A prayer in prose, headed, on the upper margin, *Oraçon;* and beginning, "O Dio d'li rey, e Segnor deli segnor, yo me confesso a tu."

X. Fol. 49. a.   *De la propriotas de la alamanças.* This tract is written in double columns; it consists of moral and religious meditations on the nature and properties of animals.   The animals mentioned are the following: —1. *Laygla.* 2. *Pelican.* 3. *Fenis* [phœnix]. 4. *Pavon.* 5. *Grua.* 6. *Gal.* 7. *Galina.* 8. *Corp* [crow]. 9. *Cing* [swan]. 10. *Pic.* 11. *Larandola.* 12. *Tortora.* 13. *Colomba.* 14. *Voutor.* 15. *Falcun.* 16. *Papagal.* 17. *Merlo.* 18. *Rosignol.* 19. *Abelhas* [bees]. 20. *Chicola.* 21. *Caladri.* 22. *Leon.* 23. *Simia.* 24. *Lop.* 25. *Mostela.* 26. *Salamandria.* 27. *Del darbon.** 28. *De lunicorn.* 29. *Cerf.* 30. *Chamos.* 31. *Pantera.* 32. *Castor.* 33. *Ricz.* 34. *De lalifant* [elephant]. 35. *Del caval* [horse]. 36. *Del buo.* 37. *De la volp.* 38. *Del can.* 39. *Del andolap* [antelope]. 40. *De la furnicz.* 41. *Serena* [syren]. 42. *Balena.* 43. *Vipera.* 44. *Aspi.* 45. *Cocodril.* 46. *Delidra* [hydra]. 47. *Serpent.* 48. *Recan.* 49. *Tigre.* 50. *Ragno.* 51. *Scorpion.*

I have thought it worth while to give this list in the

---

* The Darbon is, I believe, a fish called the Dart.

hope that it may lead to the identification of the treatise
with some Latin tract of the middle ages.   Many such
moral instructions, taken from the real or supposed properties of animals, were written in the beginning of the
fifteenth century.

XI. Fol. 70. a.   " *Aici commenczan alcunas sposicions
sobre alcuns passages de Sant M*. Sobre Johan Crisostomo.*"   This tract seems to be an abridgment of St.
Chrysostom's Homilies on St. Matthew.   The texts com-
mented upon are inserted throughout in rubric.   The
tract is written in double columns as far as fol. 74. b.,
after which it is written across the page in a single column.   The work occupies the remainder of the volume,
and ends fol. 184. a.

.   It seems very probable that this is the identical volume
which Perrin thus describes :—" Item on nous a mis en
main un livre de Poësie en langue Vaudoise auquel sont
les traittés qui suivent : une priere inscripte Novel Confort.   Une rithme des quatre sortes de semences men-
tionnées en l'Evangile.   Une autre intitulée Barque.
Et une appellée la Noble Leçon, duquel livre fait mention le Sieur de Saincte Aldegonde."*

* Perrin, p 59, where he refers to " Le Sieur de Saincte Aldegonde en son tableau," p. 153.

V.

A SMALL paper volume, 6 inches by 4, containing 104 leaves; written in a handwriting of the early part of the sixteenth century; with many marginal notes in French, in a more recent hand, the same apparently as that in which similar notes are written in the volume described, No. II. of this catalogue.

This volume belongs to Archbishop Ussher's collection, and is now marked Class C. Tab. 5. No. 25. It is in good preservation, but has lost some leaves at the end. Its contents are as follow :—

I. Page 1. *Ayczo es la causa del departiment d'la gleysa Romana;* beginning, " Al nom del nostre segnor Y⁰. X¹. Amen. La causa del nre departiment de lunita de la costuma de la romana gleysa," &c.

This tract is divided into sections, distinguished by their initial sentences being written in a larger hand; and it may perhaps be worth while to give their subjects here. The first has already been quoted, and need not be repeated; the remainder are as follow :—

Page 12. *La 4ᵃ. e ultima part de salu.*

Page 13. *Lautra part de verita es apella ministerial.*

Page 14. *La verita ministerial es departia en 3. part.*

Page 16. *Perque sian ordona li ministres exteriors e per qual fin.*

Page 20. *Li don dona ali testimoni convenivols.*

Page 21. *Qual cosa es lo ministeri principal.*

Page 23. *Lobrament de las vertucz perque es dona.*

Page 31. *Qual differencia es entre lo sacrament, e la cosa del sacrament.*

Page 35. *Del sacrament del cors e del sang d' X.*

Page 37. *Semilhament de lautra part del sacrament.*

Page 40. *De la Disciplina ecclesiastica.* This section has been printed by Perrin, as the first chapter of the treatise " De la discipline des Vaudois et Albigeois," which he has published in the second book of his " Hist. des Albigeois," p. 225. And this circumstance is probably alluded to in the following note, which appears in the modern French hand, already mentioned, in the margin of our MS. :—" Discipline, Cecy est inseré pour le commencement du traité de la discipline iusque la page 55, ou il est dict, Pourquoy il est commendé aux pasteurs de vieller." This reference is to page 55 of our MS., where a chapter occurs entitled, *Perque comande a li pastor velhar;* but Perrin has not published so large an extract from this treatise. The passage selected by him, and which forms chap. i. of the *Traite de la Discipline*, terminates on p. 42 of the MS.

Page 42. *En qual modo lo poble se deo haver.*

Page 43. *La disciplina a la beata vita uvenador.*

Page 45. *De la correpcion ecclesiastica.*

Page 54. *De la potesta ordonativa.*

Page 55. *Perque comande a li pastor velhar.*

Page 66. *De la secunda causa del nre departiment.*

Page 79. *Si li Roman sacerdot son d' la generacion de xp̄t.*

Page 81. *Qual sia la vita deli modern.* In the margin, "Vie des prestres moderns."

Page 89. *Si la vita de li present se conven cum li premier.*

Page 139. *Qual deo esser la cura papal.* There is a passage in this part of the tract which I shall transcribe, as it may serve to fix the date of the work, as well as the place in which it was composed. My eye was directed to it by the following French note in the margin, "Le Pape ne peu iuger du Royaume de Boheme." The original is as follows (p. 145) :—

"C.* xp̄t negne se rey e lo regne temporal non esser seo e non confesse si esser constitui ni iuie ni departour. D. qual done poesta a aquest aversari de xᵗ. quel liore lo regne de boemia al rey de vngaria vivent mathia rey de boemia quel done a lor aquesta poesta," &c.

The allusion here is evidently to Mathias Corvin, called the Great, King of Bohemia and Hungary, who died 6th April, 1490.

The treatise terminates on p. 185, with the following note, in rubric, from which it appears that it was transcribed from an imperfect copy :—"Ayci finis lobra non complia daquest libre per mancament de lexemplar," &c.

II. The next page was originally blank, but there is

---

* In this extract the letter C. stands for *Car*, and D. for *Donca.*

now written on it, in a hand of the seventeenth century (not the same as the French hand, already mentioned), the following note :—" Joach. Camerarius in narratione historica de Ecclesiis fratrum in Bohemia et Moravia, p. 121. Circiter annum Christi 1489." Then follows an extract from Camerarius, giving an account of the following letter to King Ladislaus. This extract* will be found in the page of Camerarius just referred to, and need not be here transcribed.

The remainder of the volume, although written in the same hand as the preceding portion of it, has a new pagination, and contains, " *La epistola al serenissimo Rey lancelau,*" beginning, " Al serenissimo princi Rey Lancelau. A li duc barons e li plus velh del regne. Lo petit tropel de li X'ans appella per fals nom falsament P. O. V. Gratia sia en dio lo payre e en y^u. x^l. lo filh de lui."

The letters " P. O. V." are interpreted by Perrin (" Histoire des Vaud.," p. 224), to signify " Pauvres o Valdes." If this interpretation be correct, it will follow that the authors of this letter disclaimed the name of Vaudois, and were therefore probably the people called *Picards*, or *Unitas fratrum*. It would seem also that the

* To this extract, on the words " Attulerunt etiam literas scriptas ab illis," is appended the following note:—" Scilicet fratribus Waldensibus quos Lucas Pragensis et Tomas Germanus invenerunt in Gallia togata, quæ nunc Romania dicitur, cum eó missi essent a fratribus Bohemis, ut referrent num aliqua in parte detegerentur aliqui qui religionem puram profiterentur absque superstitione."

treatise, " La causa del departiment de la gleysa Romana" (p. 1 of this volume), from its evident connexion with the letter to Ladislaus, and from the passage above quoted, which connects it with Bohemia, is the production of the same people, and has been erroneously attributed by Perrin and his followers to the Vaudois, properly so called, or Poor Men of Lyons.

In Freher's " Scriptores Rerum Bohemicarum," are two documents, one entitled " Professio Fidei Waldensium ad Vladislaum regem;" the other, " Oratio excusatoria fratrum Waldensium;" but neither of them seems to have any connexion with the " Epistola" before us.

The Epistle itself begins thus :—" Quanta pena sia reposta enaquilh, e li qual scandaliczan lo petit cresent en x¹ : e anczo es lo sequent la doctrina de lui meseyme, O bon Rey," &c.

The same French hand, which has already been so often mentioned, and which is probably Perrin's, has written in the margin, " Capel dit que cette confession fut presentée l'an 1508 a Ladislas Roy de Hongrie."

Lancelot, better known as Ladislaus, or Vladislaus, VI. King of Bohemia and Hungary, succeeded Mathias Corvin, already mentioned, in 1490, and died 13th March, 1516.

The letter occupies eleven closely-written leaves, and ends imperfectly, one leaf or more having been lost at the end of the volume.

It may be remarked that the volume of which the con-

tents are here given must be the identical MS. described by Perrin in the following words :—"Item nous
avons un livre fort vieux, duquel le titre est, *Æyço es la
causa del nostre despartiment de la gleisa Romana.*   C'est
à dire, Ceci est la cause pour la quelle nous nous som-
mes despartis où separés de l'Eglise Romaine.   En ce
volume y a vne Epistre, ou Apologie des Vaudois inscripte *La Epistola al Serenissimo Rey Lancelau a li
Ducs, Barons, et a li plus veil del regne.   Lo petit tropel
de li Christians appella per fals nom, falsament P. O. V.*
c'est à dire Pauvres ou Vaudois."*

It may be said that, as the MS. before us was probably
not very much more than fifty years older than Perrin
himself, and as he speaks of the manuscript in his possession as " un livre fort vieux," it is more likely that he
was possessed of the ancient original from which the
Dublin MS. was copied.   But even admitting that the
original of a letter to King Ladislaus, presented in 1508,
might be called ancient in 1618, the year in which
Perrin's book was printed, it is scarcely possible, with
that author's notions of Waldensian antiquity, that it
could be regarded as " *fort* vieux."   There exists, however, a curious piece of evidence which clearly proves
the Dublin MS. to have been the identical volume quoted
by Perrin.   In his " Hist. des Vaudois," p. 21, he cites
a passage (or rather prints a garbled fragment) from

---

* Perrin, " Vaudois," p. 58.   See also ibid., p. 224.

p. 235 of the "Livre des causes de la separation de l'Eglise Rom," and the passage certainly does occur there. It happens, however, that the person who paged the Dublin MS. made a mistake in the 120th page, which he marked 200 instead of 120; and this mistake is continued through all the succeeding pages of the volume, although it has been subsequently corrected, and the erroneous pagination erased—so, however, as to remain still legible. But in the place above referred to, Perrin has made his reference to the original and erroneous pagination, although in every other place in which he cites the book he cites it by the corrected pages. The presumption, therefore, is that this was the volume which was in Perrin's possession, and which he describes as "un livre fort vieux;" and, if so, he must be brought in guilty either of a singular degree of ignorance, or of a very lamentable dishonesty.

No. VI.

A PARCHMENT volume, 6 inches by 4, containing 123
numbered leaves; it belongs to the Library of Archbishop Ussher, and is now in Class. C. Tab. 5. No. 26.
The initial letters, titles of tracts, &c., are inserted in red
ink, and some of them are adorned with yellow paint;
but there is no other attempt at ornament in the volume.
It is written in a *black-letter* hand of the 16th century, and
is dated at the end 1523. Its contents are as follow :—

I. Fol. 1. a. A tract, headed in rubric, from its initial
words, *Si tu departires la preciosa cosa delavil;* and beginning, " *Si tu departires la cosa preciosa delavil tu
seres enayma la mia boca czoes si tu departires li vici de
las vertucz,*" &c. From this tract the volume has been
entitled in the catalogue of the library, and by the book-
binder's lettering on the back, " Liber de preciosa cosa."

II. Fol. 2. a. A tract, entitled, *De las vertucz teologials;*
and beginning, " *Ara sensec d'las vertucz teologials.
Czo es fe, sperancza, e carita.*" I am not certain whether this should be considered as a separate tract, or as
only a chapter or section of the foregoing. It quotes
Augustin, Chrysostom, Jerome, the Book of Wisdom
very frequently ; also " Terenci," " Tuli" [i. e. Cicero],
and " Seneca."

On the back of fol. 11, the treatise goes on to speak of the four cardinal virtues, "*Ara sensec d'las* 4 *vertucz cardenals*," which seems to favour the idea that the former portion of the tract, on the theological virtues, should not be considered as a distinct work, notwithstanding the separate title which the scribe has prefixed to it.

Prayer (*Ara sensec de l'oracion*, fol 23. b.), and the hindrances of prayer (*Delempachament d'loracion*, fol. 25. b.), are treated of under the virtue of *Justice*.

III. On the upper margin of fol. 29. a. there is a rubrical title, "*L'Beneuranczas;*" and on the same page is a section or chapter, beginning, "*A quilh que fameian e seteian justicia.*" This is identical with the tract entitled *De la iusticia*, in the volume No. III. above described ;[*] but in the present copy there is much that is omitted in the former, and the passages of Scripture are quoted at length, and not broken off with an "&c.," as in the former copy. The next four sections are headed, in rubric, "misericordios," "li mond decor son beneura," "li pacient son beneura," "Aquilh que suffron." These titles, however, are only the initial words of the paragraphs that follow. On the upper margin of fol. 30. a. is the heading, in rubric, "*Beneuras.*"

I am not certain whether this tract should be considered as distinct from the Treatise on the Virtues,

---

[*] See p. 27, supra, Tract XI.

Theological and Cardinal, or a continuation of it. It may be well, however, to say that that treatise is not the same as the *Liber Virtutum*, contained in the volume No. III. already described. See above, p. 24.

IV. Fol. 31. b. A treatise on the eight things upon which we should meditate every day ; beginning, " *Oyt cosas son que nos deven pensar per chascun dia.*" This short tract is divided into eight chapters, which are numbered in rubric, " *Pensier lo premier,*" " *Lo segont,*" " *lo* 3," " *lo* 4," " *lo* 5," " *lo seysen,*" " *lo septen,*" " *Loyten.*" The eight thoughts are as follow. I mention them as they may lead to the identification of the treatise with some Latin original.

1. " La premiera es pensar d'Dio."

2. " Lo segont pensier es del seo filh."

3. " Lo tercz pensier es d'la vita d'li sant, e d'la mort en qual maniera ilh aquisteron lo regne d'li cel."

4. " Lo 4 pensier es d'la nostra uita."

5. " Lo 5 pensier es d'la nostra mort."

6. " Lo 6 pensier es del dia del iudici."

7. " Lo 7 pensier es de lenfern."

8. " Loyten pensier es del paradis."

An abridged copy of this tract is contained in the volume No. III. above described.*

V. Fol. 32. b. *Sermon de* . . . The rest of the rubrical title was never added, the scribe having been, probably,

---

* See p. 39, supra, Tract XL.

at a loss for a single word by which to describe the subject of the sermon. It is a short sermon on the text,
" Cant tu seres envida a las noczas repausete al luoc plus
bas."

VI. Fol. 34. b.' A tract without title; beginning, " *Yo
entendo d'dire cal cosa sia matrimoni.*"

This tract is also in the volume just referred to, fol.
85. a. (See p. 25, supra.) The present copy, however,
is much more complete, and apparently more correct.
I should have mentioned, in the description of this
tract, as contained in the volume just referrd to, that
matrimony is distinctly spoken of as a sacrament—a
circumstance which Perrin, in the extracts he has
given from the treatise, has carefully concealed. The
fact is noted by the words "Marriage sacrament," written in a more modern hand on the margin of fol. 35. a.
of the copy now before us, opposite to a passage
which seems to be part of a quotation from St. Augustine, and is as follows:—" Car lo matrimoni es sacrament. Car el essegnald' cosa sacra. Car el significa
la conjoncion d' X⁺ cum la gleysa. Enayma di lapostol,
A quest sacrament es grant, ma yo dic en X⁺ e en la
gleysa."

VII. Fol. 38. b. A tract without title; beginning,
" *Li filh li cal naison a li payrons carnals.*" See what has
been said of this tract, in describing the copy of it which
occurs in the volume already referred to, under the title
of " De lensegnament de li filh," p. 24, above. The

present copy appears to be more complete and accurate.
It ends on fol. 42. a.

VIII. Fol. 42. a.   A tract beginning, "*Del pecca de
la dessubidiencia.   Ascuminicament del qual po primerament valar*, &c."   See another copy of this tract, noticed
p. 40, above, Tract XLIII.

IX. Fol. 44. b. A tract without title ; beginning, "*En
a quel temp herode fe pilhar e ligar e encarcerar Johan
baptista per herodiana molher de philip lo seo frayre.*"
Another copy of this tract has been noticed p. 28, above,
Tract XII.

X. Fol. 47 b.   A short tract, without title ; beginning, "*Nos vesen esser na tres greos perilh en aquisti
temp per li cal la via del regne de li cel es mot empacha.*"
This is the tract entitled "De li perilh," of which another copy is noticed p. 27, above, Tract IX.

XI. Fol. 48. a.   A tract without title ; beginning,
"*Donca nos mesquins per que tarczen de ben far.*"   A
copy of this tract, entitled "Mesquins," occurs in the volume described p. 40, above, Tract XLVII.

XII. Fol. 50. b.   Another copy of the tract, mentioned above, p. 40, Tract XLVI. ; beginning, "*Lo fellon
abandone la soa via e lo baron iniquitos*," &c.

XIII. Fol. 52. b.   A tract without title ; beginning,
"*O Segnor tu me pocz mondar si tu voles.   La saperten
al emferm ubrir lenfermeta almege e demandar benefici
d'sanita.*"

XIV. Fol. 55. a.   A tract without title ; beginning,

" *Tu sies sol pelegrin en ierusalem, e non conaguies aquillas cosas,*" &c.

XV. Fol. 57. b. *Lo fantin Y^u*, or "The infancy of Jesus;" beginning, "*Lo fantin Y^u remas en irusalem. Car moti son liqual perdon Y^u*," &c. A copy of this tract has been noticed, p. 41, above, Tract LIV.

XVI. Fol. 59. a. A tract beginning, "*Le teo payre, e yo dolent querian tu,*" &c. This tract, in the volume before described, p. 41, above, is given as a part or continuation of the sermon, *Del fantin Jesu;* whether erroneously or not I shall not determine. In the volume now before us the two tracts are apparently distinct.

XVII. Fol. 61. a. A tract beginning, "*En aquillas contras d'bellem eran pastors gardant las vigilias de la noyt,*" &c. This is a copy of the Sermon on the Nativity, mentioned p. 40, above, Tract XLVIII.

XVIII. Fol. 62. a. A tract beginning, "*E cum y^s fossa na en bellem de juda, en li dia d'herode lo rey,*" &c. This tract also occurs in the volume before described, p. 40, above, Tract XLIX.

XIX. Fol. 64. a. A tract beginning, "*En aquel temp zo es li savi atroba e adora lo fantin se partiron e retorniron en las loras contras.*"

XX. Fol. 64. b. A tract beginning, "*Li teo olh vean dreytas cosas. Czo es li olh mental e corporal bean dreytas cosas.*"

XXI. Fol. 65. b. A copy of the tract on balls and dancing, of which a portion has been published by

Perrin. It begins, "*Ayci volen parla de li bal, demon-strant premierament per testimonis de Scripturas,*" &c. There is another copy of this tract in the volume, No. III., described, p. 39, above. The two copies agree exactly, and differ from Perrin's printed copy, which has pas-sages strangely transposed and garbled. On the upper margin of fol. 66. a. a modern French hand has written the words "Du Bal."

XXII. Fol. 68 b. The tract noticed in the former volume, p. 30, above, Tract XXXVII., and published by Perrin under the title of *De la taverna.* It begins, "*La taverna es fontana d'pecca,*" &c. On the upper margin of folio 68. b. is written, in the same French hand already alluded to, the word "Taverna."

XXIII. Fol. 69. a. A tract beginning, "*Alcuns son liqual saprosumisson d'far veniancza,*" &c. Another copy of this tract is in the volume already described, p. 40, above, Tract XLIV.

XXIV. Fol. 71. a. A tract beginning, "*Lo es de saber que 4 son las raysons per las quals lome se sol desperar.*" A copy of this tract is also preserved in the former volume, p. 40, above, Tract XLV.

XXV. Fol. 73. a. A tract beginning, "*Lo segnor di per lo propheta, yo non volh la mort d'l peccador,*" &c.

XXVI. Fol. 74. b. Another tract on the same sub-ject; beginning, "*Lo nostre segnor dio celestial mege non vol la mort del peccador,*" &c.

XXVII. Fol. 77. b. A tract beginning "*Mas yo*

dic a vos que de tota parolla auciosa la qual li ome parla-
ren," &c.   This is a copy of the " Sermon d'las parollas
auciosas," noticed Tract XIII. of the former volume,
p. 28, above.

XXVIII. Fol. 79. a.   The tract beginning, " *Tot don
noble,*" of which another copy occurs, Tract X. of the
former volume, p. 27, above.

XXIX. Fol. 80. a.   A tract on usury, headed, in rubric, in the upper margin, *Sobre lusura.*   At the beginning of the tract is inserted, in rubric, the text,
" *Date et dabitur vobis;*" and the tract begins thus,
" *Dona aldemandant a tu e non volhis contrastar,*" &c.

XXX. Fol. 83. b.   A sermon entitled, " *Sermon scd.*"
[second.] " *Ayczo meseyme;*" beginning, " *Nos annes cal
cosa* x^i *amonesta al premier sermon,*" &c.   The word
Usura is written, in rubric, and by the original scribe,
on the upper margins of pages 81. a. to 84. a. inclusive.

XXXI. Fol. 85. a.   A sermon on the text, " *Yhu fo
mena de l'esprit al desert quil fossa tempta del diavol.
Mt. 4.*"   On the upper margins of the next seven pages
the word " *Sermon*" is written, in rubric, by the original
scribe.

XXXII. Fol. 88. b.   Another sermon on the same
subject; beginning, " *Yhu fo amena d'lesprit al desert,
&c.   Enaquist evangeli son notta quatre sperit: czo es,
sperit divin; sperit human; sperit maligne; sperit an-
gelical.*"

XXXIII. Fol. 92. b.   *Bon Pastor;* beginning " *Yo*

soy bon pastor. Joh. 10. *Vos d've saber que* 6 *son las propriotas del bon pastor*," &c. The next two pages are headed in rubric, " *Bon pastor.*"

XXXIV. Fol. 94. b. A sermon on the text, " *Petit e non verre mi e d'reco petit e veyre mi. Joh.* 16." The next three pages are headed, in rubric, " *Sermon.*"

XXXV. Fol. 97. b. A tract beginning, " *La femna cant ilh aperturis a tristicia, car lora d'ley ven. A questa differencia es entre li bon e li mal.*" Fol. 99. a. and the four following pages are headed in rubric, " *Sermon.*"

XXXVI. Fol. 101. a. A sermon beginning, " *Yo soy conpira alfanc e soy asimilha a la bellua e a la cenre. Joh.* 30. *Eyci es denota la misera d'la condicion.*"

XXXVII. Fol. 103. A tract, entitled, in rubric, on the top of the next page, " De la penitencia," and beginning, " *Ara di lo segnor cun vertevos ami en tot lo nostre cor,*" &c.

XXXVIII. Fol. 105. a. A tract, entitled, on the upper margin, " Sermon ;" beginning, "*Cant vos devian non volha esser fait enayma,*" &c.

XXXIX. Fol. 107. a. A tract, entitled, " *Del iudici avenador ;*" beginning, " *Cum lo filh d'lavergna sere vengu en la soa maiesta e tint li angel d' l' cun lui, M^c. 24.*"

XL. Fol. 109. a. A tract, entitled, on the upper margin, " *Sermon ;*" beginning, "*Yo fameiey e vos non dones ami amaniar,*" &c.

XLI. Fol. 112. a. A tract beginning, "*Ere vos fene*

cananea yssic da quellas en contars e cridava diczent a lui." The next three pages are headed, in rubric, " *Sermon.*"

XLII. Fol. 115. b. A sermon beginning, "*O Segnor filh d' david marceneia d' mi la mia filha es trabalha,*" &c.

XLIII. Fol. 118. a. A sermon beginning, "*Sobre a quella parolla M².* 13. *Ve vos aqual que semena issic se-menar lo seo semencz.*"

XLIV. Fol. 121. b. A tract without title; beginning, "*Crisostomo di, Tota la gloria d'dio e tota la salu d'li home es pausa en la mort d' X².*"

The volume ends fol. 123. a.; and at the end the original scribe has written, in rubric, the date, "1523;" under which, in a more modern hand, is written, in common black ink, the following note :—"Au premier iour du mois souna la tronpete." This entry does not seem to have any relation to the text of the tract to which it is appended, and is, probably, mere scribbling.

There can be very little doubt that this is the identical volume described by Perrin in the following words :— " Item vn livre en parchemin, du moyen de separer les choses precieuses des viles et contemptibles, c'est à dire, les vertus des vices."* This description, however inaccurate, contains an evident allusion to the first tract in the volume, which is entitled, *Si tu departires la preciosa cosa de la vil.*

---

* Perrin, " Hist. des Vaudois," p. 59.

Postscript to Volume No. IV.

In my notice of the volume of " Poems and other tracts," No. IV. (p. 44, supra), I had occasion to mention a poem, entitled *Nobla Leyczon*, differing wholly from the celebrated poem so called ; and I added, that I was not aware of its having been noticed by any writer on Waldensian affairs. A learned friend has informed me, that he suspects it to be the poem entitled by Morland, Raynouard, &c., *Lo Novel Sermon*. I have not had access to Raynouard's book ; but my friend tells me that the extract given by Raynouard ends with the same three lines as the poem I have described.

No. VII.

A VOLUME OF MISCELLANEOUS PROSE TRACTS.

THIS is a paper volume in 4° (7½ inches by 5¾) in a handwriting of the early part of the seventeenth century. It belongs to the collection of Archbishop Ussher, and is now marked Class C. Tab. 4. No. 17. Its contents are thus briefly noted on the first leaf, in Archbishop Ussher's handwriting :—

" WALDENSIUM

Tractatus tres, vetere linguâ Occitanicâ
conscripti.

I. Glosa sobre lo Pater nostre.

II. De las 4 cosas que son a uenir.

III. Verger de cunsolacion.

h. e.

Expositio Orationis Dominicæ. .

De quatuor novissimis.

Virga consolationis."

The book was probably transcribed for the archbishop with a view to publication, and the above was evidently the intended title-page.

1. Fol. 1. a. *Glosa sobre lo Pater nostre;* beginning, "O Tu lo nostro Payre lo quel sies en li ciel. O frayres nos deuen saber que entra totas las obras que pon esser faytas en a questa vita alcuna cosa li obra non es plus honorivol, ni plus prophetiuol ni plus legiera que orar."

F

Leger has published a portion of this tract, "Hist. des Vaudois," livre i. ch. vii. p. 40, and he tells us that the MS. from which he copied contained only the explanation of the first three petitions of the Lord's Prayer. The present copy, however, has the whole tract complete.

II. Fol. 19. b. "*Las 4 cosas que son avenir;* beginning, "*Lo es d'entendre eun chascun,*" &c. There is a copy of this tract in the volume No. III. described above ; see p. 39, supra, Tract XLI. The two copies agree in substance, but differ very widely in words and phrases, which in the MS. now before us appear to have been modernized ; the spelling is also different. The tract ends with an account of the Twelve Joys of Paradise, in these words :—" Ali qual joy nos amene Dio loquel vio e regna sencia fin. Amen."

There follow, without any titles, some short tracts which may perhaps be continuations of the treatise *De las 4 cosas.* The first of these (fol. 48. b.) begins, " *Donca lo es certana cosa que li just sleyt hauren o questa sobre dicta gloria,*" &c. : it occupies about five pages of the MS., and seems to be the same which occurs No. 3, Tract XLII. (p. 39, supra), and is there entitled " *De· lalegrecza de li salva.* The present copy, however, is somewhat longer ; but is followed, like that in No. III., by a paragraph* (fol. 51. a.)

---

* This paragraph occurs, fol. 336. a. of No. III., but has not been noticed in my account of that volume, because it is there without title, and I supposed it to be a continuation of the tract *De lalegrecza de li salva.* .

beginning, "*O Carissimes nos saven lu huic de tanti grant conoyssencia*," &c., which occupies about a page and a half. At the end of it, Archbishop Ussher has written in the margin, "fol. 337. a. (desin—" referring to the folio of No. III., on which the tract ends. Then follows (fol. 51. a.), "*Nota de li orde de Angel de Paradis;*" beginning, "*O es d'entendre que lo son con orden d' Angels en Paradis.*" This occupies nearly two pages, and at the end Archbishop Ussher has written, "*Nihil deest.*" The next leaf is blank.

III. Fol. 54. a. "*Verger de Consolation;*" beginning, "*Dar enayma dis Peyre Apostol li sant home parleron yspira per lo sant sprit de Dio.*"

This tract is mentioned by Perrin, who says, "Item, nous avons un traité notable, intitulé, ' *Vergier de Consolation*,' contenant plusieurs belles instructions confirmées par l'Ecriture sainte, et par plusieurs authorités des anciens."

The copy from which the MS. before us was transcribed was imperfect in the middle, as we learn from the following note, which occurs (fol. 68. b.) in the place where the defect is found :—" Hic decerptæ sunt duæ paginæ e libro formæ 8." Two blank leaves follow, and (fol. 74. b.) there is another defect, with the note, " Hic duæ paginæ deesse videntur in originali ;" fol. 75. a. is blank, and at the end of the Tract (fol. 83. a.) there is also written, " Reliqua pauca desunt."

This treatise is divided into five parts, the contents of which are thus described (fol. 54. a.) :—" La prima part tracta de li pecca capital; la 2ª part tracta de li autre pecca. La 3ª part tracta de las Vertuci teologials e cardinals. La 4 part tracta de las autras vertuci.   La 5 part tracta de las cosas celestials e de linfern."

Some of the matter of this Tract will be found in the Treatise entitled " Lo pecca d'la superbia," in No. III., p. 26, supra.

No. VIII.

WALDENSIAN DOCUMENTS, DIOCESE OF AMBRUN.

THIS volume (MSS. Usser. Class C. Tab. 4. No. 18) is in size similar to the former, but not in the same handwriting. It was written in the early part of the seventeenth century, and its contents are as follows :—

I. Fol. 1. a. A statement made by the Archbishop of Ambrun, A.D. 1497, of the examination of certain persons, inhabitants of the valley of Fraxinière; beginning, "Sciendum est quod anno Domini millesimo quadringentesimo nonagesimo septimo, postquam migravi e loco aut oppido *Freius* ad Ebronium, in animum induxi visitare ac perlustrare Ebrenensem diocesim meam," &c. The narrative goes on to the year 1501, and occupies nineteen pages of the volume.

I am not aware that this document, which is a narrative of much interest and importance, has ever been published; but Perrin has given an abstract of it, " Histoire des Vaudois" (livre ii. ch. 3), and has quoted in French, pp. 138–143, a part of the archbishop's account of his proceedings in the year 1501. A French copy, apparently the original of this tract, will be described shortly.

II. Fol. 12. a. The articles of the sentence of Peter Valois, a native of Frassinière; beginning, "Imprimis

tu Petre Valois dixisti et fassus es, te discessisse a loco
qui vulgo divus Andreas dicitur," &c.

In the volume (Class C. Tab. 1. No. 6) which will be
described shortly, there occurs the Process against
" Audinus Crispini, *alias* Valoy," who was the brother
of the Peter Valoy here mentioned, as appears from the
following sentence, with which the document before us
concludes :—

" Item, ad eundem modum fratrem tuum Audinum,
Thomasiam, Martham sorores tuas, sese apud eosdem
barbas confessos esse, quemadmodum tutemet fecisti."

The document is dated at the end, 1489, and is marked
" Num. 8." It does not appear, as far as I can find, to
have been ever published.

III. Fol. 15. a. A paper, dated 1488, containing short
notes of events in the history of the Vaudois. It begins,
" De discessu Valdensium ad Delphinatum. Johannes
Violinus (alias Violin) ait eos esse profectos Viennam ad
capiendum consilium."

This document occupies only two pages of the MS.

IV. Fol. 16. a. "Tractatus seu Epitome eorum quæ continentur in accusatione et lite intentata coram Reverendis-
simis dominis domino Inquisitore apostolico, atque vene-
rando officiali hujus Curiæ præsentibus, ac præsidentibus
contra Stephanum Ruffum (alias G.* le Roux), e loco vel

---

* " G," I suppose, here stands for *Gallice*, " le Roux" being the
French for *Ruffus*.

oppido quod vulgo apud Gallos vocatur La Fraissinière."
This document begins, " In primis ut cernere est ex iis
quæ in eadem lite et criminatione continentur," &c.

Perrin mentions " Estienne Roux" (p. 147), but I cannot find that the document before us has ever been published : it occupies upwards of fourteen pages of the MS.,
and is dated 1488. That it was transcribed, however,
long after that year, and by a transcriber favourable to
the Waldenses, is evident from the following note, with
which it concludes :—

" Compertum est eundem Albertum" [i. e., Albert de
Capitaneis, who had been mentioned in the document as
having examined Stephen le Roux,] " animadvertisse et
sæviisse in hanc eandem Valdensium sectam Anno
Domini circiter, 1488."

V. Fol. 23. a. The petition of certain inhabitants of
the valley of Fraissinière, addressed to the senators and
councillors of the king's council, against the Archbishop
of Ambrun, A. D. 1483 ; beginning, " In nomine Domini
Amen. Anno Nativitatis eiusdem Millesimo quadringentesimo octogesimo tertio, die vero vigesimo quinto Mensis
Augusti, Universis ac singulis hoc præsens Instrumentum
visuris, lecturis, ac audituris, Notum sit," &c.

This instrument contains copies of various documents,
letters, and papers, relating to the question at issue between the archbishop and his subjects of the valley.
The initial sentences of these documents shall be here
given :—

1. " Domine bonæ gentes de Valeria, Fraxineria ac eorum consortes litigantes et prosequentes jura sua," &c.

2. " Hic est tenor Literæ clausæ.   Hæc est superscriptio eius, Dilectissimo fratri meo Archiepiscopo d'Ambrun Regis Consiliario.   Dilectissime frater salutem.   Habitantes et Incolæ Vallesiæ, Fraxineriæ, ac Argenteriæ," &c.   This seems to be a letter from the Chancellor Viere to the Archbishop, and is dated 23rd July.

3. " Regi Domino nostro.   Humillime supp^{tes}. vestri pauperes humillimi ac fideles subditi nempe cives et incolæ Valesiæ, Fraxineriæ ac Argenteriæ," &c.

At the end is the following, which was probably the endorsement of the original document :—" Petitio sive supplicatio oblata Dominis senatoribus, ac consiliariis supremi Regis Consilii a Civibus et Incolis Fressinieriæ, contra Acta, Informationes, Rapta, et Concussiones Archiepiscopi d'Ambrun, quæ omnia facta sunt ab eodem et servis ejus in odium et contemptum litis et Controversiæ pendentis, cum intimatione vel significatione ejusdem prædicto Archiepiscopo, una cum Copia Literæ ad eum scriptæ a dominis senatoribus et consiliariis Magni sive Supremi Regis Consilii."

VI. Fol. 30. a. "Lis intentata contra duos Barbas, nimirum Franciscum de Gerundino (qui idem Barba Martinus nuncupatur), et Jacobum, qui quoque Barba Johannes vocatur, quorum Responsis et depositionibus additæ sunt multæ Calumniæ de fornicatione et Idololatria, ut constat et manifestum est ex eorundem Responsis hic annexis, quæ scriba (G. Grefier) pro sententia et arbitrio extendit et immutavit. Num. 9."

This is only the title of a document which is not itself transcribed. A copy of it, however, occurs in the volume which will be next described. See p. 79.

VII. Fol. 31 a. A letter, of which a part only has been transcribed. - It begins, "Reverendissime Pater in Deo, Domine Archiepiscope d'Ambrun, sat probe nosti controversias et lites et quæstiones quæ motæ et agitatæ sunt," &c., and ends imperfectly (fol. 31. b.) with these words "declarando ipsos bonos Christianos et Catholicos quemadmodum fuerunt habiti antequam hujusmodi accusationes et calumniæ iis civibus ac incolis imponerentur."

Then follow 51 blank leaves; and three leaves upon which some memoranda and other matter, having no relation to the Vaudois, have been written, reversing the book.

No. IX.

PROCESSUS CONTRA WALDENSES.

A FOLIO paper volume, containing a number of distinct documents, many of them original, bound together, and lettered on the back "Processus contra Waldenses." (Class C. Tab. 1. No. 6.)

The documents preserved in this volume are identical with those which are described by Morland as contained in the volumes which he has marked G. and H., and which were deposited by him in the Library of the University of Cambridge.* It does not appear with certainty that the volume before us formed a part of Archbishop Ussher's collection: it was not mentioned in the catalogue of our MSS. printed in the "Catalogi librorum MStorum Angliæ et Hiberniæ" (Oxon. 1697), and some of the documents it contains were certainly at one time, since the publication of that catalogue, in another part of the library; they appear to have been found in a loose state, and to have been bound together in their present form when the books were moved to the present library, about a century ago.

The following is a list of these documents:—

I. "No. 1. Origo Waldensium et processus contra eos facti," containing—

* See the Catalogue of the Cambridge MSS., printed in 1856, vol. i., pp. 82-88.

1. The document beginning, "*Ut vobis Rever^{mo}. in xpo patri*," &c.

This occurs in Morland's volume G. No. 3, and has been printed by Allix in the Appendix to his " Remarks on the Ecclesiastical History of the Churches of Piedmont." See also Morland, p. 215.

2. " Sequuntur examinationes factæ in materia hæresis sectæ Valdentium [*sic*] per Rev^{mum}. et Rev^{dos}. patres Laurentium Bureau Epum Siffarien., et Thomam Paschal, ac Rostagnum Archiepiscopum Ebredunen." &c.   In the margin, in a more modern hand, there is written, " Informacions prises par les commis du pape, L'Evesque de Sisteron et autres nommés par le Roy."

This paper is dated 1501, and relates to the same events as the Narrative of the Archbishop of Ambrun, which stands first in the volume last described.   It contains the Examinations of Fazion Gay, Francis Ruffus, Anthony Pau, Fazius Ripert, all of Frassinière ; also of John Lagerij (who is described as " Dominus Johannes Lagerius Vicarius de Orseria in Camposauro"), Peter Raymund, John Arnoux, Angelinus Paloni, John Barthelemy, Hugh Jacques, John Fabri, Pierre Jourdan, Hippolyte Blen, Jacques Pari, Thomette, wife of Fazius, Ripert, Marie, wife of William Bret, Jacques Bonnefoy, Hunet Julian de Valle, Thomas Granet de Valle, Anthonius Baridoni, de Castro Rodulpho, Johannes de Burgo, de Sancto Crispino, Claudius Hunbert, Honoratus de Burgo,

de Sancto Crispino, Giraud Ruffi or de Roux, and
Jacques Chambon.

At the end is the attestation and signature of the notary
" Gobaud," with the following endorsement in a different
hand :—

"Numero 1
Examinatio facta per dmn. Siffarien.
in Frassineria super eresia Valden. ;"

and in a French hand,

" Origine des Vaudois et les faicts du procureur d'Eglise
contre eux. Information prise par Vincent Gobaud."

This document occupies 28 pages. It is probably not
an original,* but has every appearance of being a contemporary copy. In the margin there are written, in
French, short summaries of its contents. These are in
the same French hand just spoken of.

II. Another copy of the document No. V. of the
volume last described, except that the petition is here
given in French. It occupies 5 pages, followed by
2 pages blank. It is endorsed on the back, "Registre
presentée au grand conseil par ceux de Freissinière sur
les attemptats de l'Archevesque d'Ambrun faicts au prejudice de la litispendance avec l'Jntimacŏn auy Arche-

---

* There are some corrections or various readings in the original
hand. The Cambridge copy may perhaps be the original. " Catal."
vol. i., p. 82, *sq.* (MS. Dd. 3. 25.)

vesque et copic de la Lettre a luy Escrite par Messieurs du Grand Conseil.

Anno Dom. 1483."

III. 2. Num. 1487. "Bulle et commission tres ample du Pape Innocent contres les Vaudois;" this title is in the French hand already mentioned, but the body of the document is in the same hand as No. I.

It begins "Albertus de Capitaneis, juris utriusque Doctor, Archidiaconus Ecclesiæ Cremonensis et Blaxensis de Berra, ordinis prædicatorum, sacre Theologiæ professor, hæreticæ pravitatis Inquisitor," &c.   It recites the Bull, "Innocentius Episcopus servus servorum Dei, dilecto filio Alberto de Capitaneis," &c.

This bull is dated 1487.   The original, with the seals, is in the Cambridge Library, No. 2, in Morland's volume G., and he has printed it in his History, book i., p. 196. See also Leger (ii. ch. 2).   It is marked at the beginning, and also at the end, ".Num. 2," and occupies 12 pages.

IV. A paper in the same handwriting as the last, endorsed on the last leaf, " Num. 3. 1483.   *Lettres de desaveu des poursuites contre leur persecuteurs.*   Copia protestationis factæ per Castellanum Vallis Loysiæ, una cum omnibus habitatoribus dictæ vallis declarantes se esse bonos et fideles, orthodoxos, præceptis ecclesiæ obedientes, et quod nullam intendunt prosequi causam in curia Christianissimi Francorum Regis.   Universitatis

vallis Loysiæ." The words in Italics are in the French
hand. It begins, "Copia. In nomine Dni nri Jesu xp̄i.
Amen. Anno ejusdem nativitatis millesimo quatercen-
tesimo lxxx^{mo}. tertio," &c. At the end is the notary's
attestation, "Facta fuit collatio de hujusmodi copia cum
proprio originali per me notarium publicum

"Paris."

This document occupies four pages and a half.

V. "Processus factus et formatus in facto sanctæ fidei
per Rev^{mum}. in xpo patrem et dominum Johannem, Dei
et Apostolicæ sedis gratia Archiepūm et principem
Ebredunen. contra Anthon. Blasii de Angrogina, Diocesis
Taurinen. habitatorem Dalphini, Sissarien Dioc^s."

At the top of the page is the word "Ihūs ;" and on the
same line, left hand margin, the letter "C," right hand
margin, "Ordina⁹." Under the C, in the margin, is the
word "Originalis," with the signature of the notary,
"N. Paris." The date of this document is 1486, and the
handwriting is the same as No. I. The signature of
"N. Paris" occurs again at the end, but can scarcely be
regarded as an autograph; neither has this document
the appearance of being an original. It is evident that
these papers were written at the same time and by the
same scribe. This paper contains several examinations
of Antonius Blasii, and occupies 19 pages.

VI. Marked "Num. 5," and in the French hand
"Bulle pour absoudre le Vaudoys au legat;" beginning,

" Alexander Episcopus servus servorum Dei, dilecto filio Georgio tituli sancti Sixti, presbytero, Cardinali Rotho-magen. &c. Cum nos hodie," &c. Dated, " Romæ apud Sanctum Petrum. Non. Aprilis." A. D. 1501. One leaf.

This is No. 2, in Morland's vol. H. Cambridge Catal., ibid., p. 87.

VII. Another bull of the same pope; beginning, " Alexander Episcopus servus servorum Dei, Dilecto filio Georgio tituli Sancti sixti presbytero, &c. Ab eo qui humani generis," &c. Dated, " Romæ apud Sanctum Petrum. Nonis Aprilis." A. D. 1501. Two leaves.

It is endorsed at the end, in the French hand, " Bulle d'Absolution en faveur des Usuriers."

This is No. 3, in Morland's vol. H.

VIII. Headed in the French hand, " Autre bulle pour absoudre de tout crime et particulierement d'heresie ;" beginning, " Alexander Episcopus, &c. Cum nos alias te," &c. Dated, " Romæ apud Sanctum Petrum. Non. Octobris." A. D. 1501. One leaf.

This is No. 4, in Morland's vol. H. All these bulls are in the same handwriting as No. I.

IX. Examinations of several Vaudois, also in the same hand, and marked, " Num. 5." The first page is marked in the margin " 1486," and contains the evidence of Peter Vole.

On the next page, " Examinatio Anthonii Blasii de

valle Angrogniæ Diocˢ Thaurinen." In the margin,
" Est alibi." On the next page, " Repetitio dicti Anthonii
Blasii," and " Alia Examinatio." Also (p. 5), " Contra
Johannam uxorem diciti Anthonii Blasii." On the next
page, " Repetitio dicti Anthonii Blasii." On p. 8, " Dicta
die et hora" [viz. 22 July, 1486], " coram dictis Do.
Ar. et Inquisitore in executione ordinationis prefatæ,
fuit exhibitus torturæ," &c. Other examinations of the
same prisoner follow, to Sept. 14, 1487, when he abjured
his heresy in presence of witnesses. This is not the
same as No. V., but it is in the same hand, and bears
the signature of " N. Paris."

There is a line drawn down every page of this document,
as if it had been cancelled.

X. The examinations of " Audinus Crispini, *alias*
Valoy, de Fraxineria, habitator Sancti Andreæ, diffamatus
de secta Valden." On the top of the page is the
word " Jesus," and in the margin " 4°. f.," under which
are the words " fregit carceres." The date of the first
examination of this prisoner is the 11th of December,
1486; his second examination was on the 30th of January,
1487 ; and his last on the 15th of May, 1487. These
examinations bear the signature (not autograph) of N.
Paris, and are in the same hand as those just described.
The prisoner at first appears to have denied that he
was a Waldensian; but at last, being " leviter torturæ
ligatus et modicum elevatus," he confessed his connexion
with the sect ; that he had been taught " quod·non erat

Purgatorium nisi in hoc mundo ;" that his father, uncle, and mother were of the sect of the Waldenses, or Poor of Lyons ; that he denied the spiritual powers of the pope, prelates, and clergy ; disapproved of the invocation of the saints, kept no feasts or fasts of the Church, gave no honour to images, had no faith in holy water, &c.

There seem to be some leaves wanting at the end of this paper. It occupies eight, of which the last is blank, and is endorsed in the same French hand as before—"Num. 6. Decres contre les Vaudoys. Audinus Crispinus *alias* Valoy. Jean Archevesque poursuivant." See Morland's vol. H., No. 1, Cambr. Catal. i., p. 85.

XI. A single leaf, headed 1488, containing short notes of events in the history of the Vaudois. It is in French, and is exactly the same as No. III. of the volume last described, except that this latter paper is in Latin.

XII. A copy of No. IV. of the volume last described (see p. 68), containing the examination of Stephen Ruffus, " alias Raoux." It occupies six leaves, of which the first and last are blank.

The upper part of this paper has been torn off.

XIII. Examinations of various prisoners, endorsed at the end—"1488. Num. 7 ;" and in a different hand, " Minutte de diverses Responses de ceux de Frassiniére ubi ne verbum quidem de paillardise. Soubs ce mesme Jean Archevesq. d'Ambrun. Veileti, Inquisiteur. Augeri Inquisiteur." Many of the persons whose examinations

G

are given in this document are the same as those that oc-
cur in former examinations.   Their names are Johannes
Violini, fil. Johannis de Campo Disderio; Joh. Violini
Gros, junior, fil. Johannis de Argenteria; Guill. Porte de
Argenteria, "ætatis c. annorum et ultra;" Joh Raymundi;
Catherina filia Berti Oliverii; Jayme filia Guill^{mi} Porte
jun^s; Poncius Violini filius Petri; Genetus Beneti, f. Lu-
dovici de valle Loysia; Michael Bertrandi alias Barba
de ffraxineria; Johanna filia Guill. ffabii de Argenteria;
Margarita filia Johannis Grossi Violini de Argenteria;
Berengaria filia Ludovici Beneti de valle Loysia; An-
thometa filia Ysoardi Aufossi; Telina uxor Ysoardi
Aufossi; Johanna relicta Jacobi Ludovici; Gena uxor
Poncii Violini.

All the foregoing examinations have the signature
(not autograph) of "N. Paris."   Then follows "Contra
mag^m Petrum Ruffi," the rest of the page having been
left blank for the accusation, which was never inserted.
On the next page, "Repetitio dicti mag^{ri}. Petri Ruffi."
Then follow accusations and "repetitions" of the following prisoners :—Johannes Audonis alias May; Jacobus
Berardi filia [read filius] Pauli de Argenteria; Guill.
Porte juvenis, fil. Eynardi; Spūs Porte f. Eynardi; Spūs
Porte f. Johannis; Anthonius Porte f. Anthonii; Pas-
queta uxor magistri Petri Ruffi.

Then follows a new series of examinations in the same
hand, headed "Jhūs.," and in the margin "xxix Aprilis
in domo Poncii Brineti coram do. Grand. in presencia do

yirati ffraxineriæ." The names of the accused are, Guilhi-
elma filia Bertrandi; Jayme uxor Petri Romani; Maria
filia Stephani Armandi; Joanna filia Johannis Alardi
de Dormilholla; Biatrisia filia Joh. Alardi de Fraysineria;
Pasqueta filia Jo. Mich. Arbaudi; Margarita filia Michaelis
Arbaudi; Cecilia filia Michaelis Baridonis; Caterina filia
Petri Pani; Michaelis Arnulphi f. Bruneti Arnulphi;
Guill. Breti, f. Michaelis Breti; Joh. Bernardi f..Gin-
gonis; Petrus Pelegrini f. Petri; Catherina relicta Guill.
Raymundi; Angelia uxor Petri Pelegrini; Johannes
Thomani f. Johannis; Johannes Raymundi f. Johannis.
Also under the date, "xxx Aprilis," Juliana relicta
Anthonii Arnulphi; Catherina uxor Peyronii Riply
de Pallono; Jacobus Riperti f. Petri; Barthol. Arnulphi
f. Bruneti; ffazius Audoni Gay f. Joh. Audonis; Michael
Arnulphi f. Bruneti; Petrus Ruffi f. Johannis.

From these inquisitions it appears that the Barbs, after
confessing their converts, were accustomed to enjoin as
penances the repetition of the Pater Noster and Ave
Maria a certain number of times; that they objected to
an oath, to the invocation of saints, and to purgatory, *p l, 3,*
which they said was only in this life. They refused also
to observe the festivals of the saints. This document
consists of 16 leaves, of which the last is blank.

XIV. "Rursus ipse arch. cupiens de premissis magis
informari, informationes continuando infrascriptos pro
secreta informatione audivit. fo. eod. Continuatio in-
formationum."

This is an imperfect document, containing an abstract of informations, with references to the folia of some register. It consists of four folio leaves, in the same handwriting as No. I.

XV. The examination of Peter Valoy. This paper is endorsed at the end, "Num. 8." It consists of ten leaves, of which the last two are blank, and the first six are torn at the top, in exactly the same way as No. XII., showing that both were placed together, and that the injury took place at the same time. They are also on the same paper, as appears from the water mark. It is in the same hand as No. I., and is dated 1489.

This must be the same Peter Valoy whose sentence is given in No. II. of the volume last described. See p. 60, supra. He appears to have been the brother of Audinus Crispinus, *alias* Valois, whose examination is given in No. X. of the present volume.

XVI. The sentence of Peter Valoy, in French. The same which was given in Latin in No. II. of the volume last described.

This paper is in the same hand as No. XI. It is on the same paper as Nos. XII. and XIII. It has at the end the signature of the notary, " N. Gebaude," and the date, " die ultima Martii," 1489, with the endorsement :—

> " Proces contre Pierre Valet [*sic*] de ffressiniere.
> Confisque ses biens, le livrant au bras seculiers [*sic*].
> N. 8."

This is in Morland's vol. H. Camb. Catal. i., p. 86.

XVII. " Proces contre deux barbes a savoir Francois
de Gerundino, dict barbe Martin, et bien de Jacob, dict
barbe Jean, aux responses des quels ont esté adioustées
des calumnies sur le faict de Paillardise et d'Idolatrie
comme appert par le sumptum de ses Reponses en brevet
y joinct, le quel le Greffier a estendu a son plaisir.

" Num. 9.

" Vn des principaux griefs c'est quils changeront les
depositions et inseroyent dedans une infinite de sales
calomnies.

" Hurre Jean Archevesq. d'Ambrun."

On the next page follow the depositions in Latin, with
this title,

" Anno Dni Mill° cccc° lxxxxii°.
Processus sive Inquisitio facta per quendam
Dmn. Berthol™. Pascalis, secum assiden.
Ven^{libus} viris Dnis Poncio Poncii, consiliario
Xp̄iani Dalph. in suo pla^{to} Gropol. et
Oroncio ejus judice Briansoni."

The signature " N. Paris" is affixed to several of the
Examinations.

This document occupies twelve leaves.   It contains
matter of very great interest and importance towards
ascertaining the real opinions of the sect of Pauperes
de Lugduno at the close of the fifteenth century.   In
the volume last described, No. VI. (p. 70), the title
of it only, or rather the French endorsement, translated
into Latin, has been transcribed.   The portion of it which
contains the examination of Francis de Gerundino de

Spoleto, commonly called Barb Martin, has been published from the Cambridge MS. H. by Allix, in his " Remarks on the Churches of Piedmont," p. 307, 4to edit.
Lond. 1690.   Cambr. Catal. i., p. 87.

XVIII. A document occupying nine leaves; headed :
" Inquisitionalis processus factus et formatus coram
egregiis et circumspectis viris dominis Anthonio ffabri
decretorum doctore, canonico Ebredunensi, hæreticæ-
que pravitatis in toto Dalphinatu et comitatibus, Vien-
nensis, Valentinensis, et Diensis generali Inquisitore, a
sancta sede Apostolica specialiter et immediate deputato;
et Christoffero de Salhiente etiam Decretorum Doctore
Canonico, vicario et officiali Valenciæ ;" beginning, "*Ad
instantiam et persecutionem honorandi viri*," &c.   It is
subscribed " Gobaudi," endorsed at the end—" 1494.
Proces contre Peyronete relaissée de Pierre Beraud de
Valence ; digne d'estre veu."

This has been also printed by Allix from the Cambridge
MS. (*ubi supr*. p. 318).   Cambr. Catal. ibid.

XIX. Another document relating to the case of Pero-
nette, occupying one page only.   It is a short paragraph,
which has been printed by Allix (*loc. cit.*), under the
title of "Sumptum ex ore Peyronettæ."   It is headed

" Jesus Mariæ filius.
Contra Peyronetam Relictam cuiusdam Petri
Beraudi alias fFernerii.   Loci Belli respectus.
A Valence l'an 1444.
Existimo fideliter scriptas responsiones."

The words in Italics are in a different hand. This document is endorsed at the end—" No. 10. Proces contre Perronete Relaissée de Pierre Beraud de Valence, digne d'estre vue."

These papers, from XVII. to XIX., inclusive, are all in the handwriting of No. I., and on paper bearing the same water mark. The next is in a different hand.

XX. The narrative of Rostain, Archbishop of Ambrun, in French. This is the same piece which occurred before in a Latin version, No. I. of the volume last described (p. 67). It begins, " *Est a presuposer, Lan mil iiij^{cc} iiij^{xx} et dix sept apres ma translation,*" &c.

This is probably the original of this tract; it is quoted by Perrin from this French copy. It consists of six leaves, of which the last is blank. On the upper margin of p. 1 are the dates "1497 et 1501;" on the lower margin, "1497, No. II.;" on the back of the last leaf the endorsement, "Num. 11, 1497." There are summaries in the margin, in a hand different from that of the document itself. The paper has a vase, or urn, as water mark.

XXI. The upper part of the next document is very much torn. The injury coincides exactly with that sustained by Nos. XII. and XV., and the paper is the same. These documents were therefore most probably all stitched together, and torn by the same hand. They are also all in the same handwriting. This document has the signature of· "N. Paris." It consists of six leaves,

of which the last is blank.   It is endorsed at the end,
" Proces et abjuration d'Antoyne Blasii.   Num. 12."

This is in the same handwriting as No. I.

XXII. A letter in a different hand, marked at the end,
" Lettre de l'Archevesque Rostain.   No. 13."   It begins,
" *Tres reverend pere en Dieu Monseigneur l'Archevesque
d'Ambrun*," &c., and occupies two pages.

XXIII. Some documents, chiefly in French, dated in
the upper margin of the first page " 12^e d'Octobre,
1501," endorsed at the end—" 1501.   Copies des Lettres Patentes obtenues du Roy Loys douziesme, par ceux
de Frassiniere.   Apres que Laurans Bureau et Thomas
Pascal eurent fait rapport de leur Commission.

" No. 14.

" Contre le Notaire Paris occupateur de patrie de leurs
biens. 12 Octobre, 1501."

This is in the same hand as the last, and occupies two
leaves.

XXIV. " Commandement du Roy pour restituer les
biens de ceux de la valoise Freissinierc."   Endorsed at
the end—" 17 Octob. 1501.   Lettres de la Cour a
l'Archevesque d'Ambrun, marquans les [confisca]tions
faites par ses devanciers.   No. 15."   In French, and in
the same hand as the last.

XXV. Another letter, in the same hand as the last,
from the court to the archbishop on the same subject,
with several marginal notes, and (in a different hand)
the certificate of " Anthonius de Medulion Breissiam et

de Rippeins Consiliarius et Cambellanus Regius, locum
tenens generalis Dalphinatus." Subscribed "Chapnisse."
Endorsed at the end—"No. 15.   Lettres du 27^{ieme} May,
1502."   It occupies eight leaves, the last of which is
blank, with the exception of an endorsement, "Num.
15."   The document last described (No. XXIV.), and
the first four leaves of the present paper, are torn in
exactly the same way as Nos. XII., XV., and XXI.

XXVI. A letter from the king on the same subject,
dated 27 May, A. D. 1502, and signed at the end, " Par
le Roy Daulphin a la relation des gens de son grand
Conseil—De Moline ;" and in a different hand—

" Curia decrevit quod supradictæ literæ exequantur
juxta suam formam, et concessæ literæ de supra, citra
tamen remissionem personarum extra terram."

This document is on the same paper as the last (water
mark, a bunch of grapes), and occupies six leaves, the
last of which is blank, with the exception of the endorsement. " 1502.   Du Regne de Loys 12. l'an cin-
quieme.   Le 25. May.   No. 16."

XXVII. Two leaves, imperfect both at the beginning
and at the end, but consecutive, relating to the examination of Odinus Crispinus.   They are probably a portion
of the imperfect document, No. X., supra.   They are in
the same hand, and on the same paper.   See p. 80.

APPENDIX.

APPENDIX.

ON THE POEMS OF THE POOR OF LYONS.[*]

No. I.

THE twelfth and thirteenth centuries were sufficiently prolific of sects and heresies. But most of them expired in the same intellectual twilight that saw their birth, and have not left to posterity any written memorials of their doctrine. Few sectarian books of those ages have yet been produced for modern critics to exercise their ingenuity upon.

But it is otherwise with respect to the congregation of Pauperes de Lugduno, or Poor Men of Lyons, which Peter Waldo formed in A. D. 1160, and which was cut off from the Church and placed in schism A. D. 1183. The sound it gave was altogether of a higher mood; and it found for itself an asylum in which it was enabled to outstay the scholastic ages, and lived to mix itself at last with the "New Learning" of the reforming ages, and lose its little rivulet in the ocean of Protestantism.

The written remains ascribed to this ancient sect have given rise to various opinions. At one time they were received with considerable but indiscriminate avidity by Protestants, who,

---

[*] These papers are reprinted from the "British Magazine," vols. xviii., xix. (1840, 1841), with the permission of the proprietor, and are believed to be from the pen of the late Hon. Algernon Herbert.

like most nations, most sects, and most families, were not un-
willing to believe themselves a more ancient race than they
really were. The full exposure of the spuriousness of those
remains, in part, has the effect (not unusual in such case) of
casting a discredit upon them all. Yet a broad line of distinction separates the frauds of the Reformation from those
simpler efforts of mediæval piety which have really come down
to us from the Pauperes de Lugduno, and which seem well
entitled to the notice of the student, both as antiquarian reliques, and as documents in the history of sectarianism.

The published documents ascribed to the Waldensians of the
twelfth century are of two obviously distinct classes. The one
consists entirely of theological tractates in prose ; and the
other chiefly of poetical or metrical compositions. *Of the former class*, one document is said to have offered the date of
1100 ; several others are said to be printed from a manuscript
written in the year 1120 ; and we are assured that another had
the date of 1230. *Of the last-mentioned class* (which is chiefly,
but not entirely, metrical) only one piece hath any sort of
date ; and the date which it exhibits forms an important feature in the present subject.

The MSS. professedly of the year 1120 were a *Confession
of Faith* in fourteen articles, and treatises entitled, respectively,
What thing Antichrist may be ; the Dream of Purgatory ; the
Cause of our† Separation from the Church of Rome ; of the Invocation of Saints ;* and *on Baptism and the rest of the Sacraments of the Church of Rome.* The antiquity of those documents
has been fully refuted. If the Confession was (as Sir Samuel

---

* Morland gives us this work as out of the MS. of A. D. 1120 ; but Leger
says its date was 1126. That, however, is most probably an error of the
press for 1120.

† It would seem, from Perrin's "Histoire des Vaudois," book ii., chap. ix.,
p. 224, that this is a Bohemian declaration, and made by persons really
having no connexion with the Vaudois, but translated into the language of
the latter.

Morland* says) "copied out of MSS. bearing date A. D. 1120—
that is to say, near 400 years before the time of either Luther
or Calvin"—it is about the only document of that character to
which the dissensions of the Church ever gave birth anterior
to the Reformation. Its catalogue of canonical books, including
those of Samuel by name, betrays a palpable forgery either of
the document itself or its date. We have before† observed
that, if the "Noble Lesson" hath a good claim to antiquity, this
production can have none; for it makes Antichrist more ancient than the doctrine of purgatory, and himself the inventor
of that doctrine, while the poem pronounces him still future,
and his coming to be looked for. The same circumstance is
equally fatal to the treatise on Antichrist. Monsieur J. Paul
Perrin,‡ writing in 1619, and perhaps the prime author of
these deceptions and forgeries, informs us that it commenced
thus: *" Qual cosa sia l'Antechrist, en datte de l'an mille cent
et vingt."* But this was either a false description of the manuscript, or was afterwards felt to be too gross and unskilful an
application of the forger's hand; for neither he himself, in the
third part of his work, nor Morland, have ventured to print
the treatise with any such heading. The unqualified expression of Zuinglian or Calvinistic opinions concerning the eucha-
rist, in the Treatise on the Sacraments, militates against the
decided weight of historical testimony. Though the Poor Men
of Lyons were accused of arrogating to themselves the power
of working the miracle of the altar, their enemies do not appear
to have laid any denial of that miracle to their charge, even
at the comparatively late period at which the inquisitions of
Thoulouse (of which the *procès verbaux* are still extant) were

* "Evangelical Churches," p. 30.
† "British Magazine," vol. xvi., pp. 607, 8. [The passage here referred
to occurs in some valuable papers, by the same author, on "Antichrist in the
13th century." As it discusses so fully the question of the date of the "Noble
Lesson," it will be inserted at the end of this Paper.]
‡ "Hist. des Vaudois," p. 57. The Italics as given above.

held. Many and clear are the internal proofs* of recency in those productions, which it is not desirable to recapitulate in this place.

The prose document of the year 1100 is a catechism for the instruction of children. Sir Samuel Morland printed it (p. 75) with no more precise account of its date than that it was several hundreds of years before either Calvin or Luther. But Monsieur Jean Leger,† a Vaudois minister, reprinted it eleven years afterwards, with these words annexed to its title, "dattè de l'an 1100." This is, therefore, the oldest prose document of the sect. Yet its language bespeaks the Presbyterian age, and the cessation of Lugdunensian Pauperism. True ministers (it says) are known *per debita ministration de li sacrament*, and false ones *per indebita*. And again, that the faithful‡ "communicate with things ministerial or ecclesiastical by the ministry duly exercised—i. e. *the word*, the sacraments, and prayer." It is evident that *the word*, thus set at the very head of all visible religion, means the system of sermon-preaching. But the preponderance of that idea peculiarly belongs to ultra-protestant reformation, and does not belong to the age or temper of Waldism. These passages resemble, and are no doubt borrowed from, the language of Calvin‖ :—
"ubicunque Dei verbum sincerè prædicari atque audiri, ubi sacramenta ex Christi instituto administrari videres, illic aliquam esse Dei ecclesiam nullo modo ambigendum est." The same catechism speaks of Antichrist in the usual tone of the modern Vaudois—that is to say, as a synonyme for the Church of Rome or its pontiff; and in that sense it repudiates "the authority, words, and benedictions of Antichrist." But this

---

* A full and recent summary of the proofs on this point may be seen in Dr. Todd's "Lectures on the Prophecies," &c., pp. 399-417. The subject had been previously handled in the "Facts and Documents, &c., of the ancient Waldenses and Albigenses," pp. 114-134.

† "Hist. Generale des Eglises Vaudoises," p. 58.

‡ Ap. J. Leger, ibid. p. 64. ‖ "Inst.," iv. c. 1.

is a real shibboleth of the spurious and recent class of documents, and at open variance with the language of the "Noble Lesson."

The origin of these false dates has been* previously indicated. The only date really exhibited in the text and body of any Waldensian document whatsoever was that in the "Noble Lesson." That date, in its most obvious and *primâ facie* acceptation, is of or about the year 1100. And therefore it was a very natural, though it was really an erroneous and impossible supposition, that the "Noble Lesson" was then composed. That year, therefore, became a notable epoch in Vaudois chronology; and these disingenuous moderns adopted it for their standard, and forged up to it.† The Protestant catechism was brought up to that identical year, and *dattè de l'an* 1100; and the major part of the false documents were brought so near to it, as to make them quite contemporary with the "Noble Lesson," and even not improbably the work of the same individual—viz., up to the year 1120.

Perhaps, if any person were to read these tracts as productions of the twelfth century, and desire specific proofs of their unauthenticity (satisfactory as it is to possess an abundance of such proofs), he would be evincing scarcely more perception of the styles and characters belonging to the different ages of literature, than a rustic invited to the tables of the great has of the flavour and qualities of wines. A man may have learned to use the vocabulary of a foreign land, but he cannot step entirely out of his own generation, and invest himself with the characteristics of a distant age. It was morally impossible for writers of the alleged date to handle so large a portion of theology, without adopting in some measure either the logical methods of the schools or the patristic unction of the Ruperts

* "Brit. Mag.," vol. xvi., p. 609. [The passage referred to is reprinted at the end of this Paper.]

† [This is now curiously confirmed by Mr. Bradshaw's recent discovery of the erasure in the Cambridge MS.]

and Bernards. If this be true in general comparison, it becomes more strikingly so in comparison with the Waldensian remains of the other class, chiefly metrical. They are different in the style of composition and the character of their doctrine. And, as it cannot be credited that both emanated from the same parties, so can it not be doubted which are the old and which the new. Besides the poetical remains, there are some prose devotions in the vulgar tongue, which appear to proceed from the genuine sect of the Pauperes of Lyons, and might, with all due allowances, be compared to the French sermons of Saint Bernard. Such are the morsels printed by Morland and Leger, under the names of "Temòr del Segnòr," "Las Tribulacions," and "Glosa Pater Noster." Their general temper will not be mistaken for the Zuinglian or Calvinistic. The first of them is in great measure directed against the love of riches and worldly possessions, and appeals to the sentiments of Saint Augustine, Saint Jerome, and Saint Gregory. Its conclusion is adorned with the following testimony of Chrysostom to the value of human virtues :—" E Sant Johan Boca d'Or di, ' que lo Segnòr a aparellia lo sio regne, a aquilli que contrasteron a li pecca, e monteron a las virtus.' " The little book of "Tribulations" is an agreeable piece of practical devotion, partly resembling the vein of the "Imitatio Christi ;" but with repeated quotations from the fathers, whose authority is placed by the side of the apostle's, "E Sant Paul di, *yo non penso*, etc. : E Sant Augustinus di, *cal ès aquesta*, etc." In another paragraph, St. Sixtus and St. Johan Boca d'Or are quoted; and the former, probably, must signify* Sextius the Pythagorean, whom Rufinus translated under the false name of St. Sixtus, bishop of Rome. The legends of the martyrdoms of St. John Baptist, St. Lawrence, St. James of Zebedee,

---

* But the words cited do not appear in Gale's edition, "Opusc. Myth.," &c., pp. 645-56.—See Schoell "Hist. Litt. Grecque," tom. v., p. 51 ; Gennadius "de Viris Illustr.," chap. xvii. ; and Miræus, ibid.

St. James of Alpheus, St. Bartholomew, St. Peter, St. Andrew, St. Matthew, and St. Paul, are given in the above-mentioned order, and as of equal authority; and St. James of Alpheus is said to have been knocked on the head "by the son* of a bishop." These productions are somewhat germane to those† "authorities of the saints" which, in the early days of the sect, Bernard Ydros compiled under the name of *Sententiæ*, and Stephanus de Ansâ translated into Romance. The words of Augustine, "vain fear is it to fear the loss of things earthly, and not to fear the loss of things heavenly," are paraphrased in the following most expressive words: "vain fear is it to fear losing the company of father and of mother, and not to fear the loss of the company of God‡ and the Virgin Mary." Near the end occurs the following quotation:—"And the Wise Man says, *Behold the life of the holy martyrs, of the men and the women, who suffered themselves to be slain, and their flesh delivered to death and martyrdom.*" The Wise Man is also appealed to for "*the three sufferings which the friends of God must have*"—viz., injuries done them by deed and word, infirmities and troubles appointed to them, and the devil who tempts them from good works; and these words are quoted from him, "I speak to you according to the patience of God;" and again, "the truly patient hopes to enjoy the brotherhood of the angels." Whencesoever those sayings of the Wise Man§ may come, it is evident that these are not the effusions of Protestantism, properly so called. The "Glosa Pater" not only abounds with quotations from the fathers, Saints Augustine, Isidore, Gregory, and Bernard (and most copiously from Gre-

---

* Which Monsieur Leger does not blush to translate "un jeune homme."

† Steph. de Borbone apud "Oudin Script. Eccles., iii., 239 ;" Martene, tom. v., 1778 ;" and Quetif "Bibl. Ord. Prædic.," i., 192.

‡ "De Dio e de la Vergena Maria ;" which Morland has the daring impudence to translate, in the opposite column of the same page, "*of God the Father, and of Jesus Christ !*"—p. 129.

§ For *Wise Man*, Morland, in his version, has thought fit to put *Solomon.*

gory), but it breathes the spirit of Spiritual Poverty, the genuine Lugdunensian Waldism. " Thy kingdom come" is explained, at considerable length, to be a prayer for the establishment of a spiritual and voluntary poverty. "Dereço lo ès entendement, *lo tio regne venga;* çoès, O Segnor! dona a nos pavretà voluntayriç," etc. To these productions no such remote date as 1100 or 1120 has been formally assigned, because they contain nothing in furtherance of the dishonest object sought for in that spurious chronology. That object was, to make out that the modern Vaudois did not owe their Protestantism, their Presbyterianism, their Pope-Antichrist, and, generally speaking, the system that now exists among them, to Zuingli, Bucer, Œcolampade, Calvin, and the divines of that age and school, but had possessed it in identical form and language from a period so distant as to exceed, by more than a generation, the very date of their founder, and the earliest external records of their existence as a religious denomination. This theory, though incredible on the face[*] of it to all who have a general knowledge of men and things, was capable of finding favour with the violent prepossessions and low tone of erudition that marked the unchurched Protestant communities; and, to give it vogue, bold fraud was sufficient. But (although they bear no forged stamp of antiquity, to pass them current with the vulgar) the above-cited remnants of prose devotion are unquestionably ancient—that is to say, they are anterior to the teaching of Luther, Zuingli, and Calvin; are conformable to the tenets that grew up among Waldo's disciples, and were composed by *Poor Men of Lyons.* The matter will be more clearly understood by keeping sight of that, their true title; and, therefore, those who might like to mystify the matter would not be sorry to keep it out of sight.

---

[*] If it were true, it is inconceivable why they should repair to Bucer and Œcolampade with humble applications for advice and instruction, instead of graciously imparting to those German reformers the complete and long-established theology of the valleys.

In 1160 there were persons who might be termed (though, perhaps, as yet they were not) Waldenses, Vaudès, or Vaudois; from that time to 1840 there have never ceased to be persons of whom such is a distinguishing appellation; and ages yet to come may speak of them by that name. But no one will venture to say that any sect of Pauperes de Lugduno is now, or has been for 300 years, in existence. The title has passed away with the opinions which directly gave rise to it, as well as with divers other tenets either introduced or retained by those who bore it. The perpetuity of the name Vaudois does not prove identity, or even similarity, of opinions and practices; yet it is compatible with such identity, and offers a probability of resemblance. But the entire disappearance of the famous and characteristic title of Pauper de Lugduno proves the intervention of a great and serious change; they are, in fact, no longer the same sect. The sect of which we read in early chronicles, councils, and inquisitions, no longer exists; and the name now usually selected to show its perpetuity is not that which constitutes the real test of the truth.

Four volumes, which are preserved at Dublin, among the MSS. of Trinity College, and which had formerly been a part of the library of the most illustrious Archbishop Ussher, contain various documents of Vaudois divinity; and, among them, certain of those which belong to the Reformation, and have fraudulently been referred to the year 1120. They contain two tracts, at least, of that class—viz., the "Dream of Purgatory," and that "On the Invocation of Saints." But the antiquity of those written copies is not calculated to remove the discredit under which their contents are labouring. That which contains the two treatises just mentioned, and is marked C. 5. 22, bears the date of 1524; and that date may be considered genuine, because it is introduced incidentally in a table constructed for finding Easter.* And another (of which the con-

* [See above, p. 24 and p. 41.]

tents are very similar in many respects, but which does not contain those treatises) is dated at the end 1523.* Since Martin Luther declared himself a reformer no earlier than in 1517, and Zuingli in 1519, it may reasonably be supposed that whatever contents of these volumes shall (upon a strict examination) be found belonging to the New Learning, and not to the ancient Lugdunensian sect, are either autographs or very early copies.

The sole evidence for referring any of the prose treatises to the twelfth or thirteenth century is external. It consists in the assertions† of Messrs. Jean Paul Perrin, Samuel Morland, and Jean Leger, that certain MSS. of them exhibited the dates of 1100, 1120, and 1230. But no such documents so dated are now to be met with. Neither does it appear certain that any one, save Perrin, ever saw the date of 1120; for Theodore Tronchin's attestation in 1656 purports only that Perrin showed him " divers *original* MSS.," words entirely devoid of meaning, and calculated to give a vague semblance of authentication, without saying anything. Perrin was, however, silent as to the date of the catechism which he printed; and it was reserved for Jean Leger to reprint it, with the daring assertion that its date was A. D. 1100.

A deep mystery and ugly suspicions hang over all the dealings of these people with Waldensian books. The written volumes which were " remises entre‡ les mains de Monsieur Morland, Commissaire Extraordinaire de Millord Oliver Cromwell, Protecteur de la Grande Bretagne, par Messrs. Antoine et *Jean Leger*, pasteurs originaires des vallées," were presented by Morland " to the public library of the famous University of Cambridge, in August, 1658." One of the pieces in volume A was expressly dated 1230, which might excite some degree of presumption that the whole volume was of that date.

---

* [See above, p. 54, Volume No. VI.].

† Perrin, " Hist. Vaud.," p. 57 ; Morland, " Evang. Churches," pp. 9, 30, 142 ; Leger, " Hist. Gen.," pp. 24, 58, 71, 83, 87, 92.

‡ Leger, " Histoire Generale," p. 21.

Yet not only other treatises in the volume, but *that very one,** seem, from their titles, to belong to the new or reformation Vaudois. A careful inspection in the Cambridge Library, by persons skilled in palæography, might clear up the case. But, alas! Monsieur Raynouard says too truly, "ces manuscrits interessans ne s'y trouvent plus depuis plusieurs années." Indeed, no confirmation can be obtained of the fact that they ever were there at all. The catalogues, which go back to the middle of the eighteenth century, are silent concerning them; and the University possesses no record or tradition whatever, either of their arrival or of their departure. The whole story of their visit to Cambridge depends entirely upon the word of Morland. Yet a work of so much splendour and pretension as Morland's "Evangelical Churches of Piedmont," ostentatiously dedicated† to "His Serene Highness Oliver, by the grace of God," &c., could not publicly announce the deposit of these religious and antiquarian treasures in Cambridge without the imminent risk (not to say moral certainty) that some persons would at least desire to look at them—a greater risk than we see any sufficient motive for running; therefore, even those who value his veracity the least will probably believe that he placed them there in the month and year he mentions. But they were removed again from thence; at what time, is entirely unknown; and it is a question, by what party, and wherefore. Believers in them have indulged in the imagination, that the Papists withdrew them during their short-lived ascendency in the reign of James the Second. But those who

* "A Treatise of the Word of God, and the power and efficacy thereof; as also how it ought to be received."

† Oliver died on the 3rd of September, 1658; and the MSS. were placed at Cambridge in August, 1658; therefore, Morland must have lodged them there at the precise point of time when his book came out of the press—and only some three weeks or so before the death of the Protector, for whose long life and reign he prays with much flattery and cant of Scripture.

are aware of the forgeries will rather conclude that the same
Puritans, under whose auspices they were lodged at Cambridge, in days of Oliverian darkness (finding them utterly
unable to pass muster as MSS. of the age ascribed to some of
them), withdrew them from the searching eye of restored
learning to some place where—not being publicly announced
to exist—they would excite little or no observation in the
republic of letters.   That such was the fact will be shown,
upon pretty strong grounds, when the "Noble Lesson" comes
under consideration, and the fate of the precious old book
(volume B) which contained it is inquired into.   Meanwhile,
it derives confirmation from that which the writer of these
pages has reasons for believing—viz., that some portion of those
documents (but not the important portions above-mentioned)
were conveyed out of the kingdom, and deposited—not in
Romish custody, such as at Paris or the Vatican, but in a
place fully as much belonging to Protestantism* as any of the
libraries of this country.   Meanwhile, the undoubted but unexplained *aphanismus* of the most important documents—if not
the only important ones, both Perrinian† and Morlandian—
leaves the whole story of their antiquity a naked assertion,
and matter of faith, not of sight.

What faith is due to the word, and what respect to the judgment of Perrin and his copyist, Morland, may be partly esti-

---

* With a view to other remarks that must presently be made, it is necessary to say that Geneva is not here alluded to.   [The author alludes to
Trinity College, Dublin, following an opinion which I once entertained.—See
above, p. 21.   But the suspicion that any of the Morland MSS. were conveyed
away to Dublin or any where else is now shown to be unfounded; Mr. Bradshaw having discovered all the MSS. in Cambridge, where Morland left them.]

† Perrin's volume, which he absurdly describes as "intitulè Livre des
Vertus," because the tract so called is the first in order of its multifarious
contents, is at Trinity College, Dublin, and has been identified by the
learned librarian, Dr. Todd.   It is catalogued C. 5, 22, and was written
in 1524.—See above, p. 101, and "Todd on the Prophecies," &c., p. 404,
note (d).

mated from the "*Catalogue of the names of all those barbes** or ancient pastors of or belonging to the Evangelical Churches of the valleys of Piemont, who have been eminent within the 500 years last past.*" It suffices to shake all faith in their pretended traditions of the valleys. In this catalogue we meet with "Mr. Arnoldo, who taught about the year 1150, from whom his disciples were called Arnoldists." Who, think you, is this good barbe of the valleys? No less a man† than Arnald of Brescia. He was a pupil of Peter Abelard, and the most furious disciplinarian reformer of those times. He declaimed against the clergy with such effect, as to raise an insurrection in Rome itself, and drive Pope Eugenius the Third out of his capital; and, like Rienzi, lost his reputation by his success. He was ignobly surrendered by Frederick Barbarossa into the hands of our countryman, Adrian the Fourth, and burnt at Rome, in 1155. It were a waste of words to argue whether this turbulent Brescian was a barbe of the Alps. The whole story is founded upon nothing more than the occurrence of the word Arnaldistæ among the various names enumerated in the famous constitution of Frederick II., or in the somewhat earlier decretal of Gregory IX. Another barbe in the same list is "Mr. Esperone, who taught about the year 1156, from whom his followers were named Esperonists." This is, in like manner, framed upon the word Speronistæ, in the constitution of Frederick; but Ducange apprises us that the true reading thereof‡ is Paronistæ, and that where we meet with Spero-

* Barbe is a Provençal word, meaning *uncle*, and is applied, by way of respect or endearment, to their pastors or ministers by the Vaudois. There is no reason to conclude that Waldo's sect invented that way of speaking, and that it may not have been a more ancient idiom in Gaul; if so, we may understand the legends of St. Patrick, the apostle of Ireland, and St. Ninian, the apostle of Pictland, being St. Martin's *nephews.*—See Morland, p. 184; Perrin, pp. 64–5.

† See Natalis Alexander, sæc. xi. et xii., p. 838, de Arnaldistis. Perrin affects to refer the Arnaldistæ to one Arnaldus Othonis (or Arnaud Hot), an Albigensian, mentioned by William of Puylaurens, c. ix., p. 672.

‡ See Ducange, in *Paronistæ.*

nistæ it is to be thus corrected : the origin of the word, and
nature of the sect, remain quite unknown.   Thus good Mr.
Esperone, whoever was his father (and Perrin* seems to father
him upon Monsieur de Sainte Aldegonde), had a misprint for
his mother.   "Mr. Josepho taught about the same time ; and
those who embraced his doctrine were in mockery called, after
his name, Josephists."   The Emperor Frederick's enumeration includes the Josephini ; and that, again, is the whole
matter of Mr. Josepho.   But his people were quite distinct
from the Waldenses, both in their rules of rigour and laxity ;
"Josephistæ contrahunt matrimonium spirituale, et præter†
coitum omnes delectationes exercent."   Bartholomew of Carcassonne, the delegate of Bartholomew, Paulician primate of
Bulgaria, is inserted in this catalogue of Pastors of the Valleys.   And Perrin‡ did not scruple to assert, that Matthew
Paris described Bartholomew of Carcassonne as being himself
the superintendent of the Bulgarian, Croatian, Dalmatian, and
Hungarian Churches of Vaudois, and called him their pope.
Thus, when occasion requires, two§ Gnostical Bartholomews

* "Hist. Vaud.," p. 64.

† Reinerus apud "Bibl. Max. Patrum," 25, 272.

‡ "Hist. Vaud.," pp. 65, 245.

§ Matthew Paris supplies us with one suggestion concerning that Paulician primate, which, in our lack of information about the Bulgarian hæresiarchate, is worthy of observation, even at the expense of a brief digression.
One Bartholomew was primate, patriarch, or anti-pope of the Hæretici ; and
the Gascon whom he employed as his vicar in Languedoc and the circum-
jacent parts was also Bartholomew.   Here seems to be more than casual
coincidence.   The Nestorian patriarch of Kurdistan is always, and *ex officio*,
Simeon.— Niebuhr, "Voyage," &c., ii., p. 270.   The Nestorian patriarch of
Kara Cathay, or Black Tartary, who combined with that hæresiarchate the
temporal sovereignty of the land of Naiman, was termed the Presbyter
Johannes.—Roger Bacon, "Opus Majus," pp. 231-32, ed. 1733.   And if the
unanimous voice of Christendom, consistent on that point amidst many errors
regarding him, may be listened to, he was so called officially, and not in a
mere personal way.   So there appears some reason to suspect that they who
pulled the strings of Manicheism in Bulgaria, affected the name of Bartholomew.

coalesce into one Vaudois barbe. Last, but not least, we will cite the name of a good Alpine pastor, who walked unseen through Old England, influenced her fortunes materially, without being once named in her history, and escaped all question or maltreatment; while the Oldcastles, Brutes, and Wickliffes, were called to an account—"Lollardo,* who was in great reputation among the evangelical churches of Piemont, by reason of a commentary he made upon the Revelation; as also for having conveyed the knowledge of their doctrine into England, where his disciples were known by the name of Lollards." Sir Samuel had previously delivered himself as follows :—" In England, they (the Vaudois) were known by the name of Lollards, from one Lollard, who was one of their chief instructors in that isle." Another catalogue, that of appellations bestowed on the Waldenses, is nearly as vile and absurd as that of the barbes; two samples of it shall satisfy us. The historian of the Vaudois, finding in the Imperial enumeration of sects the name Passagini, concerning which nothing more was at that time known, scrupled not to make the following assertion :—" Attendu† que comme pauvres passagers ils fuyoient d'un lieu en autre, ils (les Vaudois) ont été appellez Passagenes." But we are now well aware, from‡ ancient authority, that those people were a set of Judaists, practising circumcision, and keeping the Sabbath. The same author has said, "Quand ils soustenoyent que l'authorité des empereurs et rois de la terre ne depend point de l'authorité des Papes, ils les ont appellez§ Manicheens, comme constituans deux principes." And that statement relates to the charge of

---

* Morland, p. 185 ; Perrin, p. 66.

† Perrin, " Hist. Vaud.," p. 9.

‡ Bonacursus (Catharorum quondam Magister Mediolani) " de Vitâ Hæreticorum," in d'Achery, " Spicileg.," i., p. 212. It seems that in the " Const. Fred. II." we should read " Circumcisi Passagini," without any comma between those words.

§ Perrin, p. 10; Morland, p. 13.

dualism, constantly preferred against the Paulicians or Pata-
renes in all ages of their existence, from the ninth century to
the fourteenth, inclusive! If the former was a rash and un-
lucky guess, this is a shameless and wicked falsehood. It is
too evident that the affirmation of such critics and historians
is worth nothing towards establishing the date of documents
that are no longer to be seen.

The Memoir of Eminent Barbes furnishes some notices
of modern and, it may be supposed, substantially authentic
fact. "Daniel of Valenza,* and John of Molines. These two
were sent into Bohemia, to serve the Waldensian churches
that were gathered in that kingdom. But they betrayed the
churches, and wrought them much evil; for they discovered
to the enemies of the said Vaudois whatsoever they knew of
their flocks,—from whence arose a great persecution, which
occasioned the churches of Bohemia to write to the *Vaudois*†
churches of the Alps, never to employ again, in such voca-
tions, persons whose faith, probity, and zeal, were not known
by long experience." It is to be regretted that no date is annexed to this transaction, and that no copy of the alleged
Bohemian letters should be furnished. It is questionable‡

* Perrin, p. 67 ; Morland, p. 185.

† Morland cunningly substitutes *Evangelical.*

‡ The documents which the Vaudois emissaries to Bohemia translated
into Provençal, expressly state that their authors were not of the sect of
Pauperes or Waldenses, but "appella per fals nom falsament Pauvres o Valdès."—Perrin, l. ii., c. ix., p. 224 [and see p. 50, supra]. In Freher's "Script.
Rerum Bohem.," p. 238, is a document, headed " Professio Fidei Waldensium
ad Vladislaum Regem," beginning, " Nos homines depressi ;" and at p. 345, an
"Oratio Excusatoria Fratrum Waldensium." One or other of them is, perhaps,
the original of the " Epistola al serenissimo rey Lancelau," by the false Valdès.
They were the people called Picards, and, by themselves, Unitas Fratrum,
or, The Brethren : " quos per ignominiam adversarii Waldenses et Picardos
vocant. Ipsi sese . . . . Fratrum nomine appellant."—Esrom Rudiger " de
Eccl. Frat. Bohem. et Morav.," p. 6, ed. L. Camerarii. These "fratres" were
persons who separated themselves from the Taborites after 1457.—De Orig.
et Confess. Eccl. Bohem., p. 267, ibid. Casimir Oudin, under date of 1430,

whether there were any Waldensian churches in Bohemia,
though some of the sectaries who came out of the Hussites im-
properly and unwillingly received that appellation. But the
fame of the Bohemian disputes and religious wars penetrated
into the country of the Vaudois, and induced them to send
emissaries into that kingdom. As we find that a petition of
the Bohemian Pseudo-Waldenses to their king Ladislaus has
been translated into the patois of the Piedmontese valleys, and
inserted among their own documents, we may strongly pre-
sume that the two mischief-making barbes intruded themselves
into Bohemia during the reign of that sovereign. If so, the
transactions occurred after A. D. 1471, and before A. D. 1516.
Its character, avowedly discreditable, remains a mystery.
But the Bohemian document just alluded to affords reason to
conclude that the Waldenses had not as yet departed from their

has these words :—" Joannes Lukawitz natione Bohemus, professione Waldensis, ex illis qui in Bohemiâ Taboritæ dicebantur, quique simplici Fratrum
cognomine, contra alios Magistrorum appellatione tumentes, gloriabantur,
hâc quoque ætate inter Presbyteros Waldenses claruit." But, upon referring
to his "Confessio Taboritarum" (printed in Balthasaris Lydii "Waldensia,
id est conservatio Veræ Ecclesiæ, ex confessionibus cum Taboritarum, &c.,
tum Bohemorum," &c.), it will be seen that Lukawitz never says a word
about Waldensians, and uniformly terms himself and his people Taborites.
The other epithet exists merely in the title-page of Lydius's collection, and
is introduced there for motives which that title-page clearly betrays. Peter
of Pilichdorf enumerates the following countries as being entirely free from
Waldenses—viz., England, Flanders, Brabant, Gelders, Westphalia, Den-
mark, Sweden, Norway, and Prussia ; and Poland almost entirely. But he
adds, in Thuringia, Brandenburg, Bohemia, and Moravia, one thousand
heretic Waldenses have been converted within two years. And there are
hopes that more than one thousand will be reclaimed in Austria and
Hungary.—P. Pil., c. xv. As he was flourishing in 1444, and it is uncer-
tain to what time he lived, we cannot be sure that his Bohemian allusion is
not to the Picard Pseudo-Waldenses. In 1564, the Bohemians, "vulgarly
called Waldenses," sent an epistle to Sigismond, King of Poland, in which
they say that "*pious but deluded persons* take them to be Waldenses ; and
the vulgar revile them by the name of Picards."—De Orig. et Confess, etc.,
pp. 269–272. There were, however, they add, three hundred years ago or

ancient type when it was written; for its authors complain of
being falsely termed "Pavres o Valdés." And if Pauperes
was still a synonyme for the Waldenses, the latter would seem
not to have as yet essentially deviated from proper Waldism.
Similar conclusions may be drawn from the twenty-two articles* of heresy published against the Vaudois of the valley of
Fraissiniere in Dauphiné, in the winter of 1489, by Alberto
de' Capitanei, archdeacon of Cremona, and papal legate. Whoever has any acquaintance with the allegations preferred against
the sect by Alan of Lisle in the twelfth century, by Rainero
Sacconi, Stephen de Bourbon, and others, in the thirteenth,
and acknowledged by themselves in their depositions at Thoulouse in the early years of the fourteenth, whoever, in short,
knows what the poor of Lyons were, will recognise that the

more, some churches of Waldenses in Austria, near the Bohemian borders;
but they had never anything to do with them.—p. 272-3. One Stephen
(whom Perrin, p. 231, calls "Estienne homme ancien") is spoken of by him
and others as a Waldensian of Austria, and was burnt for heresy in 1468.
But since the Pseudo-Unitas-Fratrum, or Moravians of Count Zinzendorf,
represent him as a bishop, tracing his succession to the apostolic times, and
transmitting holy orders to them through the real Unitas Fratrum, we must
(if we believe them even so far as to suppose that Stephen had affected episcopacy) pronounce him and his people Pseudo-Waldenses of some sort. Besides, we have the intimation of his neighbours and contemporaries, the
Picards, that Austria had not contained real Waldenses for the three hundred years last past; and that, so far from deriving apostolic orders from them,
they had nothing to do with them at any time.—Consult [two papers on the
Episcopacy of the Herrnhuters or Moravians,] Brit. Mag., vii., pp. 499, 643.
The story in Thuanus and Dubravius about Waldo going from Lyons
to Picardy, and from Picardy to Bohemia, is a pure fable, built on no
other foundation than the word Picards. But that title was only a Bohemian
way of sounding the word Beghard, a title applied to the Fratres Liberi Spiritûs
(dangerous mystics, of whom the Bohemian Fratres were an offset), as well
as to the Beghardi et Beguinæ of the Franciscan order.—Mosheim, part ii.,
p. 637. If there were congregations of Waldenses in Bohemia, it is, at all
events, evident that the barbes failed of discovering them, since the only documents they produced were, *on the face of them*, belonging to a different sect.

* Morland, p. 216; Leger, part ii., p. 23.

articles of 1489 describe the original sect with scarcely the slightest degree of approximation* towards modern Protestantism.

The objects of the Legate de' Capitanei's censure identify themselves with the ancient sect. We can recognise in it their entire denial of the Church, and rejection of all its consecrated persons and places, coupled with their reception of Popery itself, provided it were adapted to the law of spiritual poverty, and separated from all temporal jurisdiction; their denial of the sacrament of sacerdotal confession, coupled with the enforcement of auricular confession, with penance, and absolution thereupon; their rejection of purgatory, and restriction of repentance and penance to this world; their entire prohibition of all oaths; and the charge against them of denying the validity of the sacraments as administered by the priests of the Roman Church, unaccompanied by any charge or suggestion of heresy in respect of the miracle of transubstantiation.

The applying the title of Babylon to the Church of Rome, as charged in the ninth article, was not an entirely new feature in Waldism, having been used from the middle of the thirteenth century by the sub-sect of Pauperes de Lombardiâ, whom the archdeacon of Cremona was particularly likely to have in his eye. The denial of the *validity* of sacerdotal sacraments, not merely of their *necessity* and *eligibility*, seems also to refer to the Babylonizing sub-sect in Lombardy. But even *their* doctrine of a Babylon Church was conformable to that of the Apostolics and Beguines, and had no congruity with the language of the Reformation. For in Article Four the legate charges them with holding that Sylvester had been *the last true*

---

* Not without error of a different sort. For the thirteenth charge imputes the same Gnostical orgies as were sometimes (by like error and prejudice) imputed to the Beguines.—See above ["Antichrist in the 13th century, No. viii.," p. 146-7, Brit. Mag., vol. xviii.]. But this document, in its prejudices, as well as in its correct statements, relates to the old heresies, without any traces of the New Learning.

pope; and in Article Nine, with holding that "the Roman Church *of the present time** *has become* the house of confusion, the Babylon, the great whore, the synagogue of Satan." And that was the language of the spiritualizing Romanists, who were disgusted with the actual condition of the papacy. Article Fifteen, that the Virgin and Saints are not to be invoked in prayer, is contained in the early statements of Stephanus de Borbone sive Bellevillâ. The reason for it ascribed to them by the Legate de' Capitanei, viz., that Mary and the saints are too far off, and cannot hear us, agrees well with the one given in Peter of Pilichdorf, that they are too much absorbed in the enjoyment of their own† beatitude to attend to us. But it is a reasoning vastly distinct from the language of the spurious "Invocation of Saints," and would have sounded most heterodox in the ears of its author.

It is therefore, upon the whole, sufficiently clear that the people in question continued to retain the characteristics of the Waldism of the middle ages, down to the close of the fifteenth century.

An entire new-modelling of religion in the churches of the west was attempted in the early years of the sixteenth century. At that time the community of the Waldenses was altered from its old model to one resembling that of the Calvinists. The change was effected with the rapidity and precipitation that belongs to all great revolutionary eras; for we find Vaudois documents, composed on the new principles, and written as early as A. D. 1524. In A. D. 1530 (the year of the Confession of Augsburgh), two barbes, Monsieur George Morel‡ of

---

* Cunning Morland translates it thus—" *The Church of Rome is* an house of confusion," &c.

† " Tantis impletos esse gaudiis, quòd nihil possint cogitare de his quæ in terris fiunt, et per consequens non esse invocandos a nobis."—c. 19, p. 282.

‡ Morland, p. 185 ; Perrin, p. 67. The latter is so loose and unsettled in his style, that he sometimes calls them Morel and Masson, and sometimes Maurel and Masçon. [See above, No. II., p. 8, *sq.*]

Fraissinieres, in Dauphiné, and Monsieur Pierre Masson of Bourgogne, "were sent into Germany to communicate upon religion with Bucer, Œcolampadius, and others. Pierre Masson was taken prisoner at Dijon." Some correspondence of Bucer and Œcolampadius with them* is in print. This year, 1530, may be regarded as a great epoch of change in the sect. To that time we may probably enough refer the composition (if compositions they be) of many of the works that have been fraudulently antedated. We are led to that observation by Perrin's own account of the famous *Confession of Faith*. The date of A. D. 1120 was not affixed *by him* to that document. That palpable falsehood was reserved for his successors. But his description of the document is given in these terms—"Extracted from the book entitled ' Spiritual Almanack,' and from the ' Memoires of George Morel.'" The book so (as above) entitled is a composition most indubitably modern; and the George Morel here mentioned is the very same person who went for doctrine to Bucer and Œcolampade. From this we can easily judge at about what time, and under what circumstances, the Protestant-Vaudois writings came into existence.

There is, however, one remark due in justice to those documents. They do not by any means appear to be forgeries. There does not appear to be a word in them that indicates the desire to personate other authors than their real ones, or to imitate another age, or affect another date, than their real one. They offer no more internal evidence of such an attempt than they do of antiquity, but seem to have been written, by whoever did write them, in simplicity of purpose. And when they are qualified as spurious, forged, or the like, we must only be understood to say that the ancient dates (such as 1100, 1120, and 1230) were afterthoughts and forgeries. The authors themselves had no more idea of those years in their minds than

* Perrin, " Hist. Vaudois," pp. 46, 7, 211-16 ; [and see the volume No. II. described above, p. 8, *sq.*]

of the Hegira or the æra of Dhulkarnein. The idea of setting up an apostolical succession of faith and testimony (not of
ministry), by the aid of an unfathomable and immemorial
Waldensianism, was not in their contemplation. This observation applies to so much of them as is printed. And there
exists no reason at present for thinking that any treatises were
composed for the purpose of deception.

Lately, in speaking of those compositions, we guarded ourselves by saying, " if compositions they be." For it is uncer-
tain whether a large proportion of them may not be translations,
executed by Morel and others, from German, or from the Latin
of German authors. One of the documents of the Vaudois,
though it has been absurdly spoken of as an original in the
Piémontese, is manifestly the translation of a Bohemian document. It is the Epistle* of the Taborites (Pseudo-Waldenses)
of that country to their king Ladislaus. And the translators
have made so free with that monarch's name, as to term him†
el serenissimo rey *Lancelau.* The declaration entitled *Causa
del nostre department de la Gleisa Romana* is another transla-
tion‡ made in Bohemia. Among the tractates falsely ascribed
by the Protestant-Vaudois to the Waldenses Proper, one at
least appears to be no composition of their own, but a version
of something written in the northern parts of the Continent.
For we read that " disorderly fastings§ are especially those
upon viands more rare, more precious, and delicate, such as
are beasts of the sea, *figs, dried grapes, almonds,* by which the
poor are despoiled, and the rich pampered, and alms subtracted;
whereas, if they fasted upon more light and common food,

---

* See Perrin " Hist.," p. 58.

† Not only Lancelau in Provençal, but Lanzilao in Italian, and Lancelot
in French, are used for translations of Ladislas. It is questionable whether
there exist any such name as Lancelot, otherwise than as French for Ladislas.

‡ So Monsieur Perrin's notice of it leads us to imply. [See above, pp. 47,
50.]

§ On Baptism, &c., ap. Morland, p. 177; and ap. Leger, part i., p. 69.

they could more lightly and easily minister to their families and the other poor." One may readily suppose that Smyrna figs, Malaga raisins, and sweet almonds, were not altogether so cheap and common in Saxony or the Marches of Brandenburgh, in the first half of the sixteenth century, as modern traffic has made them; and that even now there are many decent but humble families there who could not live upon them with that severe attention to economy into which the writer is disposed to resolve the principle of fasting. But it would seem strange to warn the people of Piedmont and Dauphiné, sitting beneath their own vines and their own fig-trees, against the use of figs and grapes, ay, and even of the spontaneous and scarcely cultured almond; and that, not as being an indulgence to the palate, but on the ground that their costliness operates as a wrong towards the poor. Some of the Vaudois valleys, indeed, are too high in the Alps for the vine to flourish; but most of them* are described as yielding wine and fruits in abundance.

Thus much has been said upon the subject of the prose class of writings attributed to the Poor of Lyons, and upon the demerits of those puritanical impostors who have endeavoured to deceive the world concerning them; not with the idea of throwing any important light upon a subject already understood, but chiefly as a prelude to the consideration of the rhythmical remains of the ancient Pauperes de Lugduno, which cannot be entirely separated from that of the above-mentioned chronological forgeries.

* See Jean Leger, "Hist. Generale," pp. 3-5.

PERRIN'S HISTORY OF THE VAUDOIS.*

As the author of the foregoing paper has (it is believed very justly) spoken of Perrin, as "perhaps the prime author of these deceptions and forgeries," the Editor is induced to add a few lines on the subject of Perrin's work. The circumstances of its concoction and publication are somewhat curious, and are probably unknown to most of those who read the popular accounts of the Vaudois, which quote Perrin, and his ignorant followers Leger and Morland, as authorities. Who is, and who is not responsible for any one particular statement or opinion contained in Perrin's book, it might be hard to say ; but as to the work generally, whether we maintain it to be a fair and sincere history, or a book of lies and forgeries, it is certain that we are not to consider it the offspring of a simple and solitary pasteur in Dauphiny, who believed whatever was told him, but as the work of the French Protestant Church, and a very curious work too.

Some who have been accustomed to consider Protestantism as a free and easy system of private judgment, encouraging men to think, and speak, and write just what they please,—and who have been shocked at the notion of inquisitions, indexes, censorships, and all the other stumbling-blocks which Romish tyranny has laid in the way of marching intellect,—may be sur-

* [British Magazine, vol. xviii. (Dec. 1840), p. 614. This paper is inserted here from its connexion with the foregoing and with the controversy respecting the authenticity of Waldensian history. It is from the pen of the Rev. S. R. Maitland, D. D., then Editor of the British Magazine. The remarkable facts which it establishes as to the authorship of Perrin's book are particularly interesting, when it is borne in mind that the MSS. now in the Library of Trinity College, Dublin are shown to have been in Perrin's possession, and to have been quoted as the authorities for his " History."]

prised to see how vigilant and arbitrary the Reformed Church of France was on this point. As early as their first National Synod, held at Paris in May, 1559, it was decreed :—

"Les ministres ni autres personnes de l'Eglise ne pourront faire imprimer aucun Livre composé par eux, ou par autrui touchant la religion, ni en publier sur d'autres matières, sans les communiquer à deux ou trois ministres de la parole, non suspects."[*]

This was pretty strict; but the Synod of Orleans, in April, 1562, went further :—

"Les Imprimeurs, Libraires, Peintres et en general tous les fideles, notamment tous ceux qui auront charge en l'Eglise, seront averti de ne faire aucun chose de leur art, office ou emploi, qui depende des superstitions de l'Eglise Romaine, ou qui les favorise. Et quant aux faits particuliers, et ensemble à correction qui y echerroit, ce sera au consistoire d'en juger."—*Ibid.*, p. 27, No. XX.

Still more directly did the Synod of Rochelle, in June, 1581, come to the point :—

"Les ministres et les fideles ne publieront à l'avenir aucuns de leurs écrits imprimés ou autrement sur les matieres de religion, de politique, de conseils ou autres choses de quelque importance, sans la permission expresse et l'approbation du Coloque de leur eglises."—*Ibid.*, p. 153, No. XLVIII.

By the time of the Synod of Montauban (that is, June, 1594), it had come to be thought necessary that the Church should not only prevent such books as it did not like from being published, but that it should get such books as it did like, written by men of the right sort :—

"On choisira dans chaque province des personnes propres pour répondre aux écrits des aversaires, sans néamoins ôter la liberté aux autres freres d'y emploier les dons et les talens que Dieu leur aura communiqués; le tout aux fraix de la Province, où ladite réponse sera faite. Et quant à ceux qui s'ingerent de faire imprimer des livres, sans avoir anparavant communiqués aux Coloques ou Synodes, suivant la discipline, ils seront grièvement censurés et leur écrits suprimés."—*Ibid.*, p. 178, No. I.

[*] Aymon, "Synodes Nationaux des Eglises Reformées de France," tom. i., p. 6, No. XXIX.

Authors, however, have always been rather a wilful race, and the press a difficult engine to manage; and in June, 1598, the Synod of Montpellier was obliged to decree :—

"Sur la plainte de diverses provinces touchant la licence que se donnent les imprimeurs de mettre toutes sortes de livres en lumiere, les ministres des églises où il y a imprimerie, sont averties de ne permettre pas qu' aucun livre soit imprimé, qu'il n'ait auparavant été examiné et aprouvé."—*Ibid.*, p. 219, No. XXVII.

These decrees of National Synods, and more, which might be quoted,* are sufficient to show how completely the French Protestant Church took the management of its literature into its own hands. We very justly consider the Church of Rome, with all her apparatus for correction or suppression, as responsible for those books of her members which she allows to circulate; and, in like manner, if there were nothing more specific to be produced, we might fairly assume that Perrin's book was, as a matter of course, examined and approved in the Coloque, or in the Provincial Synod, to which he belonged, and was at least so far published with the sanction of the Church. But there is, in fact, a great deal more ; and quite enough to show that this book about the Vaudois was a particularly laborious and deliberate act of the Church, represented not merely by Coloques, or Provincial Synods, but by one National Synod after another.

Perrin attended the National Synod held at Rochelle, in March and April, 1607, as one of the deputies for the province of Dauphiné ; and it seems that he had at that time made some progress in his history ; for it was then decreed—

"Monsieur Perrin est exhorté de continuer son travail pour achever la veritable Histoire des Albigeois et des Vaudois; et pour lui aider, tous ceux qui ont des Memoires, ou de leur Doctrine et Discipline, ou de leurs Persecutions, sont chargés de les lui envoier au plutôt que faire se pourra."—*Ibid.*, p. 313, No. XXXIV.

* As those of Alais in 1620. *Ibid.* ii., p. 151, No. XXI. ; of Charenton, 1623, ii., p. 278, No. XI. ; and Alençon, 1637, ii., p. 566, No. VIII.

It appears that, instead of attending the National Synod at Maixent, rather more than two years after (May and June, 1609), Perrin sent a letter, and the following decree was made :—

"Sur les Lettres du Sieur Perrin, accompagnées de celle de la Province du Dauphiné, par lesquelles ils font la deduction de ce que ledit Sr. Perrin a fait pour écrire l'Histoire des Albigeois, de laquelle il a marqué le dessein et le but dans sa lettre ; la Compagnie en étant contente, l'exhorte de continuer son travail, et pour lui aider à l'achever on a prié les sieurs Ferrier, Durand, Benoist, de Castelfranc et Vignier, de chercher tous les memoires qui'ils pourront trouver pour les lui envoier ; afin qu'il le publie au plutôt, et pour cet efet la Compagnie lui remboursera ses fraix, et le recompensera de ses peines."—Ibid., p. 361, No. VII.

One would, of course, like to know something about all the persons who were thus assigned to assist Perrin, and directed to act as purveyors of documents for his work; but should it appear that any one of them was a rogue, it may not be worth while to inquire much about the rest.   Now it is but too clear that such was the character of the first man on the list, M. Jeremie Ferrier, who makes a considerable figure in the history of these Synods.   At the Synod of Gap, in 1603, where he is described as "Professeur en Théologie à Nimes," he acted as "Ajoint" to the Moderator.*   He filled the same high office at the Synod of Maixent in 1609, at which this decree, appointing him to help Perrin, was made; but at that of Privas, in 1612, he comes under notice as the subject of heavy accusations :—

"Principalement pour avoir quitté l'eglise de Paris sans congé contre la promesse qu'il avoit faite de la servir, comme aussi pour avoir beaucoup negligé sa charge de Professeur en Theologie n'aiant pû l'exercer tandis qu'il a fait divers voiages en cour et aux assemblées politiques, contre l'ordonnance du Synode National de St. Maixent : n'aiant donné aucun ordre à personne de remplir sa charge pendant son absence.   Semblablement pour s'etre ingeré dans la recepte et le maniment des deniers academiques, dont il s'est trouvé avoir entre les mains plus qu'il de lui etoit dû, la somme de 3103 liv. 5. s. 6. d.   De meme pour avoir consenti à la publication des

* Ibid., i., 255.

lettres du Capitaine Gautier, qu'il devoit plûtôt suprimer que de s'en servir pour exciter des querelles qu'il n'a pû apaiser sans s'engager à deguiser plusieurs choses d'une façon mal seante a son ministere. Pour lesquelles causes et autres, il lui a été ordonné d'ecrire des lettres satisfactoires à ladite eglise de Paris, et de se vuider les mains de la susdite somme: et de plus, afin d'obvier a tous les ombrages, noises, et soupçons, on lui defend de se trouver dans les assemblées politiques et generales, durant l'espace de six ans, et en lui conservant l'honneur de son ministere, on ordonne qu'il l'exercera dans une autre province, telle qu'il sera jugé plus convenable de lui assigner, pour la gloire de Dieu, et l'edification de l'eglise."—*Ibid.*, 413, No. XVI.

He seems, however, to have been supported by a considerable party; for "Les Sieurs d'Aguillon et Barniers, du Corps des Magistrats de Nimes, avec Arnaud Guirand, Second Consul, Vestric Favier du Corps de la Maison de Ville, et les Sieurs Suffren et Chambrun, Pasteurs de l'Eglise du dit Nimes, Deputés par la Consistoire de la dite Eglise," appeared at the Synod to pray that they might be allowed to keep their minister.* They sought in vain; and the pasteurs Suffren and Chambrun were very near getting suspended for the part which they had taken in the business. However, to make the story short, the accused appears to have been contumacious; and, attached to the acts of the National Synod just mentioned, we find the "Excommunication et Deposition de Monsieur Jérémie Ferrier," by the Provincial Synod of Lower Languedoc, under the sanction of the Synod of Privas.† After reciting the various complaints that had been made, and

"Aiant donc dûement et pleinement été informés des mauvais comportemens dudit Ferrier, du mepris audacieux qu'il fait de la discipline, des propos injurieux et insolens qu'il a prononcés contre les Assemblées Ecclesiastiques, de son trop grand attachement à ce present siècle, du recours qu'il a eû à de mauvais et indignes moiens, des rebellions et desobeissances enormes, qu'il a commises contre le St. Ordre institué de Dieu, aiant aussi apparu qu'il a entierement abandonné le saint et sacré ministere, et qu'il a protesté avec serment qu'il y renonçoit;"—*Ibid.*, 462;

and having in vain given him an opportunity to express his

---

* *Ibid.*, p. 416.   † *Ibid.*, p. 461.

contrition, if he had had any, they proceeded to excommunicate him as " un Homme Scandaleux, Incorrigible, Impenitent, Indisciplinable." At the next Synod, which was held at Tonneins, in the year 1614, he is placed in that which forms one of the most curious appendages to the acts of these Synods, viz., the "Role des Ministres deposés et apostats."

"Au Bas Languedoc, Jeremie Ferrier, ci-devant Pasteur et Professeur daus l'Eglise et Universite de Nimes, personnage de haute stature, aiant les cheveux noirs et frisés, le teint olivâtre, les narines ouvertes, et les lèvres fort grosses, a été censuré plusieurs fois, et ensuite suspendu pour ses malversations et rebellions, aiant abandonné la sainte ministere, il fût excommunié de nos Églises le 14 de Juillet, 1613, desquelles il s'est entierement separé à l'âge d'environ 38 ans."—*Ibid.*, tom. II., p. 49.

Such was one of the persons appointed by the Synod of St. Maixent, in 1609, to help Perrin, and to get documents for him. In pursuing his personal history we have outstripped that of the work which it is our principal business to follow. We must therefore go back five years (to 1609), when Ferrier and the other assistants were appointed by the Synod of Maixent. It will be remembered that two years *before* that, Perrin had made some progress in his History ; and we shall find that three years *after*, at the Synod of Privas (the same which censured Ferrier), Perrin made his appearance, and presented his book. The five colleagues before appointed to him may be supposed to have done their best, or their worst, and the work was now to be further reviewed by another set :—

" Le Sieur Perrin, aiant aussi présenté son livre de l'Histoire des Albigeois et Vaudois, son dit Écrit a été mis entre les mains de Mrs. les pasteurs Roussel, de Cuville, de Beau, Petit et Joli, Pasteurs, afin qu'ils en fassent leur raport devant cette compagnie, laquelle a donné pour les Fraix faits par ledit Sr. Perrin, la Somme de trois cens Livres."—*Ibid.*, tom. i., p. 404, No. III.

At the same time the Synod issued this further direction :—

" Le Sieur Perrin, sur le Raport qu'on a entendu de ceux qui ont vû son Travail sur l'Histoire des Albigeois, est exhorté, suivant l'Avis des Commissaires, d'en faire une Révision, et de le présenter ensuite, au Synode du Dauphiné, afin que le voiant limé suivant l'Intention de cette Compagnie, il puisse être mis en Lumière."—*Ibid.*, p. 429, No. X.

After *two years more*, during which we may suppose that the new commissioners were employed in the limation of the work committed to them, the National Synod of Tonneins (May and June, 1614), issued the following decree :—

" Le Synode de Dauphiné est chargé de voir l'Histoire des Vaudois et Albigeois, recueillie et dressée par le Sieur Perrin, qui est chargé d'en envoier un Exemplaire à chaque Province d'abord qu'elle sera imprimée."—*Ibid.*, tom. II., p. 11, No. VI.

All this the reader may think very leisurely proceeding ; but in such matters it is best not to be in a hurry; and therefore *after three years more*, at the Synod of Vitré, held in May and June, 1617, the said commissioners reported as follows :—

" Les Deputés de la Province du Dauphiné, ont fait entendre à la Compagnie que leur Synode a examiné l'Histoire des Vaudois et Albigeois, recuellie par le Sr. Perrin, mais qu'elle n'a pas été imprimée et distribuée selon l'Ordre qui en avoit été donné audit Sieur Perrin, par la Synode National de Tonneins ; On a ordonné que ladite Histoire sera envoiée à Messieurs les Pasteurs et Professeurs de l'Église et Université de Geneve, qui seront priés par le Synode du Dauphiné de la voir.   Et quant à la demande faite au nom dudit Sr. Perrin, de quelques deniers pour l'impression de son livre : la compagnie y aura égard lorsqu'on fera la distribution des deniers provenans de la Liberalité du Roi.   Cependant il est enjoint à la province du Dauphiné, de procurer l'Impression dudit livre, sans attendre la Gratification qu'on doit faire audit Sr. Perrin, outre ce qui lui a été donné par le Synode National de Privas."—*Ibid.*, p. 87, No. IV.

After all this one really might suppose that the work was in the press, and would be speedily published; but still one cannot be too careful to avoid the evils of precipitate publication. On the other hand, however, there is a possibility that a manuscript may be worn to rags, and surely this one must have had a very narrow escape, for it is not until more than three years again, after this report, that we find the Sr. Perrin at the Synod of Alais, informing that assembly, not only that his book was actually printed, but that he had it in contemplation (encouraged perhaps by the ease and rapidity with which he had knocked ·off a small portion), to write an Universal History of the Church, from the creation of the world to the time present—a matter which the Synod somewhat quaintly referred back to his own prudence and conscience. But their article must be given :—.

" Le Sieur Jean Paul Perrin, Pasteur de l'Église de Nions en Dauphiné, s'etant présenté devant cette compagnie, pour lui rendre compte de l'Impression de l'Histoire des Vaudois et Albigeois, et aiant declaré qu'il est maintenant occupé à écrire l'Histoire Universelle de l'Eglise qu'il suivra depuis le commencement du monde jusqu' à present; La Compagnie l'aiant loüé de ce qu'il entrepend un si grand ouvrage, et remercié de la peine qu'il a prise de mettre en Lumière ladite Histoire des Vaudois, remet à sa prudence et conscience à juger du fruit que l'Église peut tirer de ses autres écrits, sans lui en préscrire aucun necessité. Et sur ce que ledit Sieur Perrin a représenté qu'il est chargé d'un grand nombre d'enfans, et qu'il suplie la Compagnie de donner au moins quelque Subvention à l'un de ses Fils, lequel aiant été debauché par les Jesuites, et s'etant ensuite converti, donne maintenant une grande Espérance de pouvoir servir utilement l'Eglise de Dieu : la province du Dauphiné est exhortée d'y avoir egard selon la Charité, et selon le Mérite dudite Sr. Perrin."—Ibid., p. 185.

Thus the work was reported as actually printed at the synod held between October and December, 1620. It has been already stated, that some progress had been made in its composition as early as the year 1607. It is certainly very ridiculous to see such a mountain, or rather such a chain of mountains, labouring for a dozen years to bring forth such a mouse as Perrin's little book; but, strange as all this is, there is something in the synodical history of this work which is still more strange. We have seen how this Synod of Alais took the matter of its publication; and who would expect to find the very next national synod (that of Charenton, in 1623), without the least reference to Perrin or his book, requesting another person to undertake a history of the Albigenses, just as if not a word had ever been said on the subject? Yet it is, in fact, with special reference to the decree of the Synod of Alais, already quoted, and as a remark upon it, that the Synod of Charenton decrees:—

" Sur le Canon qui regarde la composition de l'Histoire des Albigeois, cette Assemblée étant bien informée de l'Érudition et de la Capacité du Sieur Tilloit, Pasteur dans l'Église de Sedan, décréta qu'il seroit prié d'écrire ladite Histoire, et on exhorta les Provinces de lui envoier tous les Mémoires qu'elles avoient sur ce Sujet."—*Ibid.*, p. 248.

What this could mean, except that some circumstances or other had led them to distrust Perrin, and repudiate his book, it seems hard to say. If anybody can put a more charitable construction on it, let him do so ; but let him also bear in mind, that the very next Synod (that of Castres in 1626,) issued the following order :—

"On ordonna de suprimer tous les Écrits qui avoient été délivrés par Monsieur Perrin, pasteur de l'Église de Nions, et par Monsieur de Mirabel, décédé, à la Province de Bourgogne, et que les Députés de ladite Province avoient ensuite délivrés à ce Synode."—*Ibid.*, p. 351, No. VIII.

The exact meaning of all these orders, issued at various times during a period of nearly twenty years, it may not be possible fully to explain. From the foregoing sketch, however, it seems plain that, though in the spirit of poetry, and, perhaps, of misguided affection, M. Gamon might prefix verses to his friend Perrin's book, addressing him as—

" Grand Thésorier de mémoire,
Trompette de la vérité,
Qui par le clairon de l'Histoire
Fais résonner l'antiquité,"

and might thus claim for him the undivided honour of the work, yet we must not allow the muse of the said "Christophle Gamon, Ancien de l'Église d'Annonay" to bewitch us into a belief of any such thing ; many others must share the credit, or the discredit, of the work. If it has falsehoods and forgeries, they are not to be ascribed to haste of composition, or want of books, or of opportunity for inquiring as to the genuineness of manuscripts, or to be accounted for as the mistakes of a simple and incompetent individual. Yet it is to the facts connected with this book that we must look for an explanation of a great part of the mystery which hangs over the rhodomontade that is popularly called the history of the Vaudois.

[After the foregoing paper had been in type, I was reminded by Dr. Maitland, to whom I had sent a proof sheet, that he had reprinted it eleven years ago in his "Eight Essays on various Subjects," *Lond.* (Rivingtons), 1852. Had I recollected this circumstance, I should probably have contented myself with referring the reader to that work; but as the article was actually in type, and especially as it has so close a connexion with the subject of this volume, and with the paper that precedes, "On the Poems of the Poor of Lyons," I have allowed it to stand in its original form, with only a few verbal corrections which Dr. Maitland had himself introduced into his second edition of it. I have not thought it necessary to annex the note on the history of *Esaie Ferrier*, which Dr. Maitland has added, in the "Eight Essays," p. 195, as the 'curious reader' can consult that volume for himself; his trouble will certainly be repaid, especially if he carries back his eye to Essay VI., on "The Waldenses and Albigeuses," which will be found to put the historical question in a very clear light.]

DATE OF THE NOBLE LESSON.

[THE following extract having been more than once referred to in the preceding pages,* is here inserted from one of the papers entitled "Antichrist in
the Thirteenth Century" (Brit. Mag., vol. xvi., pp. 605-610). Its object is
to show that the doctrine of Antichrist, and of the near approach of the last
times, contained in the poem called "Nobla Leyczon," is taken from the
prophetical speculations of the Abbot Joachim, and consequently that the
poem must be later than the first ten years of the thirteenth century, during
which period Joachim's principal writings became known.]

Among those who believed in the prophesying of Joachimus
Abbas, and consequently lived in fear and hopes of an approaching end, we must number the schismatical sect called
the Waldenses. One of the most ancient and interesting
monuments of that sect is the Provençal poem entitled "La
Nobla Leyczon," or, "The Noble Lesson." In it they declare
that the last time is at hand, and that from thenceforth they.
must devote themselves wholly to following and pleasing
Christ, and watching diligently for the day of Antichrist's
coming.

This declaration immediately raises our desire to know the
date of the poem; and it is given in these words,

"Ben ha mil e cent ancz compli entierament;"

that is to say, eleven hundred years are now entirely complete.
Upon this ground it has been generally supposed that the
"Nobla Leyczon" was written presently after the year 1100.†
The contrary may, however, be proved.

The sect in question were condemned by the Church, and
brought as offenders before its tribunals, under the name of

[* See pp. 95, 97.]
† "La date de l'an 1000 qu'on lit dans ce poeme merite toute confiance."
—Raynouard, "Choix de Poesies," tom. ii., p. cxlii.

Waldenses, which they received from a certain Waldus or
Waldo, at no earlier time than the middle of the twelfth century. Some have supposed that their society was of a much
earlier date, and called Vallenses, from occupying certain valleys of the Alps; but that their later appellation of Waldenses
was invidiously preferred by their adversaries, as giving to
them the appearance both of recent and heretical origin. If
that be a fact, it will appear, like other facts, from its evidences; but we have nothing to do with it at present, one
way or the other; we are merely concerned with the date of
this particular poem. It contains the following passage :—

> " Que non volha maudire, ni jurar, ni mentir,
> Ni avoutrar, ni aucir, ni penre de l'autruy,
> Ni venjar se de li seo enemis,
> Ilh dion qu'es Vaudes e degne de punir
> E li troban cayson en meczonja e engan."*

The question whether this poem was composed at the very
outset of the twelfth century, or at least half a century later,
resolves itself into the question—whether the singular noun
substantive Vaudes stands for Waldensis, or not. No impartial philologist will hesitate to answer that in the affirmative.
In the Provençal language, the Latin *vallis* was expressed *val*,
plural *val;* or in the oblique cases, *vals;* or it was expressed
vau, as Vaucluse, Vallis Clausa—plural, *vaus.* There exists
neither authority, nor analogy, nor rule, by recourse to which
such a word as *vaudes* can be derived from *vallis.* The *Vaudes*
of the Occitanic or South-Romance dialect, was *Vaudois* in the
North-Romance or Lingua D'Oui, now called French. But
the name of Vaudois is not confined to the sect called in Provençal Vaudes; it is that of the inhabitants of the Pays de

---

* " Qui nonvult maledicere, jurare, aut mentiri,
   Stuprare, occidere, aut surripere de alieno,
   Aut ultionem petere de suis inimicis,
   Dicunt quòd Waldensis est et dignus qui puniatur
   Et occasionem illi parant mendacio et fraude."—vss. 369-73.

Vaud, in Switzerland ; and that country was called,* in Latin,
as early as the tenth century, Pagus et Comitatus *Waldensis*.
In the German dialects it is called der Wadt, der Graffschaft
Wadt, and die Waadt, or Waat.† This name is the same as
Wald in high Dutch, meaning the forest or woodlands ; and
Müller,‡ in speaking of the capital town, says—"Lausonium
in *der Wald* an der Lemanischen See;" that is, Lausanne in
the Forest by the Lake of Geneva.   There was really such a
people as the Vallenses; they are so called in the "Notitia
Imperii,"§ and they inhabited Sedunum, or Sion, in the
Graian Alps : but their country is called in French, Le Valais ;
in modern Latin, Vallesia, or Valesia;‖ and in German, Wallis,
Landwallis, or Wallisserland.   Now, will any one believe that
the combined names, Waldensis and Vaudois, in geography
have one etymology, and in history have another?   It is ex-
ceedingly palpable that the author of the "Noble Lesson"
complains of his brethren being handed over to punishment
under the opprobrious name (as Catholics esteemed it) of
Waldenses.   Consequently, we are arrived at the conclusion
that this work is either a forgery by virtue of its date, or that
the words in question have a very different meaning from that
which is usually assigned to them.

We should be loth to adopt the former conclusion. The work
is covered with the down of genuine and sincere antiquity ; and
is either no forgery or a most masterly one.   Considered with

---

* See Müller, "Geschichten Schweizerischer Eidgenossenschaft," i., p. 255.

† Müller, ibid., and p. 473; Busching Geographie, xiv., p. 140.

‡ Tom. i., p. 117.

§ Cit. Ferrarius ed. Baudrand.   The "Notitia" was composed after the
Hunns had conquered Illyricum, and before they destroyed Concordia ; that
is, between A. D. 445 and 453.

‖ We read in Reinerius, "contra Waldenses," c. 7, "Bibl. Max. Patrum
Lugdun.," tom. 25, p. 272, that "Valesii seipsos et hospites suos castrant."
Whether the fanatics he alludes to were in the Valais, or in the Duchy of
Valois in Picardy, cannot be determined from his words.

respect to the times of the Waldenses, it is difficult to conceive the motive for any one of them producing this simple effusion under a false date. And if we consider it in reference to the times following the Reformation, when the Calvinists made themselves busy about this ancient sect, we may see at a glance that it proceeds from no such workshop. It contains nothing inconsistent with the historical character of Waldism, or in any way favourable to its ideal portrait as drawn by Protestant hands. Among Christian duties it enumerates—

> " Purement se confessar senza alcun manca,*
> E qu'il faczan penitencia en la vita present,
> De junar, far almonas, et aurar au cor bulhent,
> Car pur aquestas cosas troba l'anma salvament."

The distinction between mortal and venial sin is more than once alluded to. No clergyman hath power (saith the Lesson) to pardon a mortal sin, for that belongs to God alone; and no pope† has had that power—*since pope Silvester !* It is in fact a document for the Calvinists to make the best they can of, since it is extant, but not one that they could ever have desired to forge.

Closer examination will show that the date of this poem has been misunderstood, and that the vulgar acceptation of it would involve us in difficulties altogether insurmountable. The "Noble Lesson" says—

> " Ben ha mil e cent ancz compli entierament,
> *Que fo scripta l'ora*, car sen al derier temp ;"

---

* Verses 419-20. Concerning Waldensian auricular confession, see above [Brit. Mag., vol. xvi.], p. 267.

> " Fideliter confiteri sine ullâ negligentiâ,
> Et facere pœnitentiam in vitâ præsenti,
> Jejunare, dare eleemosynam, et orare cum corde ferventi,
> Nam propter has res anima invenit salutem."

This was rather a stiff morsel for the Church of Geneva to swallow.

† See verses 409-12.

K

and it further observes, that from thenceforth it must be their
sole study to follow Christ, and to do his good pleasure, and
to be well advised of the time when Antichrist should come.*
Therefore its chronology, if the whole of it be taken together,
not only states the eleventh century to be just completed, but
it affirms the year 1100 to be the hour *written*, or *foretold in
Scripture*, as the time of the end, and that of Antichrist's imminent approach.   But there is no passage of Scripture that
can be employed, or that ever was employed, to show that a
consummation should happen either at the outset or even in
the course of the twelfth century.   The smallest of the prophetic numbers, and consequently the earliest date, if we think
fit to turn those numbers to chronological uses, is the celebrated 1260.   That number was actually applied to such
uses, and with serious effect, while the old Waldensian sect was
in activity; and no other number (that we know of) was so
employed.   Therefore, since they themselves tell us expressly
that they were not merely guided by the moral signs of the
times and the gathering of clouds overhead

("Tot jorn veyen las ensegnes venir a compliment"), .

but by the word of Scripture pointing out the time numeri-
cally, it becomes morally certain that they spoke with reference
to the completion of the twelfth, not of the eleventh century,
and to the approach of the great and fatal years 1256 and
1260.   The whole of a century is governed by the year of its
commencement, and each of its successive years bears the name
of that year prefixed to its own units or decads.   Eleven hundred ninety-eight, eleven hundred ninety-nine—it was still
eleven hundred.   But as soon as the clock struck twelve on
the night of the 31st of December, 1199, those who were

* " Autra ley d'ayci enant non deven plus aver,
   Sinon en segre Yeshu Xrist e far lo seo bon placer,
   E gardar fermament czo qu'el a comanda,
   E esrer mot avisa cant venre l'Antexrist "—vas. 454-7.

watching the flight of time could exclaim, now we have entirely done with the year 1100 (that denomination of time is "entierament compli"), and we have opened a new score with the year 1200. That is the meaning of the verse in the "Noble Lesson;" and it was composed in an early year of the thirteenth century.

Oliver Cromwell, being friendly to the distant Presbyterians of Piedmont, did not send Colonel Pride to purge them, but despatched a more sleek and civil messenger to inquire into their divinity, ecclesiastical history, and ancient documents. One Samuel Morland, an ingenious mechanician and inventor of hydraulic engines, was selected as the fittest man to pump them. He brought home and published some Waldensian MSS., all said by him to exhibit the date of A. D. 1120. One of them was entitled "Qual cosa sia Antichrist?" another "Purgatori* Soima;" two more, upon "Invocation of Saints," and "On Sacraments;" and another (not printed by him), "Causa del nostre departiment de la Gleisa Romana;" and, the most important, the "Confession of Faith in Fourteen Articles." They appear to be forgeries of but moderate skill and ingenuity. As regards the first of them, which was headed "What *thing* may Antichrist be?" (thus setting aside the idea of his personality), the authors of the document seem to have forgotten that Antexrist and Xrist† were the words [? manner of writing] used in the ancient Provençal of the Waldenses. These productions set forth the‡ remote date of 1120, being some forty years before Waldenses existed by that name. We are now furnished with a clue to all this. That interesting monument of ancient days, the "Noble Lesson," seemed to the cursory observer to present the date of

---

* Somnium Purgatorii. See Morland, "Evangelical Churches," pp. 9, 80, 142.

† So, in the same tongue, Xtofle for Christopher.

‡ It seems to be implied that the "Causa del nostre," &c. was decorated with the same date as the others; but it is immaterial.

1100. They really believed that Waldensian records ascended to that year; and so they thought they were doing the thing with discretion and modesty by assuming the near, but subsequent, date of 1120. Examination of the case proves that 1200, or a trifle more, is the date really belonging to the "Lesson." Therefore, future editors of Morland should say in the errata, "for 1120 read 1220."

The doctrine of Antichrist in the "Noble Lesson" in itself suffices to explode the incredible confession published in Morland. In that production (art. ix.) the word Antichrist is employed to denote simply and generally the Church of Rome, according to the conventional phraseology of puritanism. Purgatory, it says, is a fiction invented by Antichrist. The "Qual Cosa," &c., is a laboured expansion of the same idea; its Antichrist is merely the papal authority and church in general. And this is offered us for the language of A. D. 1120. Yet the "Lesson" informs us that in 1100 (to take the date even as the forgers understood it), when the Church of Rome was old, and its dogmas established, Antichrist was still looked for and to come, a formidable power, undefined, but *necessarily* distinct from the papacy. The doctrine of the ancient Vaudes of the year 1200 was one based upon the old catholic doctrine of Antichrist, and adapted in some of its details to the scheme of prophecy of which Joachim of Curacio was the original and sole contriver.

To hold that the twelve hundred and sixty days of prophecy were significant of that same number of years, computed from the nativity of our Saviour, was, *pro tanto*, to be a Joachite. For no man ever propounded such a doctrine* before Joachim; and no one seems to have adopted it after him, except those

---

* Nay, it is not too much to say that the idea of their being *any* "scripta ora" or predicted chronological epoch *whatsoever* originated with him; and that the allusion to such a prophetic epoch is in itself strong internal evidence of a date subsequent to that of his "Liber Concordiæ."

who gave credit to his pretensions. But the "Noble Lesson" is yet more Joachitic than that amounts to; for it says that *the entire completion of the eleven hundred*, that is to say, the year 1200, is the scriptural hour. Now it is indisputably false that Scripture names any such time or number. But, taking the Abbé Joachim's interpretation of the forty-two months as so many generations of thirty years, and adopting as an authoritative construction of prophecy his doctrine of the sixty years, or two generations of transition, the year 1200 was the "scripta ora" at which the latter tribulations were to begin, and when the rise of the Patarene Bestia with ten horns, or mixt and mystic Antichrist, was to be looked for. It seems to result from this examination that the Waldenses of his day, and subsequent to it, believed in the predictions of the Calabrian, and were confirmed by them in their rejection of the orders and discipline of the episcopal church.

One word more upon this head. The schemes of Joachim aimed at an entire subversion of the secular church, in order to replace it by a remodelled pontificate of unlimited power, to be exercised by the Angelic popes in the third "status mundi" and reign of the Holy Ghost. Let us see whether Waldism, as it appears in its genuine and antique remnants, is much at variance with this. It seems to have set as little store by priest or bishop as he did. But how, as to popes? Popes, down to Silvester inclusive, had the power of pardoning mortal sins; not the privilege of declaring or pronouncing valid absolution conditionally, but that very power of pardoning which is inherent in God himself. Down to Silvester, there were Angelic popes, or something very similar. And if so, why might there not, as the new light spread itself and the transition years advanced into the third status, be a renewed series of Angelic popes? But, again, why Silvester, of all men? and what made *him* the last of the popes who could bind and loose all things in heaven and earth? He was the last bishop of Rome who was independent of the imperial power; for it was he that received the Emperor Constantine into the church, and placed the church under his protection. Therefore her connexion with the Joachitic Babylon seems to have been the event which deprived the Joachitic Jerusalem of her spiritual efficacy. The Protestant theory, or that of independence upon Rome, was not that which the sect desired; but a pure popery, unalloyed with any admixture of the power civil and imperial. These reasons exist for thinking that they followed the Abbot of Flore (who seems never to name or allude to them) further than the mere adoption of his prophetic chronology. Complete rejection of the episcopal priesthood, coupled with inordinate reverence for the papal office *in its state of perfection,* forms a notable coincidence. That they did not share his zeal and affection for the papacy in its actual state may readily be admitted.

ON THE POEMS OF THE POOR OF LYONS.

No. II.*

THE religious poems that have come down to our age from the Poor Men of Lyons are these seven: "The Noble Lesson," "The Bark or Boat," "The New Discourse," "The New Comfort," "The Eternal Father," "The Contempt of the World," and "The Gospel of the Four Seeds." The first of these, in 479 verses, has twice been printed entire; and it seems to furnish the most important share of information concerning the character and tenets of the sect, although it is inferior to some of the others in poetical spirit. Of the six remaining poems, the reading world possess no more than what Monsieur Raynouard has extracted, by way of specimen, in his "Choix des Poésies Originales des Troubadours," printed at Paris, in 1817. And the imperfect form in which he has given them, however it might be suited to *his* immediate purpose, is much to be regretted by us; the more so, because his object was merely philological illustration, without reference to religion or its history; and, consequently, the portions omitted by him as tedious or unpoetical may have been precisely those that were best adapted to *our* purpose.

Two manuscripts of the "Noble Lesson" exist; and three are spoken of :—I. The first was in Morland's volume B., among the MSS. received by him from the Messieurs Leger, and deposited at Cambridge, in August, 1658. It was "in parchment, and that in a very ancient but excellent character." The volume is said to have contained in all twenty-six pieces, under nineteen heads or divisions. But the whole of these

* [From the British Magazine, vol. xix. (Jan. 1841), p. 11.]

documents have been, in some unexplained manner, spirited away, ἀκλειῶς ἅρπυιαι ἀνηρείψαντο. II. The second was deposited by Jean Leger* in the library of Geneva, on the 10th of November, 1662, and is esteemed by the present librarian to be of the twelfth century. It is on parchment, in ancient Gothic characters, and remains to this day where he placed it.† III. The third is a copy written on paper, and preserved among Ussher's MSS. in Trinity College, at Dublin. It is considered to be in the same handwriting as the book which bears date 1524 [see p. 43, *supra*]; and therefore may be either of that date, or of any other within the lifetime of the same amanuensis. It is probably a mere transcript from the older parchment text, and void of all authority and value; but if carefully examined, it might illustrate the progress of knavery and falsification. Where the old text has "cant venre l'Antexrist"—i. e. "when Antichrist shall come" (declaring his futurity), this paper copy exhibits "el temp de l'Antexrist"—i. e. "the time of Antichrist" (leaving his presence or futurity ambiguous); whereas Jean Leger, departing from all the three texts, and in fact perpetrating a downright forgery, prints‡ it "a fuire l'Antexrist"—i. e. "to shun or avoid Antichrist," which almost implies his presence. Where the old text rejects all the popes "subsequent to Sylvester," the transcript expunges

* "Hist Generale," etc., part i., p. 23, 4.

† Monsieur Raynouard errs in representing that the Geneva library obtained from Leger any other Vaudois MSS. besides the book in question. Monsieur Gerard, the librarian, in his receipt given to Leger, most expressly states that this book, No. 1, was in the Vaudois dialect; and all the other loose MSS. contained in the *liasse*, or bundle No. 2, were Italian and French. But those words of the receipt which so state it are omitted in* Raynouard's quotation, and their place supplied by the abbreviation *etc.*

‡ Part i., p. 30. The same author has omitted all the lines from verse 66 to 286; and again all those from verse 413 to 455; without any intimation to his readers either in words or by mode of printing, that he was not presenting a continuous passage. Whoever examines the poem will see the motives of this artifice.

those words, and so makes it an absolute rejection of all popery. The character of such a copy cannot be misunderstood.

Morland's volume, B. (by his account), also contained the other poems, with the exception of "Contempt of the World" and "The Four Seeds," whereof he has made no mention. The Geneva codex contains them all; and so does the paper copy at Dublin.

But there is strong ground for suspecting that no more than one genuine and original text exists; and that the Cambridge and Geneva MSS. are indeed one and the same. Volume B., a volume so curious and valuable that only Saracens or Vandals would burn it, has vanished; and it must (probably) be existing somewhere. The truth of the matter (so far as it may be surmised from circumstances, and from the behaviour of a deceitful person), appears to be, that Monsieur Leger gave the book to Morland between the years 1655 and 1658 inclusive; that Morland placed it in Cambridge Library in 1658, while the Protector was dying; took it out again before the king's restoration, and gave it back to Leger; and that Leger placed it in Geneva Library in 1662.

When a man of credit, and employed by the state, prints a statement that he has at a certain time lodged certain documents in a given public library, we do not usually consider ourselves possessed of evidence in favour of that fact, but as simply possessed of the fact itself.* But Monsieur Leger, in

---

* [The remark is perfectly just; and as it regards the argument, very important; but I lay hold of the words "a man of credit" as a peg on which to hang a few remarks on the credit which is really due to Morland. The reckless manner in which some writers have quoted him, as well as Perrin and Leger, as if they were first-rate authorities, absolutely requires that the truth on this point should be brought forward and borne in mind. We may reasonably, as well as charitably, hope that in a wretched old age, embittered by poverty, blindness, and a bad wife, when, supported on the alms of an archbishop, he used to play "himself psalms and religious hymns on the

1669, speaks in another tone:—"That all the above-named originals (he says) were delivered to the said Sieur Morland, and by him deposited in the famous library of Cambridge, *we do not need any more solemn voucher or proof* than the declaration of it which he inserts with the list of them, prefixt to his history, printed in London in 1658." No living soul *could*

theorbo," he was a better man than when he was one of Mr. Secretary Thurloe's tools, and according to his own account betrayed his employers. It was his boast and his ground of claim that, when employed in a confidential station by Cromwell, he had given private information to the king. That such a man, when he was sent out to get up a history of the Vaudois, would stick at trifles, is not to be imagined. It was all right to take what he could get in the way of documents, while the Protector was protector, and as right to throw them overboard when the king was, or was like to be, king. He seems to have been a vain weak man, with some talent for mechanics, but as to his politics, with some spice of craft and knavery, very little better than

"——————————that tool
That knaves do work with, called a fool."

For though he did perhaps receive as much from the king as his services deserved, especially in a gold medal from his own royal hands, yet, if not the king, some of the king's party, had filled his head with such extravagant conceits, that he ran through what he did get in keeping up a style fit to receive what he expected. They had promised him the garter, and advised him by all means not to ask the king for anything whatever, for he meant out of his own royal generosity to do something for him, far beyond anything that he could imagine; and they so wrought on his wife, that she fell down on her knees before him in the garden, and begged him of all love to swear that he would not ask for anything, for she had good assurance that she was going to be made a duchess. This is stated on the authority of his own autograph letters. Some interesting information respecting his mechanical as well as political proceedings, may be found in "A Brief Account of the Life, Writings, and Inventions of Sir Samuel Morland," published by Johnson at Cambridge, and Whittaker, London, and supposed to be from the pen of Mr. Halliwell. By the way, did the author of this paper ever give attention to the preface to Morland's work on the Vaudois? It seems impossible that he could have written it himself; and if he did not, one would like to know who did.—ED. OF BRIT. MAG.]

have then disputed the veracity of Morland. For if the disappearance of the MSS. had been discovered, Leger could not have spoken thus on the subject, in this as well as other passages; and if it had not, there was nothing in the declaration of Morland to move any scepticism. But this is the language of a conscious man, well knowing that their deposit at Cambridge had been transitory, and that they were not there at the moment when he was writing. By disclaiming the need of further vouchers and proofs, he reminds us to examine the transaction narrowly. Thus do the guilty very often betray themselves; for unaccused innocence never professes to be innocent.

If the book remained at Cambridge but a few months or weeks, some people must have seen it, and would bear in mind its general appearance. When a black duck with a white neck dives under water, and some yards off there comes up a black duck with a white neck, it is naturally supposed to be the same duck. And the like conjecture would arise if a manuscript vanished mysteriously from one library, and shortly afterwards an exactly similar one made its appearance in another library. Let us observe how honest Jean Leger handles this rather ticklish topic :—" Extrait d'un Traité intitulé la Noble Leiçon datté de l'an 1100, qui se trouve tout entier en *un livre* de parchemin ecrit a la main, en vielle lettre Gothique, *dont se sont trouvés deux exemplaires*, l'un desquels se conserve a Cambridge et l'autre en la Bibliotheque de Geneve." Of poems and other works copies are made; and each copy must be written on vellum, paper, or some particular substance, and in some particular character. But here the work itself, and the copies made of it, are strangely mixed up together. The words might signify that there was (in some unnamed place) one parchment and black-letter original, from which two copies (of unnamed materials and character) had been made, and sent to Cambridge and Geneva; if indeed they have any proper and grammatical meaning, it is that.

But Monsieur Leger's intention was, to insinuate that he had found two twin-sister manuscripts of the same poems, equal in age, and similar in all things, and had sent one to England and the other to Geneva. The improbability of such a circumstance, the questions it was not unlikely to call forth, and the monitions of conscience, deterred him from saying it out plainly and grammatically, and caused him to stammer it forth in such prevaricating phrase.

$$\Theta\epsilon\lambda\omega \; \tau\acute{\iota} \; \tau' \; \epsilon\acute{\iota}\pi\epsilon\hat{\iota}\nu, \; \dot{a}\lambda\lambda\acute{a} \; \mu\epsilon \; \kappa\omega\lambda\acute{\nu}\epsilon\iota$$
$$'A\iota\delta\acute{\omega}\varsigma.$$

If the above-cited words are ambiguous and suspicious in themselves, they become still more so when we consider how they are employed by him. They introduce a long garbled extract of the "Noble Lesson," occupying four pages. He had previously informed* us that it, and all his other specimens, were taken from original MSS. But, *in point of fact*, he has copied the text, as in Morland's previously printed edition (to the existence of which he makes no allusion), with some alterations out of his own head. The words in question are to serve the reader for his immediate information, whence the extract is taken. Yet no one reading them can guess whether he took it from the Cambridge MS. or from the Geneva MS., or from some common original. Sure never did man (unfettered by consciousness) express himself on such wise.†

---

* In p. 25.

† [The Editor is not sorry to be thus imperatively, though not perhaps at first sight obviously, called upon to mention the "Granger Society," which has been recently formed under the presidency of the Marquis of Salisbury. Its object is, " to publish a series of ancient English portraits, and family pictures, accurately copied from the originals, and engraved in the best style of art," in a manner and form which will no doubt be cheerfully explained to any one who applies to W. J. Thoms, Esq., Sec. *pro tem.*, 25, Parliament Street. Of the value of portraits as keys to the works (whether written or acted) of those whom they represent, there cannot be two opinions. Put Bishop Burnet opposite Archbishop Laud, let them look at each other, and look at them both ;

Curious as was the coincidence of one man furnishing two libraries with two similar and most ancient MSS. of the same works, from valleys of which the extent was small and the literature scanty, it did not move their fortunate discoverer to give any details of it.   But it rather operated to seal his lips in mystery.   Black-letter parchment No. 1 was obtained by him and Antoine Leger, and given to the commissary of Cromwell before 1658; but there is no hint of *where* it was found. Black-letter parchment No. 2 was found in the valley of Pragela in Dauphiné, and taken to Geneva in 1662; but not a syllable of *when* it was found.   The truth is, that No. 1 was procured by Leger in the valley of Pragela; and that No. 2 was procured by him before A.D. 1658; and that whatever can truly be predicated of one may be predicated of the other.

The contents of the Cambridge MS., as described by Morland, do not tally with the account of the existing state of the Geneva MS., as collected from what Leger and Raynouard say. There is no printed index to the contents of the latter.   For we know Mons. Leger's brief enumeration to be very grossly defective; and Monsieur Raynouard's professedly relates only to the poetry.   We will first give the reader a view of the points in which the two supposed MSS. are described as tallying.

and if you do not learn the specific facts, which you may obtain from studying their lives or their works, yet you will get a commentary on them almost as valuable as the facts themselves.   In like manner, look at the large portrait of Leger prefixed to his book on the Vaudois.   It appears to be well executed, and has all the air of a likeness, but what a thing it is! One might almost defy any one who has as much feeling of physiognomy as most children of eighteen months, to believe anything on the word of the original.   It seems as if it were put at the entrance for a "cave canem."   Even before one had read his impudent ignorant book, one would be inclined to parody the trite lines, and say,

  " If on his fame some dark suspicions fall,
      Look in his face, and you'll believe them all."—ED. OF BRIT. MAG.]

The Morland MS.	*The Geneva MS.*
1. Glosa Pater, or the Explication of the Lord's Prayer.	Explication de l'oraison Dominicale.
3. Doctor, or divers passages, etc.	Le Docteur.
7. Novel Comfort.	Lo Novel Comfort.
8. Novel Sermon.	Lo Novel Sermon.
9. La Noble Leyçon.	La Nobla Leyczon.
10. Pair Eternal.	Lo Payre Eternal.
11. Barca.	La Barca.
12. An Explication of the Ten Commandments.	Des X Commandements.
13. An Explication of the Articles of the Apostles' Creed.	Du Symb. des Apôtres.
19. Several Sermons upon several texts of Scripture.	Quelques Sermons.

In these ten points the black-letter manuscript at *Geneva* corresponds with the black-letter manuscript *nobody knows where.* The nine following, which are in the index to Morland's volume B., have not been quoted as existing in the Geneva volume that contains the poems, and therefore we cannot assume that they are contained in it. But as we possess no index of the contents of it, there is no reason to assume that they are absent from it. They all appear to be old Waldensian, and not Protestant-Vaudois.

2. Trecenas.	16. On the three Theological and the four Cardinal Virtues.
4. Penas.	
5. Li goy de Paradia.	17. On the goods of Fortune, Nature, and Grace.
6. Epistle to the Faithful.	
14. A treatise on Vice and Mortal Sins.	18. On the Six Honourable Things in this World.
15. Concerning the Seven Gifts of the Spirit.	

As we can pronounce nothing concerning the presence or absence of these nine articles, they show neither discrepancy nor conformity. Lastly, the following four are quoted from the Geneva book, which are not named in Morland's index, of

which two are Waldensian poems, and two are of the Protestant-Vaudois tracts fraudulently antedated :—

> Lo Despreczi del Mont.
> L'Evangeli de li Quatre Semencz.
> Du Purgatorie Songè.
> Des Traditions.

When we consider that Morland can scarce have credit for
being able to read correctly a page of old Provençal MS. in
Gothic letters, it would excite no great surprise if his list of
the various contents of such a volume was incomplete ; especially as he did not publish any of his four poems, Nos. 7, 8,
10, 11, or quote a line from them, or show any indications of
having read them. His index was probably defective in respect of the two poems, owing to his not observing where one
copy of verses ended, and a fresh one commenced. However,
the occurrence of two Protestant tracts in the Genevese volume
is more remarkable; there is no reason in the world to suppose that they who abstracted so precious a document from
Cambridge held it quite sacred, and took no precaution to alter
its contents, by unstitching it, and then doing it up again,
either in the same or in a different binding. It is apposite to
remark, that the MS. books of Morland, already* mentioned
as having been carried out of the country and deposited in the
hands of Protestants, are most fully ascertained, by those who
have had access to examine them, to be *in the binding of the
country* in which they now are. One of the treatises, super-
numerary in the Geneva book, as compared with Morland's
index, had been the article 6 of Morland's lost volume A., entitled "A Treatise against Tramettament, or Traditions and
Ordinances of Men, as not consonant to the Holy Scriptures."
Upon the whole, there is great reason to believe that the
volume now in Geneva Library is, in its essentials, the same

---

* Brit. Mag., vol. xviii., p. 607. [See the passage referred to, p. 104,
supra. But the volumes G. and H., portions of which I once suspected to
have found their way to Dublin, were never mislaid or missing at Cambridge.]

which was for a few months at Cambridge, during the last illness of Oliver, and in the brief Protectorate of Richard. The dates harmonize perfectly; and the interval of time is no greater than common prudence would dictate to less practised hands. We trace the agency of the same individual throughout, and we observe in his language repeated indications of a self-betraying consciousness. The manuscripts are described in the same terms, and as of the same materials and writing. The conformity between their multifarious contents is great and striking. One of them is mysteriously and unaccountably gone; which establishes the *corpus delicti*, and so smoothes the way to the ascertainment of person and place. Lastly, the opinion to which all this tends, that there exists, and long has existed, but one* Waldensian copy of the poems of the sect, is supported by the language of J. P. Perrin† concerning them: "Item, on nous a mis en main un livre de Poesie en langue Vaudoise, auquel sont les traités qui suivent: Une priere inscripte Nouvel Confort. Une rhithme des quatre sortes de semences mentionnés en l'Evangile. Une autre intitulée Barque. Et une appellée la Noble Leçon. Duquel livre fait mention le Sieur de Sainte Aldegonde."

The various readings that at first seem to diversify them may ultimately tend to identify these books. It is morally certain that Morland could not handle Piémontese or Provençal poems in a Gothic codex of 450 years ago, either as a translator, or as a reader. In fact, he never attempted to touch the older and finer poems. But it had been arranged that he should print and translate the "Noble Lesson;" because that work was indispensable to the party, for its precious words "mil e cent ancz," the groundwork of all their chronological chicane. The Legers must have furnished him with a transcript of it in common writing, for the use of the printer; and

* Of which Ussher had a Protestant-Vaudois transcript, of moderate correctness.

† "Hist. Vaud.," c. vii., p. 59.

also with a translation into French, to give him some idea of the meaning. But the said transcript was inaccurate and slovenly, with deviations from the text, where it was hard to make out. The defects of the transcript are much aggravated by the printer, and by the editor's incapacity to correct the press. Such seems to be the fact respecting Morland's text. For two such ancient MSS., as we are told of, would be, if not of equal, of comparable authority, and would present some alternation of good readings. But the Cambridge text is condemned throughout by its *curiosa infelicitas*. Its copyist has, with the minutest number* of exceptions, marred whatever he changed. Sometimes the rhyme is entirely destroyed, and sometimes the sense. And, what should weigh most with us, he had no perception of the metre, or rhythm, and seldom fails to do it injury. Whereas the old Waldic scribe, writing when that mode of teaching was still in use, should have known the cadence of this popular recitative. In collating Morland's text, it is to be feared Monsieur Raynouard wasted his learned pains on trash; as when some schoolmaster, who has set a truant boy the first Eclogue to write out, collates page after page of blotted blunders, just to ascertain that it is really Virgil, and not Johnny Gilpin. It may well be questioned if such mean scholars, as they who primed him were, could themselves read the MS. correctly; and equally so, whether he could correctly read their copy. Jean Leger was probably the person who furnished him with the transcript that was sent to the press. For that author has printed a large portion of the "Noble Lesson," with the fraudulent suppression of thirty-seven lines that were incompatible with his theory; and in order to close up and hide that deep gash in the text, and obtain a tolerable juncture of the two lips of the wound, it was absolutely necessary for him

---

* Perhaps no others besides vss. 130 and 348; in the former of which the words inserted (similar to those in vss. 11, 170, 340, and 367) are indifferent; and in the latter seem rather preferable, provided that "a mal tenir" will bear the meaning given to it.

to expunge the word *sinon*, *except*, in *v.* 455,* and substitute
mas, *but;* and he accordingly did so. Now we find it so written
by the English editor. The word had been substituted afore-
hand, with a view to the garbled extract that Leger meditated
printing, and perhaps had already made; and we see his hand
in it. The manuscript copy on paper, which belonged to Ussher,
and seems to have been made full three centuries ago, agrees
with the genuine codex; and we find nowhere, but in printed
editions of a non-forthcoming manuscript, that reading of which
Leger's trickery stood in need.

The case of the variations may be better appreciated by observing Monsieur Leger's conduct upon the same subject, but
on another occasion. He gave (as we have observed) specimens
artfully garbled and re-joined, from the "Noble Lesson;" and
announced it as original MS. text. But he really reprinted
the same text of it which Morland had already printed. Yet
how did he do so? He freely altered it, whenever it suited either
his taste and judgment, or his sinister ends. Out of eleven
alterations, important enough to be worth reckoning, only one
(that in *v.* 76) coincides with the manuscript. The rest are
all entirely out of Monsieur Leger's own brain. They are as
follows :—

English Text.	*Leger's Extract.*
v. 12. a esti.	o escri.
15. ben *omitted.*	ben *inserted.*
29. car.	lo.
76. cayçon.	rason.
357. alcun.	moti.
368. sel ama.	se troba.
372. punir.	murir.
373. ban.	ben.
385. se.	sal.
398. soç.	sols.
457. cant venrè.	a fuire.

* Being line 3rd of Leger's "Hist. Gen.," p. 30.

Raynouard, alluding to the pretended two ancient manuscripts, spoke approvingly of "the kind of variations they present" (p. cxliii), and regarded it as a proof of authenticity in the poem. What would he say of *this* kind of variations? It is the same kind, and from the same hand. The truth of the case is, that Leger did not adopt the text out of Morland's pages, but out of a duplicate of the same apograph as he had furnished to Morland: subject to the benefit of his own *curæ secundæ*, conjectural corrections, and interpolations. The *mas* in *v.* 455 had been provided for in the first instance; but the bold and flagitious forgery *a fuire*, in *v.* 457, was an afterthought. Thus much may suffice to illustrate the matter of the variations.

Though nothing may have been said upon it, it were hard to suppose that no misgivings upon this subject should ever have crossed the minds of the Genevese. Raynouard* published the Genevese text of the Vaudois poetry from an exact copy of the old manuscript, which Monsieur Favre Bertrand of Geneva made for him; from whom he received, at the same time, "quelques renseignements trés détaillés et trés-utiles." In speaking of the (supposed) two manuscripts of the Noble Lesson, he calls attention to an apparent distinction between them. "I am led to believe (he says) that the Cambridge manuscript had been taken from a copy more ancient than that which had served as an original to the Geneva manuscript; for in that of Cambridge we read *au* for *with*, coming from the Romance word *ab;* and in that of Geneva we read *cum* instead of *au.*"† Considering what all the Romance tongues, as well the great modern languages, as also these humbler dialects and patois originally were (viz., the provincial Latinity of the common folk, vulgar Latin, no doubt, but mere Latin, which

---

* "Choix de Poésies," etc., 2, p. cxlii. It need scarce be said, that these remarks are made with all due respect for his peculiar merits and his fourscore years of learning.   † Ibidem, note (2).

have, by gradual change, and admixture of barbarisms, been deflected into their present forms), it must strike our ears as a proposition somewhat paradoxical, that the word *au*, or indeed any word whatsoever, is a more ancient word for *with* than *cum*. But whatever estimate the reader may incline to form of the value of this reasoning, he will be a little surprised to hear that the fact upon which it is founded does not appear to have any existence. The following computation is believed to be a correct one, viz. that the English edition of the Noble Lesson contains the preposition *au*, *with*, exactly seven times; that is to say,* in *vss.* 89, 205, *bis*, 318, 329, 421, 475. And in every one of those places, without exception, the Geneva MS., as copied by Monsieur Favre Bertrand, exhibits the same word. The Geneva MS., in which it is said, "we read *cum* instead of *au*," contains *au* seven times in the Lesson, and *cum* just twice; that is to say, *cum* in *v.* 343, and *con* in *r.* 300. And in both these instances the English edition may be said to tally with it; for in *v.* 300 the preposition has been entirely omitted by the copyist or the printer, to the destruction of the sense; and in *v.* 343, it is plainly printed thus,

"E li home e las fenas lical eran *cum* lor."

Whether this observation has been hazarded by Monsieur Raynouard, or whether it be one of the *renseignements* for which he is indebted to Monsieur Favre Bertrand, it may be pronounced to be, in every point, utterly devoid of the shadow of foundation. The correspondency of the two (pretended) manuscripts, in respect of the preposition *with*, appears to be perfect.

The manuscript was lodged in Cambridge library but about three weeks before the death of Oliver Cromwell; and it is not

---

* The numbers of *vss.* refer to Raynouard's edition, being the only one in which they are numbered. That numeration agrees with the version about to be subjoined; but not with Morland's edition, in which the verses have not been correctly distinguished.

probable that it remained there much longer than till the spring of 1659, when it became apparent that Richard was unable to govern the country. After the Restoration, it is obvious that Morland and his party could have no power of getting any documents abstracted from the University library; and in all probability, the Puritan librarian to whom he consigned it, and from whom he obtained it back, was then sent (as the saying is) to the right about. If he was not, he kept his place by changing his principles; and would never have compromised himself by surrendering his treasures to the Geneva faction. Besides, a great and somewhat sudden change came over the spirit of Samuel Morland himself, upon the king's return. He forgot all about "the Mene Tekel upon the walls of the palaces and banqueting-houses" of the royal family; and recollected how he had always opposed and abhorred the plots of Cromwell and Thurloe against the king's sacred person. Morland then ceased to bewail the tribulations of the poor Vaudois, or (as he used to say) to be "grieved for the afflictions of Joseph." But he got himself a baronetcy,* a pension of £500 a year, and the places of gentleman of the bedchamber, and civil engineer to the king. And, in this latter capacity, he devoted the mechanical talents, in which no man surpassed him, to adorning palaces, on whose walls he no longer saw the writing of God's finger. He even went over to "the tabernacles of Edom and the Ishmaelites, Amalek and the Philistines, with them that dwell at Tyre," and exhibited his inventions, and offered his services, to Louis XIV. It follows, from this state of the case, that Sir Samuel Morland, Bart., &c. &c. &c., would by no means have been likely, himself, to strip the Cambridge library of the valuables with which he had had the merit of endowing it. The courtier of Windsor and St. Germain's would, perhaps, have manifested but an imperfect recollection of Monsieur Jean Leger's features, had they chanced to meet one another again.

---

* See " Biogr. Univ.," art. *Morland*.

But, at all events, he would not have robbed his own country, and its institutions, to which he had now attached himself, in order to accommodate the Calvinists of Geneva. We may rest pretty well satisfied, that the missing books were got back out of Cambridge library, and one or more of them returned to Leger (by whom they had all been originally furnished), in the interval between the death of Oliver and restoration of Charles; and before Morland had changed his politics, or knew that he should have an opportunity of so doing with advantage.

DR. GILLY'S FIRST LETTER ON THE "NOBLE LESSON" AND WALDENSIAN MSS.

[THE foregoing paper, and the conjecture it contains, that the MS. containing the Waldensian Poems had been dishonestly abstracted from the Cambridge Library, drew forth the following letter from the late Dr. Gilly, addressed to the Editor of the " British Magazine" (vol. xix., p. 156). Dr. Gilly calls the conjecture alluded to "a monstrous charge;" and now that we know the facts of the case, that none of the MSS. were ever disturbed, not even by librarian curiosity, from the place in which Morland placed them, the epithet seems fully justified. We learn, however, from this part of the controversy how easy it is to prop up a charge of this kind by plausible circumstances; and the correspondence is worthy of a place in this Collection for the sake of this lesson, independently of the historical facts which it elicits.—J. H. T.]

DEAR SIR,—I am very glad to see that your columns continue open to a discussion on the various branches of the Waldensian question, although they contain many opinions contrary to my own.   We shall strike out, I hope, some sparks of truth at last, if we will but investigate the subject with forbearance, and not use hard words towards those who think differently from ourselves.   " *Constant imputation of motives spoils the manly bearing of a controversialist.*"   To this sentiment, expressed so well in your last Number, (Brit. Mag. vol. xix. p. 8,)* I respond most heartily; and therefore I venture to protest against expressions which occur in your pages in relation to the Waldensian MSS.; such as—" *these disingenuous moderns adopted it for their standard, and forged up to it*" (ibid., vol. xviii., p. 603); "*progress of knavery and falsification*" (ibid., vol. xix., p. 12);

* [The passage here referred to occurs in an article on " The Controversial Spirit of the Reformation under Edward VI." Dr. Gilly, in his letter, as it originally appeared, always quotes the Brit. Magazine by its *numbers*. But as these were noted only on the paper covers, and have disappeared in the bound up work, I have changed his references into the volume and page.—J. H. T.]

"Protestant-Vaudois tracts fraudulently antedated" (ibid., p. 16).

There may have been errors in abundance in the production and use of these MSS.; but carelessness, haste, eager anxiety to make out a case, ignorance, inadvertencies, mistakes in transcribing and printing, wrong reasoning, and the many infirmities of our nature, will account for not a few of the delinquencies which are too incautiously set down to *knavery*.

The metrical compositions ascribed to the Waldenses of the twelfth century are now occupying the attention of one of your correspondents, and in your last two Numbers (vol. xviii. p. 601, xix. p. 11) they are called the "Poems of the Poor of Lyons." The principal of these is the Noble Lesson, "La Nobla Leyczon," said to be a document of the year 1100, from a date which it seems to offer in two of its lines:—

> "Ben ha mil e cent ancz compli entierament,
> Que fo scripta l'ora, car sen al derier temp."

> "There are already a thousand and one hundred years fully accomplished,
> Since it was written thus, for we are in the last time."

(Morland's Translation.)

> "Bien a mille et cent ans accomplis entièrement,
> Que fut écrite l'heure que nous sommes au dernier temps."

(Raynouard's Translation.)

Now, whether the "Noble Lesson" be a document of the year 1100 or thereabouts, or of a later period—whether it be a poem of the Sub-Alpine Waldenses, or of the "Poor Men of Lyons," is still an open question; but it is no small satisfaction to me to find that the charge of its being a forgery seems to be withdrawn, and that its authenticity is acknowledged as "a simple effort of mediæval piety," "as an antiquarian relic," and as the genuine document of some sectarians of a remote period anterior to the Reformation. For my own part, I believe the "Noble Lesson" to be of a more ancient date than the British Magazine and its correspondents are inclined to allow, even of the early part of the twelfth century; and perhaps we may approximate more nearly to each other's opinions, if we will turn our attention to the following points of investigation, and examine them fully and candidly :—

I. Which is the most ancient copy of the "Noble Lesson" now existing in MS. ?

II. What is the declared opinion of persons who have been in the habit of examining old MSS. as to the age of that which is considered the most ancient?

III. What is the character of the *hand-writing* of the oldest copy of this poem?

IV. Has it any especial marks of antiquity, such as accents ?*

V. Is it found in company with other poems of a similar character, which will assist the inquirer in forming his opinion ?

VI. Is it composed in that dialect of the Romaunt, or Provençal, which may be called Gallico-Provençal, or Pedemontano-Provençal?

VII. Are there any words or inflections in the "Noble Lesson" which bear traces of Lombard, Saracenic, or Arabic origin ?†

VIII. Are there any marks or features, by which it may be ascribed to the *beginning*, rather than to the *end*, of the twelfth century ?

IX. When was the dread of the approaching end of the world (on which the "Noble Lesson" dwells so impressively) most felt, at the beginning, or towards the close of the twelfth century ?

X. Is there any internal evidence, that the "Noble Lesson" was written before certain Romish novelties were introduced at the end of the twelfth century ?

* "Je regard ce signe (un accent) comme une preuve d'antiquité."— Raynouard, p. cxxxii.

† Ladoucette, in his "Histoire, Topographie, Antiquités, Usages, Dialectes des Hautes Alpes," shows that the valleys in the Cottian Alps, where the Waldensian poems are said to have been written, were occupied for a long time by Lombards and Saracens.—pp. 45, 257, 264, 300, 512.

Raynouard's name and authority having been introduced into this discussion, it is as well to cite the passages which bear on it from that writer's "Choix des Poesies Originales des Troubadours," Paris, 1817.

"Si l'on rejetait l'opinion de l'existence d'une langue romane primitive, c'est-à-dire d'un idiôme intermédiaire qui par la decomposition de la langue des Romains, et l'établissement d'un noveau système grammatical, a fourni le type commun d'apres lequel se sont successivement modifiés les divers idiômes le l'Europe latine, il serait difficile d'exliquer comment, dans les vallées du Piémont, un peuple séparé des autres par ses opinions religieuses, par ses mœurs, et sur-tout par sa pauvreté, a parlé la langue romane à une epoque très-ancienne et s'en est servi pour conserver et transmettre la tradition de ses dogmes religieux; circonstance qui atteste la haute antiquité de cet idiôme dans le pays que ce peuple habitait·

"Le poëme de *La Nobla Leyczon* porte la date de l'an 1100."—Raynouard, vol. ii., p. cxxxvi.

"La secte religieuse des Vaudois est donc beaucoup plus ancienne qu'on ne l'a cru généralement."—Ibid.

"La lecture des poésies religieuses que je publie donnera une idée suffisante de leurs dogmes.

"Quant à l'idiôme dans lequel elles sont ecrites, on se convaincra que le dialecte Vaudois est identiquement la langue romane; les légères modifications qu'on y remarque, quand on le compare à la langue des troubadours, reçoivent des explications qui deviennent de nouvelles preuves de l'identité.

"Il me reste à parler des manuscrits des ouvrages en dialecte Vaudois.

"Samuel Morland avait déposé en 1658 à la bibliothèque de l'université de Cambridge plusieurs manuscrits dont le catalogue est au commencement de son histoire.

"Ces manuscrits intéressants ne s'y trouvent plus depuis plusieurs années.

"La bibliothèque de Genève possède trois manuscrits Vaudois. Celui qui est coté No. 207 contient les poésies religieuses et morales; il m'a fourni les pièces qui sont imprimées de la page 73 à la page 133."—*Ibid.*, p. cxl. to cxlii.·

"*La Nobla Leyczon.*

"Ce poëme, qui est une histoire abrégée de l'Ancien et du Nouveau Testament, m'a paru assez important pour-être inséré en entier. J'ai conféré le

---

· "J'ai dû au zèle à la sagacité et à la bienveillance de M. Favre Bertrand de Genève une copie exacte des pièces que je publie, et quelques renseignements très détaillés et très-utiles. Il me tardait d'offrir à ce littérateur distingué l'hommage public de ma reconnaissance."

texte du manuscrit de Genève avec celui du manuscrit de Cambridge*
publié par Samuel Morland.

"La date de l'an 1100 qu'on lit dans ce poëme mérite toute confiance.
Les personnes qui l'examineront avec attention jugeront que le manuscrit n'a
pas été interpolé; les successeurs des anciens Vaudois, ni les dissidents de
l'église romaine qui auraient voulu s'autoriser des opinions contenues dans ce
poëme, n'auraient eu aucun intérêt à faire des changements; et s'ils avaient
osé en faire, ces changements auraient bien moins porté sur la date du poëme
que sur le fond des matières qu'il traite pour les accommoder à leurs propres
systêmes dogmatiques. Enfin le style même de l'ouvrage, la forme des vers,
la concordance des deux manuscrits, le genre des variantes qu'ils présentent,
tout se réunit en faveur de l'authenticité de ses poesies; M. Sennebier jugeait
que le manuscrit de Genève est du XII⁰ siécle."

I have long been in correspondence with a friend, Mr.
Metivier, on the subject of the "Noble Lesson," who does not
concur in all my views of its antiquity; but his intimate acquaintance with the Romaunt dialects renders every remark of
his worthy of notice. He writes thus on the subject:—"The
idiom of the 'Noble Lesson' is also essentially the same as that
of the remaining MSS. I only remark the substitution of *au*
(analogous to the Provençal and Catalan *ab*) for *per* or *cum*,
which last I think occurs only once [twice?] *Ce* (que) for
car would be another peculiarity, if the copyist had not, as I
suspect, misinterpreted the *o* or *ç* in the MS. In the prose
MSS. I do not find *que* for *car*. *Que* always, *car* never, is the
Catalan rule. I have marked several altered or transposed
rhymes in this Genevan copy; a clear proof that there existed
a more ancient *oral or written original*. I do not think Morland's copy the most ancient. The use of the explicit *illi*,
instead of the implicit *ilh*, inclines me to the supposition that
the Genevan MS. is older than Morland's. The prose MSS.,
some of which are so modern, invariably expand *ilh* into *illi*.

---

* "Je suis porté à croire que le manuscrit de Cambridge avait été fait
sur un exemplaire plus ancien que celui qui à servi pour la copie du manuscrit
de Genève; dans le manuscrit de Cambridge on lit *au*, avec, venant d'*ab*
romane, et dans celui de Genève on lit *cum* au lieu d'*au*."

The irregularity of the metres rather favours your hypothesis of the early date.—G. METIVIER."

It will be observed that Mr. Metivier differs from Mr. Raynouard, as to the comparative antiquity of the Cambridge and Genevan copies; but he makes a similar observation as to the substitution of *au* for *cum*. With regard to the objections in Brit. Mag., vol. xix., pp. 19, 20 [pp. 147, 148, *supra*], I should say that there must be an omission, or misprint, in the note containing Mr. Raynouard's remark about *au* and *cum*, for certainly there does not seem to be any foundation for the statement as it there stands.*

Your correspondent, in the continuation of his article, "On the Poems of the Poor of Lyons" [pp. 135–150, *supra*], accuses Morland of having himself withdrawn some of the lost Cambridge MSS. from the library, particularly vol. B., and of having given it back to Leger. "The truth of the matter (so far as it may be surmised from circumstances, and from the behaviour of a deceitful person) appears to be, that Monsieur Leger gave the book to Morland between the years 1655 and 1658, inclu-

* The following extract from Champollion Figeac, another philologist, will show that his opinion also was in favour of the Waldensian MSS. :—

"Mais il ne faut pas oublier, que dans des temps peu réculés le Piémont n'eut d'autre langue que celle de la France méridionale, de l'Italie et de l'Espagne, c'est-à-dire le *roman*. Ce fait n'est contesté par personne, et on en trouve une preuve irrécusable dans les livres qui nous restent de la secte des *Vaudois* qui habitaient les vallées du Piémont. Ces livres consistent en quelques manuscrits très-rares en France et partout ailleurs, si ce n'est en Angleterre où doivent exister (à Cambridge) plusieurs manuscrits envoyés en 1658 à Olivier Cromwel, qui les avait démandés aux pasteurs Vaudois."—Note, p. 24, "Nouvelles Recherches sur les Patois ou Idiômes Vulgaires de la France, par J. J. Champollion-Figeac, Conservateur-adjoint de la Bibliothèque Publique de Grenoble, et Professeur de Litterature Grecque à la Faculté des Lettres de l'Academie de Grenoble." [Dr. Gilly's remark, that "there must be an omission or misprint in the note containing M. Raynouard's remark," &c., must mean M. Raynouard's note, and that the author of the paper on the Poems of the Poor of Lyons was right when he said that there was no foundation for the statement as it there stands.—J. H. T.]

sive; that Morland placed it in the Cambridge library in 1658, while the Protector was dying; took it out again before the king's restoration, and gave it back to Leger; and that Leger placed it in the Geneva library in 1662" [p. 137, *supra*]. Strange enough, your correspondent, in his previous article, Brit. Mag., vol. xviii., p. 607 [p. 104, *supra*], assigns as the reason why some of the MSS. were withdrawn from Cambridge, that they would not "pass muster as MSS. of the age ascribed to some of them before the searching eye of restored learning." Now it so happens that the book at Geneva, containing the "Noble Lesson," &c., is a collection of MSS. which will bear the most severe investigation.

The monstrous charge of stealing from Cambridge, to restore to Leger, rests on the supposition, that the book which still remains in the library of Geneva, and from which the "Noble Lesson" in Raynouard's volume was transcribed, is the same which Jean Leger gave to the library in 1662; but I have in my possession a letter from Mr. Favre Bertrand, which distinctly states, on the authority of the librarian himself, that the book in question was *not* given by *Jean* Leger in 1662, but by *Antoine* Leger in 1661; also, that the volume given and described by *Jean* Leger was different from that deposited by *Antoine* Leger; and that Jean Leger's gift is no longer in the library,—does *not* "remain to this day where he placed it." Your correspondent may possibly adhere to his accusation against Morland, and say, "Well, then, he gave the book to *Antoine* Leger; and there it is, transferred from Cambridge to Geneva." Let the matter be thoroughly sifted; and for this purpose I subjoin a copy of M. Bertrand's letter,* with his account in full of the little book containing the "Noble Lesson." A comparison of Mr. Bertrand's list of the Waldensian MSS. remaining in the Library of Geneva, with Morland's catalogue

* In that letter you will find some of the "*renseignments*" which Mr. Bertrand had communicated to Raynouard, and of which your correspondent [p. 148, *supra*] seems to entertain some suspicions.

of those abstracted from Cambridge, will be useful in this controversy :—

"J'ai l'honneur, Monsieur, de vous* envoyer la notice des MSS. Vaudois qui sont dans la bibliothèque de la ville de Genève, et que vous avez desiré connoitre. Je serai fort heureux si elle peut vous être de quelque utilité. Veuillez, Monsieur, agréer l'expression de mon entier dévouement.

"*Genève*, 10 *Juin*, 1832.   GM. FAVRE BERTRAND."

"*Manuscrits*, No. 207. Il renferme des écrits en langue Vaudoise tant en prose qu'en vers. Son format est petit, in 12mo, d'environ 4 pouces de hauteur, sur 3 pouces de largeur. Il est écrit sur velin et paroit être du 12me siècle. Il contient :—

"1°. Incipit *Prologus in secundo libro exposicionum Canticorum Salomonis*.

"Il y a sept livres de cette exposition mais le premier manque, et le volume commence par le second. Cet ouvrage occupe 221 pages, il est en prose Vaudoise ; le titre seul est en latin.

"2°. Ayci commencza la Barca 336 vers.

"3°. Ayci comencza lo Novel Sermon, 408 vers.

"4°. Ayci comencza lo Novel Confort, 300 vers.

"5°. La Nobla Leiczon, 472 vers.

"J. Leger (Histoire des Eglises Vaudoises) a publié deux longs fragments de ce poëme, ou en trouve aussi quelques morceaux dans d'autres livres, mais le seul ouvrage dans lequel il à été publié entier est la *Choix de Poesies des Troubadours, par M. Raynouard*. Il est imprimé (tom. ii. pp. 73—102) d'après une copie que j'ai faite sur le MS. de Genève. On trouvera dans le même volume des extraits de toutes les poésies que renferme ce MS.

"Dans l'intérieur de la couverture de ce MS. on lit une note d'une ecriture peu ancienne qui detaille les ouvrages qu'il contient et ajoute qu'*il appartient aux eglises reformées des vallées du Piémont, lesquelles prient de le leurs conserver en la bibliothèque de Genève.* Cette note se trouve pleinement confirmée par un petit carnet dans lequel E. Girard, Bibiothècaire vers le milieu du xvii. siècle, inscrivoit les acquisions et les dons, qui augmentoient la bibliothèque. On y lit,

---

* Having requested my friend, the Rev. Richard Burgess, to procure information from Geneva on the subject of these Waldensian MSS., and having lost the envelope of this letter when my house was on fire, two years ago, I cannot say whether Mr. Bertrand addressed himself to Mr. Burgess or to me.

"' Livres qui ont été donnés à la bibliothèque dès que j'en ai eu la charge 1656.

E. GIRARD.

*   *   *   *

"' Le 17 8bre 1661, Mr. Leger, Pastr. et Profr. le jour avant son decès m'a remis pour être gardé pour les eglises de Piémont un petit livre MS. intitulé les Expoóns du Cãtique des Cantiqs de Salomon en lettre antique. Et les poëmes intit. la Barca, Novel Sermon, Nobla Leisson, lo Paire Eternel, lo Novel Confort, lo Dispressi de la Mort, deli quatre Semens, et de la Penitenza, en langage ancien Vaudois. Manuscrit en parchemin, est en l'armoire.'

"On voit que le livre remis par Léger est évidemment le MS. No. 207, et qu'il s'agit ici d'*Antoine Leger*, qui avoit été à Constantinople, et qui s'y étoit assez intimement lié avec le patriarch Cyrille Lucar. Il mourut effectivement en 1661. (Senebier Hist. litter. de Genève, tom. ii. p. 131.)

"Dans *l'Histoire des Eglises Vaudoises par Jean Leger*, (mort vers 1670), p. 78, on voit qu'il avoit remis à la bibliothèque de Genève des papiers concernant les Vaudois, et un volume qui renfermoit *la Noblu Leiczon* et *lo Novel Confort*, mais qui du reste etoit *different** de celui qui porte le No. 207,

---

* That this difference between the book now remaining at Geneva, and the one which Jean Leger gave to the university there, may be thoroughly understood, I subjoin Leger's own account of it:—"Outre les pièces ci-devant mentionnés et remises à Mr. Morland, et par lui données en garde en l'université de Cambridge, ayant encore recouvert dans la vallée de Pragela, un volume in 8 fort epaix, où sont en langue Vaudoise, en caractères très-anciens, et *en parchemin*, les beaux traités de la Noble Leiçon, du l'urgatoire Songé, des Traditions, de l'Invocation des Saints, du Nouveau Confort, du Docteur, de l'Explication de l'Oraison Dominicale, du Symb. des Apôtres, et des X Commandements, et quelques Sermons, je les ai mis en depost en la Bibliothèque de Genève, et en ay tiré le suivant temoignage de *Mr. Gerard*, Bibliothéquaire. ' Je soussigné declare avoir reçu des mains de M. Leger, cy-devant Pasteur és Vallées, 1. Un livre de parchemin-manuscript in 8, contenant plusieurs traités de la doctrine des anciens Vaudois, en leur propre langue. 2. Un liasse de plusieurs autres manuscrits importants des affaires des dites vallées, partie en langue Ital. partie en langue Françoise, que je conserve en la Bibliothèque de cette cité, pour y avoir recours au besoin, en foi de quoy, &c. A Genève le 10 Novembre, 1662, signé *Gerard*, Pasteur, Principal du Collège, et Bibliothéquaire.' "—Leger Hist. Gen. des Eglises Vaudoises, p. 28.

In Vol. xix. p. 12, note [p. 136, *supra*], your correspondent accuses Leger of having " omitted all the lines (of the Noble Lesson) from line 76 to 286, and again, all from 418 to 455, without any intimation to his readers either

dont je viens de montrer clairement l'origine. Le Bibliothècaire, Gerard, donna à Jean Leger un reçu de son livre le 10 Nov. 1662, c'est à dire un peu plus d'un an après le depôt de l'autre MS. par Antoine Leger. Le volume deposé par Jean Leger ne se retrouve plus dans notre Bibliothèque.

" Jean Leger donne aussi la liste des ecrits Vaudois qu'il avait remis à Samuel Morland, envoyé de Cromwell auprès du Duc de Savoye. Ils furent deposés à l'université de Cambridge, en Août, 1658, mais maintenant ils n'y sont plus, et le MS. de Genève est unique.

" Jean Leger fait encore connoitre les ouvrages Vaudois, qui servirent à Perrin pour composer son *Histoire des Vaudois et Albigeois* (Genève, 1618), mais dans ces indications il n'est fait aucune mention de *l'Exposition du Cantique de Salomon.* A la suite de la Nobla Leiczon on trouve encore :—

" 6. Lo Payre Eternal, 156 vers.

" 7. Lo Despreczi del Mont, 115 vers.

" 8. L'Avengeli de li 4 Semencz, 300 vers.

" 9. De la Penitenza. Traité on prose de 24 pages qui termine le volume."

" *Manuscr.* No. 208. Ecrit sur papier petit in 8°. Sur le dos de la relieure on lit *Controv. Vaud.* Il est du 14ᵉ ou 15ᵉ siècle. Il renferme des traités en langue Vaudoise et en prose sur les *Articles de Foi,* les Sept Sacremens, les Dix Commandements, *la Penitence, le Jeune, le Purgatoire, l'Invocation des Saints, la Puissance donnée au Vicaire de Christ.*

" Lorsqu'on a fait relier ce volume, on a mal reparti les cahiers ; ce qui fait que les traités sont mal en ordre, et se trouvent intercalés. La fin et le commencement de ce volume manquent.

" *Le Traité du Purgatoire* repond à quelques differences près, à celui dont Jean Leger (p. 33) a publié un fragment sous le titre *del Purgatori Seuma,*

---

in words or by mode of printing, that he was not presenting a continuous passage," and adds, " Whoever examines the poem will see the motive of this artifice." I cannot agree to this. I have referred to Leger, and I find that he begins his manuscript from the ' Noble Lesson' by speaking of it twice as a specimen or extract, "*commençunt par un echantillon,*" "*extrait d'un traité intitulé La Noble Leiçon.*" He then inserts the first forty-four lines, and, leaving a vacant space to show that he had omitted some lines, introduces the next extract by a heading in these words:—" *Et plus bas parlant de l'estat auquel Dieu a crée l'homme ;*" he proceeds, as your correspondent has described, making insertions and omissions at pleasure, without marking where the passage is continuous or not ; but he intimates from the first that he is only giving extracts, and at the end of all he says, " this specimen will suffice"—" Cet échantillon suffira."

qu'il annonce comme tiré du livre de l'Anti-Christ, daté de 1126.   Leger (p. 85, et suiv.) a aussi publié une partie de l' *Invocation de li Sanct.*   Mr. enebier (*Catal. des MSS. de la Bibl. de Genève,* p. 463) semble avoir pris le traité de *la Potesta* pour un ouvrage sur l'Apostasie.

" *Manuscrit* No. 209.   Petit 8° écrit sur papier.   Voici ce qu'en dit Mr. Senebier (*Catal. des MSS.,* p. 463).   'Les Conseils des Barbets.—Ce MS. incomplet renferme divers morceaux de Theologie et de Morale, en patois Vaudois; il me paroit du XV siècle.'

" Sur le dos du livre on lit, *Conseils des Barbes,* et au bas de la première page, *Conseils des Barbes touchant les heritages.*   Le mot *Barbe,* qui signifie *oncle,* se donnoit dans les vallées aux pasteurs du pays.

" 1.   Le MS. est incomplet au commencement ; on lit en tête des *recto* des premiers feuillets *pistola* ou *pistoleta.*   Le premier feuillet parle des heritages. Mais les suivans traitent d'autres sujets, tels que le rancune, le mariage, &c.

" 2.   A la page 16 commence un autre ouvrage, ayant le titre de *Pensiers;* il occupe quatre pages et demi.

" 3.   *De la Penitenza e del juni,* en 18 pages.

" 4.   *Pecca,* en 103 pages.   C'est un traité des Péchés. Il y a un chapitre sur chaque péché, et le tout est précédé de deux pages et demi sur l'aumône, DE LIMOSINE.   Ce traité est terminé par *la Oracion de Manasses.*

" 5.   *Glossa sobre lo Pater nostre,* en 42 pages. Leger ('Hist.,' p. 40-46) en publié une partie.

" 6.   *De las 4 Cosas que son avenir,* en 82 pages.   Ces quatre choses, dont chacune est traitée à part, sont la mort, le jugement, les peines d'enfer, les joies de paradis. Jean Leger ('Hist.,' 1 part, p. 23, B., No. 45) cite deux ouvrages, intitulés *Las Penas et li Goy de Paradis* qui vraisemblablement sont des parties du traité de *las 4 cosas.**   . . . ." [cætera desunt].

I wish to direct particular attention to the fact, that extracts of the Exposition of Solomon's Song are bound up in the Genevan book containing the "Noble Lesson," but that no mention is made, either in Perrin's or Morland's catalogue, of the *Song of Solomon.*   Morland speaks of "the Proverbs of Solomon, and Ecclesiastes" as being in vol. E.   It is also worthy of notice, that the MSS. No. 208 and 209 in the Genevan library, which contain some of the treatises mentioned

---

* The pages of Mr. Bertrand's letter containing the continuation of the catalogue were destroyed or lost when my house was damaged by fire.

M

in Morland's Cambridge MS., vol. B, are written on *paper*, whereas Morland's were on *parchment*.

I am persuaded, by these and other internal evidences contained in the Genevan MSS., that all the ingenious reasoning which your correspondent has employed, to fix upon Morland the suspicion of having taken the MSS. away from Cambridge to give them to Leger, will go for nothing. But, to do my best towards solving the mystery, I will endeavour to procure, if the conservators of the Genevan library will permit me, a complete transcript of the contents of the little book containing the "Noble Lesson," and other poems, and to have them collated with the various existing copies of the same compositions, under the hope that such collation will lead to more satisfactory conclusions than those at which we can arrive at present. I have seen the Genevan book, and examined the MSS. which it contains, and can vouch for the accuracy of Mr. Bertrand's description of it. A fac-simile of the seven first lines of the "Noble Lesson" is given in page 139 of my "Waldensian Researches."

Here I may take the opportunity of observing, that Dr. Todd has done me some little wrong in his "Lectures on the Prophecies relating to Antichrist." From the general tenor of his style, I believe it was unintentional ;* but he represents me as continuing to entertain all the opinions, which I expressed in my first publication on the Waldenses, whereas my second publication—"Waldensian Researches," printed 1831 —contains a modification of some of my former statements. It has escaped him also, that I took the first opportunity to point out the loss of the most ancient of the Waldensian MSS. out of the Cambridge collection. Compare Dr. Todd's notes, pp. 403, 408, with "Excursions to the Mountains of Piedmont," p. 22, second edition, 8vo, 1825, and "Waldensian Researches," pp. 132–156.

[* My mistake was occasioned by my having used the first edition of Dr. Gilly's "Excursions to the Mountains of Piedmont." See above, pp. 20, 21. —J. H. T.]

Dr. Todd, or the writer on the Poems of the Poor of Lyons, or any other critical scholar who has access to the volume of Ussher's MSS. in the library of Trinity College, Dublin, would be doing service to the cause if he would supply you (for publication in the "British Magazine") with a detailed account, or catalogue raisonné,* of the MS. Class C, Tab. 5, No. 22. That volume, as Dr. Todd informs us, in page 404 (note), of his recent work, "*contains all the tracts mentioned in Perrin's account* (p. 58) *of the contents of his MS., and in the same order. The first tract in the volume is entitled,* '*Liber Virtutum,*' *and begins,* '*No es justa cosa efort.*'"

I wish to be informed also if the Dublin library contains a copy of the Waldensian New Testament, mentioned as the first in Perrin's catalogue. "*Premierement nous avons en main un Nouveau Testament, en parchemin, en langue Vaudoise, très bien ecrit, quoy que de lettre fort ancienne.*"—French Ed., p. 57.

It will help to bring us to an understanding if we can trace the history of this " New Testament in the Waldensian language." Raynouard and Champollion-Figeac identify the Romaunt, or "*langue Romane primitive,*" with the Waldensian tongue. But we must endeavour to distinguish between the vernacular version of the New Testament well known to have been made by Waldo and " the Poor Men of Lyons," and the translation alleged to have been made by the Waldenses of the Cottian Alps,—that is, the Waldenses of the valleys of Piedmont and Dauphiné. I subjoin a list of copies of the New Testament which are ascribed to the Sub-Alpine Waldenses:—

The copies mentioned by Perrin, Morland, and Leger, which I need not here describe.

" Novum Testamentum lingua Pedemontana-Vallensi per Barbetum quemdam, seu ministrum Vallensem, translatum. Codex in 12° scriptus post annum M. C. *Bibl. civica Tigurina,*

[* The suggestion contained in this passage led to the publication of the Catalogue of the Dublin Waldensian MSS., which is now reprinted.—J. H. T.]

Ottius." Le Long, Bibliotheca Sacra, vol. i., p. 369. [*Paris*, 1723, fol.]

" Novum Testamentum ad usum Valdensium, sc. quatuor Evangelia, septem Epistolæ Canonicæ, quatuordecim Epistolæ Sancti Pauli et Actus Apostolorum. Deinde Proverbia Salomonis, Ecclesiastes, Canticum Canticorum, priora decem capita libri Sapientiæ et quindecim priora Ecclesiastici. Codex spissus in 4to integer, in quo nihil deest; in membranis à quadringentis annis circiter exaratus, at versio antiquior, *sicut ad me scripsit Dⁿ. Thomassin de Mazaugue filius senatoris Aquensis, penès quem extat hoc exemplar,* quod usui Valdensibus fuisse, multis probari potest argumentis, præsertim ex Oratione Dominicâ, quæ eadem est, duobus verbis duntaxat mutatis, ac in codice Joannis Leger, pag. 40, Hist. Valdensium. Hoc exemplar etiam describit epistola D. Remerville de S. Quentin, scripta anno 1704, et edita in collectione quæ vulgo dicitur *Piéces Fugitives d'Histoire et de Litterature,* 2 *partie, anni* 1704, p. 270." Le Long, Bibl. Sacr., vol. i., p. 369.

It is worthy of remark, that Le Long does not throw any discredit on the testimony of Perrin and Leger upon the subject of the Waldensian MSS.; on the contrary, he argues in defence of the antiquity of one of them. Natalis Alexander also notices this copy described by Le Long, in his " Vindiciæ Librorum Deutero-canonicorum, V. T. Supplementum ad Hist. Eccles.," p. 75; and he seems to think that the copy mentioned by Remerville de St. Quentin was not the same as that described by Thomassin de Mazaugue. Natalis Alexander therefore believed in the antiquity of this codex, written, " *lingua partim Pedemontana, partim provinciali.*"

There is also a MS. book, containing the New Testament in the Waldensian language, preserved in the library of Grenoble. It so happens that about a month ago I received an account of this relic (the existence of which has been disputed), in a letter, of which the following is an extract, most kindly addressed to me by the librarian of the Grenoble library, in answer to one which I had writen to him for information on the subject:—"Le MS. dont vous me parlez se trouve encore actuellement dans la Bibliothèque de Grenoble sous le No. 488. C'est en effet une traduction du N. T. en dialect Vaudois. Ce manuscrit, dont l'authenticité n'a jamais été révoquée en doute, est, à ce qu'on croit, du treizième siècle. Il est sur velin, et il a des lettres initiales coloriées, ainsi que des ornements. Son format est petit, in 4to un peu oblong. Quelques pages ont souffert mais assez légèrement."

Upon receiving this most interesting communication, I immediately requested to be favoured with a fac-simile of the precious MS., which has since arrived, and it is now before me. The fac-simile exhibits passages from the third chapter of St. Luke's Gospel; of course without our division into verses. The handwriting resembles that of MSS of the thirteenth century deposited in the library of Durham cathedral; and the translation has the following characteristic commencement of the chapter:—"*Mas la parolla del segnor fo faita*," &c. The passage does not begin as our version does—"Now in the fifteenth year," &c.; but, if rendered into English, would read in this order:—"But the word of the Lord came unto John, the son of Zacharias, in the Wilderness, in the fifteenth year of the reign of Tiberius Cæsar," &c.

I might here speak of a MS. which is noticed in the will of an Englishman who died in 1345:—"Etiam bibulam meam in Romanam linguam translatam." (See "Testamenta Eboracensia," part i., p. 10, Surtees Society, 1836.) This may, however, have been one of the copies of Waldo's translation, or that which the translators of the Rhemish Testament mention in their preface; "More than two hundred years ago, in the days of Charles V., the French king, was the Bible put forth faithfully in French, the sooner to shake out of the deceived people's hands the false heretical translations of a sect called the Waldenses."

I must again repeat that I hope we shall soon have, in one of your early Numbers, a detailed account from Dublin of the

"*Small Paper Volume*" (mentioned by Dr. Todd, p. 407, " Lectures on Antichrist") "*written in the beginning of the sixteenth century, very similar to the volume alluded to in note,* p. 404." If this volume contains " La Nobla Leyczon, La Barca, Lo Novel Sermon, Lo Novel Confort, Lo Payre Eternal, Lo Despreczi del Mont, el l'Evangeli de li quatre Semences," they may be compared with Morland's description of volume B, said to have been deposited at Cambridge, and with the little MS. book in the library of Geneva, No. 207. I should also feel much obliged if the writer of the article on the " Poems of the Poor of Lyons" (Brit. Mag., vol. xviii.) would tell us more plainly, in your next Number, where he thinks he might find a portion of the lost Cambridge documents. " He has reasons," he says, " for believing that some were conveyed out of the kingdom and deposited in a place belonging to Protestants" (Brit. Mag., vol. xviii., p. 609).*

The various readings of the copies of Waldensian MSS., especially of the " Noble Lesson," to which allusion has been made in this controversy, are viewed by me in a very different light from that in which they are seen by your correspondent. To my mind they prove the existence of several old codices of the " Noble Lesson," and are an answer to those who write about " the frauds of the Reformation," and who bring such sweeping charges of forgery against Perrin, Morland, and Leger. If it is " morally certain that Morland could not handle Piémontese or Provençal Poems, in a Gothic Codex of 450 years ago" (see Brit. Mag., vol. xix., p. 16),† is it not improbable that " *such mean scholars*" as your correspondent calls the Legers, who primed Morland, and furnished him with transcripts and translations of the MSS., should have been able to give various readings, *ad libitum*, in anything like a colourable form, to copies of MSS. of old Piedmontese and Provençal poems? I admit that there are marks enough of blundering inaccuracy, and want of erudition, in the publications of the three above-

* [*Supra.* p. 104.]   † [*Supra,* p. 143.]

mentioned writers; and I do not defend Morland and Leger, where they offer such glaring mistranslations as those which you have adduced; on the contrary, I will notice them all when I treat the question at length; but, since they give the original passages in an opposite column, it is only fair to remark that they themselves have supplied us with the means of correcting their own errors.

Your correspondent mentions *three* manuscript copies of the "Noble Lesson." I am inclined to speak of *five* :—

I. The Genevan copy transcribed for Raynouard's volume by M. Bertrand, and still remaining at Geneva. This I believe to be the Book of Poetry in the Vaudois language, described by Perrin, p. 59, and mentioned by St. Aldegonde, 1 Tab., p. 153.

II. The lost Cambridge copy of volume B, transcribed by Morland.

III. The copy of which extracts are given by Leger, "Hist. Gen. des Eglises Vaud.," p. 26-30.

IV. The copy preserved among the Ussher collection of Waldensian MSS. in the Library of Trinity College, Dublin. This Dr. Todd and the correspondent of your last two Numbers describe as a transcript of the beginning of the sixteenth century—i. e., one hundred years older than the book of Perrin, who is at the head of the supposed gang of forgers.

V. The copy (to which nobody, as far as I know, has before made any reference) from which Ladoucette took his extract in his "Histoire des Hautes Alpes," p. 299, which extract, short as it is, has a reading which differs greatly from the others.

Among the various readings* to which I am inclined to attach importance, as proving the existence of more than one

* Almost every line in Leger's and Morland's transcripts contains a variation from the Genevan MS. To suppose that all these were to answer a purpose is really too much. Of the first forty-four lines there is only one of Leger's which corresponds entirely with the Genevan copy, and only two of Morland's.

ancient copy, from which transcripts have been made, let me direct attention to the following :—

I. Genevan.*	II. Cambridge or Morland.	III. Leger.	IV. Usher's, as cited by Dr. Todd, "Lectures on Antichrist," p. 443.	V. Ladoucette.
Title, Leyczon.†	Leyçon.	Leyçon.		
Line 6, ancz.	an.	an.		
" 29 and 30 form one line only in Morland and Leger.				
" 216, paure (poor).	pura (pure).			
" 370, aucir.	sucire.	aucire.	…	occir.
" 372, Ilh dion.	Illi diçon.	Illi dison.	…	loz dison.
", 372, e degne de punir.	e degne de punlr.	e degne de murir.	…	loz feson morir.
" 457, Cant venre l'antexrist.	Cant venré lenteXrist.	à fuire l'anteXrist.	del temp d'lantexP̄t.	
" 460, Aquilh.	Aquilli.	Aquilli.	Aq̄lb.	

* The Genevan MS. is not accentuated, if Raynouard's copy be correct. Morland's and Leger's have accents.

† In the copies of Leger and Morland the ez of the Genevan MS. is invariably changed into ç, and the final h into li; as filh, aquilh (Gen.), fili, aquilli (Morland and Leger.)

In justice to Perrin, whom you, Mr. Editor, have handled with some severity (Brit. Mag., vol. xviii., p. 620) [see p. 116, *supra*], I think it right to say that I have found proof of his credibility in several points where his *veracity* has been doubted. Gilles, the native historian of the Waldenses, states that many MSS. enumerated by Perrin were sent to him from the valleys of Piedmont; and he gives the name of the Piedmontese pastor who was deputed to arrange them, and to make translations of them for Perrin's use. (See Gilles, " Hist. Eccl. des Eglises Refor. du Piemont," p. 383.)

The same author gives the date of the letters from Bohemia for which your correspondent asks (vol. xviii., p. 610), [see p. 108, *supra*], viz., the 27th June, 1533; and the particulars of the transaction, in which Daniel of Valence and Jean de Molines were implicated, according to Perrin (p. 67). He gives the substance, also, of those letters on which your correspondent observes that " it is to be regretted no copies have been furnished." (See Gilles, pp. 33–35.)

I may be allowed to select another example of the manner in which I have tested Perrin as to his history and documents. In pages 110 and 111 he writes thus of the Waldenses:—
" Eglises vrayment reformées de temps immemoré, car encor qu'en ladite vallée il y ait à preset des vieilles gens, et non en petit nombre, qui approchent, et quelques uns qui ont passé, cent ans. Si n'ont ces bon viellards jamais appris de leurs pères et ayeuls qu'il y ait eu de leur temps aucune messe chantée en leur pais."

Perrin's book was published in 1619. Claude Seyssel, Archbishop of Turin, who visited the Waldenses of the Piedmontese valleys in 1517,* boasts that he was the first prelate in the

---

* Your correspondent thinks that it was an artifice of the Protestant-Vaudois, after the Reformation, to carry up the Waldenses to an origin before Waldo; but Seyssel, who was in the valleys before the Reformation, informs us, fol. v., that the heretics of the valleys had all along been ascribing an anti-

memory of man who had visited them episcopally. Two of his expressions are strong enough :—" *Et eam ob causam, nullus hominum memoria eorum prelatus ad vallium illarum penetralia accedere vix fuerit ausus ; me tamen,*" &c., fol. ii.—" *Spe fideque pleni, ad ipsa loca nostris antecessoribus maxima ex-parte (ut diximus) inaccessa, Deo authore profecti sumus,*" fol. iv.— " Claud. Seysselli adversus Sectam Valdensium Disputationes:" Paris, 1520.

In 1406, the Dominican, Vincentius Ferrerius, preached to the Sub-Alpine Waldenses; and he declared, in a letter to the General of his order, that, for forty years before, no Catholic preacher had been heard in the valleys.—(See " Præf. Ricchini ad Monetam.," p. xvi.) Claude Seyssel, in his work, alludes repeatedly to books and writings in the vulgar tongue, by which the Waldenses were confirmed in their hostility to the Roman Church.* See especially, fol. iv. and v.

I am afraid this letter is already too long, but I cannot lose the opportunity of stating, in reference to your correspondent's date of 1160† for the institution of Waldo's fraternity of " The Poor Men of Lyons," that 1173 was the year in which Waldo first came into notice. This is distinctly represented in the only *contemporary* document which gives us detailed information of Waldo's first impulse and consequent proceedings. The Lyonese merchant happened to hear a troubadour reciting a

quity to their sect similar to that which, according to Reiner, was claimed by the Leonists.

* Is it not a strange coincidence, when taken in connexion with the alleged antiquity of the Waldensian MSS. that when Ecbert wrote against certain heretics, whom he called Cathari, about the year 1160 (before Waldo), he remarked, " Muniti sunt verbis sacræ Scripturæ quæ aliquo modo sectis eorum concordare videntur."—See " Bibl. Patr.," vol. iv., p. 2, p. 78. The Cathari against whom Ecbert wrote came from Italy, and may or may not have had some communication with the Sub-Alpine Waldenses ; but if one community of dissenters had its writings at that early period, so might another.

† [Brit. Mag., vol. xviii., p. 601 [*supra*, p. 101].

poem of Alexis, and, singularly enough, a Romish legend produced impressions which led to a movement in opposition to the Roman Church. I refer you to "The Chronicle of Laon," published in Bouquet's "Recueil des Historiens," vol. xiii. p. 682.

This document escaped even Ussher's notice (perhaps from not having been in print before Bouquet's collection), and has never been brought forward, as far as I know, by any writer on Waldo and the Poor Men of Lyons. The passage begins thus :—" *Currente adhuc anno eodem Incarnationis* 1173, *fuit apud Lugdunum Galliæ, civis quidam, Valdesius nomine, qui per iniquitatem fænoris multas sibi pecunias coacerverat,*" &c. Those who would make themselves well acquainted with Waldo's true history, and with that of "The Poor Men of Lyons," should first consult contemporary authorities only, in the following order :—

Chronicon Anonymi Canonici Laudunensis, sub annis 1173–1178. Bouquet, vol. xiii.

Gaualteri Mappei De Secta Valdesiorum, xxxi. MS. Bod. 851. A part only of this is in print, published by Ussher. De Chr. Eccl. Succ., c. viii. p. 268.

Stephen de Borbone, who derived his information from Waldo's fellow-labourers in the work of translating and transcribing MSS. Apud Echart Pr. Or., Scr., vol. i. p. 162.

I am, dear Sir, yours faithfully,

W. S. GILLY.

DURHAM, *Jan.* 8, 1841.

ON THE POEMS OF THE POOR OF LYONS.

POSTSCRIPT* TO No. II.

SINCE the second portion of this paper was printed, some further and very surprising information has been communicated to the public concerning the ancient MS. or MSS. of the poems. It is contained in the letter of Monsieur Favre Bertrand, of Geneva, to Dr. Gilly, and quite recently published by the latter in the Correspondence of the " British Magazine." The ancient manuscript book deposited by Morland at Cambridge, in 1658 vanished unaccountably. But we now learn† with surprise that the manuscript book deposited by Jean Leger at Geneva, in 1662, disappeared in like manner. It is not to be found at Geneva; and no account can be given (at least none is given) of the mode of its disappearance. The book *ne se retrouve plus*. Such a fatality as these transactions exhibit will scarcely find a parallel in the history of literature ; and if the principal actor in them was honest, he was strangely unfortunate. Two similar volumes produced by the same individual, and lodged in two places, distant from each other, and both secure—yet both of them evanescent, and melted into air !

However, there is at Geneva now a visible manuscript of these poems, agreeing in age, materials,‡ and written character, with the description we have received of the two invisible ones. But Monsieur Bertrand says it is duodecimo, whereas the missing Geneva volume is described as having been an octavo. This

---

* [Brit. Mag., vol. xix., p. 257.]

† [See Dr. Gilly's Letter, p. 160, *supra*.]

‡ Monsieur F. Bertrand, indeed, calls it *vellum ;* but Girard, who received it from one of the Legers, terms it *parchment*. Therefore, whichever it really is, it is the same substance that the Legers called parchment.

makes a third ancient codex, agreeing in many grand points with the other two. And who brought this one to Geneva? Monsieur Antoine Leger, who, jointly with his nephew Jean, gave the Cambridge one to Morland. The librarian Girard,* (in a list of the donations that had been made to the library since he had the care of it, and of which list the date does not appear), enters it as a donation made by Antoine in October, 1661, and on *the day previous to his death*. Just about one year before the nephew deposited *his* book at Geneva, and took Monsieur Girard's receipt for it. All the three manuscripts (if they ever existed) appertain to the same family.

One thing, at any rate, we may take for granted. The nephew, John, must have known all about his uncle's curious old copy, must have frequently examined it and compared it with his other two, and must have shed some pious tears when he heard of the deathbed scene on the 17th of October, 1661. When he went to Monsieur Girard in November, 1662, to present him with his own copy, Girard would no doubt exclaim, "Ah! it is but this time twelvemonth, that your poor dear uncle brought me such another book. Here it is. Now we are quite rich in Vaudois poetry." Not a bit of it. When Jean Leger published his work in 1669, he knew nothing of the third manuscript which his dying kinsman had bequeathed to the library of Geneva. In the heading prefixed to his extracts from the "Noble Lesson," he informs his readers that there had been found two ancient copies of that poem, of which one was at Cambridge, and *one at Geneva*—viz., his own; while Girard's signature came forward to prove that there were two copies at Geneva, that of 1661 and that of 1662. Strange! that his living uncle should never have named the other book to him. Stranger, if possible, that the last act of his dying kinsman should never, in the course of eight years, have reached his hearing. Most strange, incredible, and morally impossible.

---

* Or Gerard, as he is called in the "Histoire Generale," &c.

Evil so abounds upon earth that it must continually be in our thoughts. And Charity is so inseparably united to her heavenly sister Truth, that she must very frequently become aware of its presence. But it is her peculiarity, signified in the Gospel, not to think evil from enmity and malice, or believe in its existence from the odious *wish* that it should be found existing. The author of this paper, having it for his object to vindicate the authenticity of these poems, can have no wish whatever to diminish the number of vouchers for their antiquity. Nothing would satisfy him better than that several such copies should exist, or have existed. And it is only disbelieved because it appears to be unworthy of credit, and because the statements present clear traces of prevarication. When Leger was offering to the world his cunningly garbled specimens of a production not as yet recognised by the learned, it was certainly not his interest or desire to lower the proofs of its genuineness, or diminish the number of old contemporary documents demonstrative of that fact. We see him constantly exerting every nerve in the opposite spirit. Therefore, we may be fully satisfied that, when he assures us that Geneva contained but one old MS. of it, he speaks the whole truth without suppression. And though we may think he has made two books out of one, we are sure he did not reduce three into two. Either the deposit made by Anthony in 1661, or that by John in 1662, is a fiction; but the other is a true history (inasmuch as one copy is forthcoming), and we are disposed to regard it as an authentic passage in the life and adventures of Morland's volume B.

With this alternative before us, it is difficult to make a choice. If Girard* was dead in 1669, when J. Leger printed his receipt for the volume of 1662, we should possess no assurance that the aforesaid receipt ever existed except in type. That

* Monsieur F. Bertrand only says that he [Girard] was librarian " about the middle of the seventeenth century ;" and more, perhaps, is not known of him.

theory would sink the volume in question, and set up that of Anthony in the previous year. But it involves a decided act of forgery; and it is perhaps safer to believe that the receipt was really given in 1662 in exchange for the book which the younger Leger had brought. In that case the subsequent but undated entry in the list of donations, by Monsieur Girard, would become the point in these incredible narrations upon which we must lay our finger. The incorrect entry stood un-contradicted by any public documents in Geneva. And if any one inquired for the MS. mentioned in the receipt given to Jean Leger, the same answer as we now receive was then in readiness—" How extraordinary ! how very distressing ! *il ne se retrouve plus.*" Nobody could say, " I knew Monsieur Antoine intimately, and he never said a single word about his valuable donation." For he gave it into the hands of Monsieur Girard *on the very day preceding his death.* Since Leger could only boast that " deux exemplaires se sont trouvés" in all, of which only one was at Geneva, and falsehood manifestly exists, it appears to belong rather more probably to Girard. Some other motive than the mere wish to multiply ancient MSS. must be supposed to have existed. That motive may possibly have been the great alteration the book had undergone, by unstitching it, and shuffling and changing the contents. For the book of Anthony, in 1661, was far from coinciding in its contents with that of John in 1662. The whole matter is, however, involved in such complete mystery, that nothing affirmative can, with any degree of confidence, be pronounced upon it; and those who will may freely elect to believe in the library entry, and in the book of 1661, rejecting Monsieur Jean's receipt and his book of 1662. Those who *can,* will feel pleasure in believing the whole story as it is told them.

It may be remarked that, if the various reading of this patois were proofs of distinct MSS., we should here have conclusive evidence that Raynouard *did not* publish from the present Geneva text (*quod est absurdum*); for Monsieur Girard, in his enumeration of its contents, has treated us to some remarkable variations.

The impression created by the state of the case, and specially by the language of Perrin citing Saint Aldegonde, that this was an unique and almost sacred volume, the sole ancient codex, is strongly confirmed by the entry concerning it; which states that it was "remis pour être gardé pour les Eglises du Piémont." It was not Leger's: it does not now belong to the Genevese; nor does it belong to any one of the Vaudois Valleys. But it is a volume kept, as in the ark of the covenant, for all the tribes of Israel.

ON THE POEMS OF THE POOR OF LYONS.

No. III.*

NONE of the extant poems of the Poor of Lyons, or, at the most, but one, could be applied to the purposes of psalmody; but they were composed as vehicles of instruction in sacred history, and of moral precept. Such a method of teaching was peculiarly suited to the wandering habits and empaupered condition of their first leaders. And the very form in which these poems present themselves would lead us to suppose that their authors still retained the primitive simplicity of their sect.

But the chronological allusion contained in the poem, which (for that reason) had been selected for publication, makes a clear profession of antiquity. It cannot, however, avail to establish so high an antiquity as it appeared, and was fondly imagined to do; and, consequently, cannot lend any effective support to those other dates which were so constructed as to harmonize with it. For either it must be as inauthentic as they are, or else its meaning has been misapprehended.

The passage in question is near the commencement, and in these words :—

> " Ben ha mil e cent ancz compli entierament,
> Que fot scripta l'ora ; car sen al derier temp."

> " Well has eleven hundred years been completed entirely,
> Which was the hour written; for we are at the last time."

---

† The English editor has given the line thus—
> " Que fo scripta lora, car son al derier temp."
> " Since it was written thus—*For we are at the last time.*"

He probably takes lora as equivalent to the French alors or lors; and evidently supposes 1 John, ii. 18, to be quoted. But, first, the authors could

The first question we have to ask upon this is, whether the "Noble Lesson" was indeed composed in or about A. D. 1100. And we are compelled to answer that question peremptorily in the negative.

Firstly, the authors of it declare themselves to be reviled under the appellation of Vaudes. That noun was used in the singular, and accented* on the last syllable, Vaudés. In their translation of the epistle to Ladislaus† they spell it Valdés. And sometimes they formed it in‡ the plural, Vaudési or Valdesi. The futility of the attempts to derive that word from *vallis*, a valley, has been§ demonstrated in the British Magazine already. It is evidently the same word that is so well known in Spain as the name of several families, and in like manner accented on the last, Valdéz. Señor Valdéz or Dominus Waldensis is‖, in effect, the same name as that of the English Lord

never have hazarded such a proposition as that John meant the twelfth century when he said, "*even now*, . . . it is the last time." Secondly, there is no such word as lora in the language of these poems. It has no meaning, except as an elision of la ora ; as in the " Novel Confort"—

"Car vos non sabe l'ora que Xrist deo venir."

Thirdly, the Romance Latin is as exact in its genders as the ancient ; and fo scripta could not be said by a Vaudois to express fo scripto, any more than fuit scripta could be said by Tully or Virgil for fuit scriptum. Morland's interpretation is altogether absurd and barbarous.

* See Leger, " Hist.," p. 28.   † Perrin, " Hist.," p. 224.
‡ See Leger, p. 154.
§ Brit. Mag., vol. xvi., p. 606, 7. [See p. 127, *supra*.]
‖ It is customary to call him Peter Waldo, as if it were the nominative, declined in *onis*, which was a common name enough. But perhaps the truth in this case may be, that he was de Waldo, in the ablative. His appellations of Petrus Waldensis, Waldius, Waldus, Don Valdensis, Valdesius, and Valdes (which latter occurs in the ablative in W. Mapeus, " a primate ipsorum Valde," and is completely identical with the Spanish Valdez), may be considered equivalents for de Waldo, as Lugdunensis is for de Lugduno. And they are of the best antiquity. The first person, perhaps, who names him (Alanus de Insulis in sæc. xii.ᵐᵒ), calls him Waldus. Peter of Pilichdorf contra Waldenses (circa A. D. 1444), says that in *civitate Walden* quæ in

Forester, and the French Count de Laforêt. Waldenses they were called, when this poem was written. But the fraternity which received that appellation was not formed until the year 1177, being three or four years after Waldo embraced voluntary* poverty. Thus it is brought down seventy-seven years lower than its pretended date. To which it may be added, that Poor of Lyons was the genuine and primitive appellation of this sect, and that no instance of their being called Waldenses has as yet been discovered† anterior to 1192.

Secondly, it contains an account " of the three laws that God gave to the world" (v. 437, et seq.), viz., that of nature, that of Moses, and that of Christ, after which was to be none other. But the doctrine of three consecutive laws of God, and states of the world and church, originated with Joachim, abbot of Curacio and Flore, and from him it was derived into various channels of sectarianism. The Vaudés differ from him in

finibus Franciæ sita est [versus Alamanniam, in one MS.] fuit quidam civis dives. "Bibl. Max. Patrum," xxv., p. 278. The tract "Contra Pauperes de Lugd." (also ascribed to Peter of Pilchdorf, but palpably by another hand) says, surrexit quidam *e regione Waldis* Petrus nominatus (Ibid. p. 300). This opulent landholder (for such he was) may have received his appellation from some private estate or domain, of which geography can take no cognizance. But considering the expressions above used—viz., in finibus Franciæ sita, versus Alamanniam, and regio Waldis; and considering that Lyons was the birth-place, and Burgundy the cradle of this sect; it is probable that the Pagus Waldensus or Pays de Vaud, der Wald an den Lemanischen see, situate in the Burgundia Transjurana, was that from which he took his title. The Waldenses of Languedoc came into that country from Burgundy, as appears from authentic documents.

* The writer of this is greatly obliged to Dr. Gilly for pointing out the Chronicon Laudunense, with which he was entirely unacquainted. It seems, in the absence of equivalent evidence to the contrary, conclusive that Peter's own vow of poverty was made in 1173, and that he first began to have associates in 1177. And the generally received date for the first of those events—viz., 1160, must give way.—Recueil des Historiens de France, xiii., 680-2.

† In which year the statutes of Otho, Bishop of Toul, term them hæretici qui vocantur Wadoys.—D'Argentré, *Collect. Jud.*, 1, p. 82.

making the natural or patriarchal the first, the Mosaic the second, and that of Christ and his apostles the third and last. But they evidently formed their triad after his theory had been published. The same abbot taught that each of the three laws was under a different Person of the Holy Trinity, and assigned to the* three Persons three distinct attributes, to be manifested in the three laws respectively—to the Father, power; to the Son, wisdom; and to the Holy Ghost, charity. But the Noble Lesson says—

> " These three, the Holy Trinity,
> Should be prayed unto as one God,
> Full of all wisdom, and all power, and all goodness,"

which† three attributes the New Comfort thus distributes to the Divine persons—

> " The power of the Father, and the wisdom of the Son,
> And the goodness of the Holy Ghost."

So it seems they had adopted his heresy of tritheism, as well as his notion of three states, though they did not apply either the one or the other in the mischievous way he had done. But the year 1181 is the earliest in which the abbot of Curacio can be said to have promulgated his theories. In this manner we bring down the poem eighty-one years from its alleged date.

Thirdly, it complains that they were marked out as objects of persecution by their name of Waldenses.

> " Ilh dion qu'és Vaudés e degne de punir."‡

But it does not appear from history that the see of Rome had

---

* Joachim Psalt. Decem Chord. 240, b.   In Apocalyps, 5, b.

† See Brit. Mag., vol. xvii., pp. 1, 2.

‡ See Nobla Leyczon, v. 350–373. In v. 372, Leger has put *murir*, death, instead of *punir*, punishment. The manuscript, the Dublin transcript, and even Morland, are against him. It was a wanton act, committed to embitter a passage, of which the force really operates to destroy his own theory of dates.

ever pronounced any condemnation on the Poor Men of Lyons, or instituted any persecution of them, anterior to the bull of Lucius the Third, in A. D. 1183. They were (said Stephanus[*] de Borbone, sive Bellavillâ) excommunicated by John Bellesmains, Archbishop of Lyons; and judged schismatic and heretical by a council anterior to the [fourth] Lateran. But Joannes a Bellis Manibus, Archbishop elect of Narbonne, was transferred to Lyons by Lucius the Third[†] in the course of A. D. 1181; which proves that the fourth in Lateran was the council above alluded to by name, and that of Lucius III.[‡] the one said to have preceded it. "Pope Lucius (saith Conrad[§] of Ursperg) placed them in the number of heretics;" which expresses in a positive way what the silence of history confirms negatively—viz., that the bull of Lucius was the first penal animadversion[‖] on the Pauperes. Therefore we have now degraded the aspiring date of the poem in question by no less than eighty-three years.

---

[*] Apud Martene, Thesaurus, tom. 5, p. 1778. Quetif, *Bibl. Ord. Predic.*, 1, p. 192.

[†] For the proofs of this see Gallia Christiana, IV. p. 130. It follows that the year 1180, mentioned by Stephen of Bourbon, *cannot* be right; and 1183 is, probably, the year he means. Their excommunication by Archbishop John was probably in execution of the papal bull, though he places it first in the sentence. Quære tamen.

[‡] It is not necessary to infer from his words, that Lucius held a general council, or a provincial synod of the whole Gallican Church. The pope's ordinary council, serving for the ancient diocesan and patriarchal synods, will suffice to explain them.

[§] Cit. Bossuet, *Hist. des Variations*, L. xi.; Raynouard 2, p. cxxxviii.; Maitland, "Facts and Documents," &c., p. 398.

[‖] The same is declared by Esrom Rudiger. Lucius Papa Tertius ut hæreticos . . . illos cætus est execratus, de Ecclesiis Fratrum in Bohemiâ, p. 9. Antiquissimum monumentum in quo expressa fit mentio hæresis Pauperum de Lugduno ipsum decretum est Lucii Papæ tertii anno 1183. Du Plessis d' Argentré, *Collect. Jud.*, 1, p. 82.

We have next to inquire, Is the line a forgery? or is the assertion in it a lie? or has its import been misápprehended? The first-mentioned supposition would save all further trouble. We have no credible evidence that more than one genuine MS. has existed within memory. Looking to that one MS., we are given to understand that it is not interpolated by modern hands. Monsieur Raynouard's words, "Les personnes qui l'examineront (ce poeme) avec attention jugeront que le manuscrit n'a pas été interpolé," seem indeed to appeal only to the moral evidences of non-interpolation furnished by the poem itself; not to any actual and searching examination of the ancient parchment. But as Monsieur Favre Bertrand transcribed the whole, with a full knowledge of the importance of this line, and conveyed it to Raynouard with no intimation of its being supposititious, or having undergone alteration, it is fair to conclude that it is (to all appearance) an integral part of the text. It is a question of fact, which requires to be, and we hope soon will be, narrowly examined. Meanwhile, it behoves us, not in verbal courtesy alone, but in all sincerity, to accept and believe that the antique text *bond fide* stands thus.

It comes next in order to inquire, whether this poem may not have been composed in its present form at, or anterior to, the time (whatever that may be) at which this old MS. was penned; and whether its author may not have falsely represented it as yet a century older, and so practised a literary imposture. To this supposition three answers suggest themselves. *First*, that the character of this production, and of the others that accompany it, is simple, manly, and virtuous, betraying no aim or purpose but the diffusion of what they held for truth. *Secondly*, that the poor of Lyons had no inducement to the practice of this deception. We cannot discover any end that the poet would gain by persuading his hearers or readers that those verses were written in A. D. 1100. We should refrain

from charging the author of this interesting work with a falsehood that would be gratuitous,* and is not accounted for.
Thirdly, if we were disposed to fasten upon him such a design,
we should find it difficult to account for his ignorance and incapacity in the execution of it. His case was not like that of the
Vaudois-Protestant date-forgers. For this MS. is very ancient,
since some have judged it to be of the twelfth century. Therefore the poet must have lived when all the main traditions of
the sect were tolerably fresh. And the date of Peter Waldo
and that of the papal persecution could scarcely have been unknown to him. Whilst engaged in antedating his own work,
of which the date was private, by nearly a century, he would
not have clumsily betrayed his own fraud by antedating both
the founder and the persecution, of which the dates were notorious and public.

Since we admit (until duly advised to the contrary) that the
verse is genuine, and acquit its author of any dishonesty, but
at the same time well know that it was not composed within
eighty-three years of A. D. 1100, it remains to find some
sense in which the words in question can be true. Such an
explanation has been already suggested in a former volume.†
And nothing has since occurred to induce the abandonment of
that suggestion. The whole of a century is governed by the
year of its commencement, and each of its successive years

---

* Some persons had in the thirteenth century (as Sacconi states) begun to
trace the origin of this community to Pope Sylvester's time, or earlier. And
Peter of Pilichdorf, who was professor of theology in A. D. 1444 (Fabric., Bibl.
Med. Latin, ed. Mansi. D'Argentré, Collect. Jud. 1, p. 84), accuses the Waldenses themselves of tracing their own origin to the days of Sylvester. No
such spirit manifests itself in their printed remains. And the mention of Pope
Sylvester in v. 409 of the " Noble Lesson," while it shows the origin and ex-
plains the growth of the Sylvestrian fable, proves at the same time the author's entire innocence of it. It may be observed that both those authors
speak chiefly in reference to the Waldenses in Germany.

† [Brit. Mag., vol. xvi., p. 607. See the passage alluded to above p. 129.]

bears the name of that year prefixed to its own units or decads. Therefore the line—

" Ben ha mil e cent ancz compli entierament"

may be taken to mean that the century of years of which 1100 had been the denominator was entirely completed, and the fresh century, of which 1200 was the denominator, actually commenced. It is no light argument to this purpose that syntax is violated by putting the singular verb *ha* instead of *han.* " Eleven hundred years *has* been, not *have* been, completed." In that respect the Romance tongue is as regular as the Latin, and does not subjoin singular verbs to plural nouns. The poems, it is believed, offer no other instance of *ha* for *han.* Therefore those who would hastily rejoin to us, " The words will not grammatically express your meaning," must remember that they will not grammatically express anything; but that the tendency of the grammatical license employed is synthetical, and to place the 1100 years (if we may so say) algebraically *sub vinculo.* What should we think, if we read anywhere " Undecies centum anni completum est ?" The case is the same; and the expression made use of seems anomalous and unique.

We are to understand that it was composed in, or shortly after, the year 1200, and that its author regarded that epoch as " the hour written of" or foretold, as introducing the " last time," and all after which was but the remnant of time, " el remanent," to be marked by the world's downfall, " el chavon," and to be spent in expectation of the* great Antichrist's advent. But we have also seen him borrowing from Joachim the idea of three states, and partly tainted with his tritheism. Now, the doctrine which we have been led (by other considerations) to ascribe to the author of this poem happens to be purely that of Joachim, and which has no where been met with but in that abbot's original speculations. He taught that

* See verses 454–60.

A. D. 1200 *was* the beginning of the time of the end, and A. D. 1260, its consummation; and that the intervening sixty years *were* a remnant of time, not properly belonging either to his second or his third *status mundi*, and to be characterized by the downfall of the secular church, the tyranny and persecutions of the beast, and lastly, by the manifestation and brief (but too long) reign of Antichrist. And this he taught, not as a prophet himself, but as a spiritually gifted interpreter of the scriptural prophecies. Therefore the year 1200 was really scripta l'ora, according to the scriptural exposition of the very man of whose ideas we had detected a portion in this and another of the poems; and according to that of no other man (his disciples excepted) that ever lived. Herein, it must be admitted, there is considerable confirmation. And unless it should so befall that future scrutiny of the MS. were to shake the authenticity of the passage, we shall probably do well to acquiesce in the above conclusion.

No difficulty will arise from the[*] statement, that "Monsieur Senebier (the Genevese librarian) judged the MS. of Geneva to be of the twelfth century." He was a naturalist, distinguished by a voluminous work on vegetable physiology, and similar productions. Although it is no proof against his being practically skilled in antiquarian research, those two pursuits have seldom, if ever, been followed to the highest degree of eminence by the same individuals. They seem to require different habits of mind and of study, and to lead to, if they do not require, different intimacies and habits of social intercourse. But if we allow to his judgment the amplest authority that such decisions can possess, it will amount to nothing. For an opinion that only assigns it to the twelfth century is satisfied by the hypothesis that it was written in 1190 or 1199. But, when these opinions are broached, we must never forget that a book was written *by a man*, and that man was neither

---

[*] Raynouard, "Choix de Poesies," 2, p. cxliii.

born the day before he wrote it, nor (most likely) did he die the day after. Consequently, to say that a given book was probably written in 1180, is, by implication, to say that it was probably written in 1150 or in 1210. Because it is perfectly probable, that the same scribe who was sixty years old in 1180 may have written it when he was only thirty; or that he who was thirty years old in 1180 may not have written it till he was sixty. It is therefore abundantly manifest, that such a judgment as that pronounced by Mons. Senebier entitles us to claim many years of the thirteenth century, when all we have strict occasion for is its commencement.

DR. GILLY'S SECOND LETTER ON THE WALDEN-SIAN MSS.

[THIS Letter was drawn forth by the Postscript to No. II. of the Papers "On the Poems of the Poor of Lyons," p. 172, *supra*.   It was printed in the Brit. Mag., vol. xix., p. 387, *sq.*]

MY DEAR SIR,—Surely the writer "On the Poems of the Poor of Lyons" might adopt some more likely mode of ascertaining facts, than by indulging in such suspicious and injurious surmises as are contained in the last Number of the British Magazine.   The whole mystery of Leger's production, and use of copies of "The Noble Lesson," is as surprising and perplexing to me as it is to him, and I have felt the difficulties of the case in all its bearings.   The appearance and disappearance of some of the MSS., the apparently irreconcileable accounts given by the parties concerned with them, the memoranda of the librarian Girard, on the deposit of the MSS. in the library of Geneva—these are all subjects of wonder.   But, instead of wasting time in endless conjectures, had we not better resort to an accurate inquiry on the spot, where there are yet some remains of the MSS. which have occasioned this controversy; and where some traces may yet be left of the proceedings of the Legers, and Girard, and Morland?   There is at least one ancient codex of the "Noble Lesson" in existence, and somebody may be found to scrutinize it with a sharp eye, and to report if it exhibits any, and what, marks of interpolation, and what are its several characteristics.

Your correspondent says,* "*We have next to inquire, Is the line—*

'Ben ha mil e cent ancz compli entierament'

---

* Brit. Mag., vol. xix., p. 263 [p. 182, *supra*].

*a forgery? Looking to that one MS., we are given to under-
stand that it is not interpolated by modern hands. Monsieur
Raynouard's words, 'Les personnes qui l'examineront (ce
poème) avec attention jugeront que le manuscrit n'a pas été
interpolé,' seem indeed to appeal only to the moral evidences
of non-interpolation furnished by the poem itself, not to any
actual and searching examination of the ancient parchment."
"It is a question of fact,"* your correspondent continues,
"which requires to be, and we may hope soon will be, narrowly
examined."*

Why, I repeat, does he not take measures to have the MS.
examined by a witness in whom he can confide? In my last
letter to you,* I stated that I had myself seen the Genevan
book, and had examined the MS., and could vouch for the accuracy of M. Bertrand's description of it. The persuasion on
my mind is, that the MS. of the " Noble Lesson" has not been
tampered with. But I may not have looked into it with the
searching eye of habitual suspicion, though I went to the library of Geneva on purpose to examine it. And who am I ?
A partizan, a prejudiced person. Well, then, I subjoin a fac-
simile sent to me from Geneva ; it contains four lines ; one of
these has the date in the MS., the line concerning which it is
asked, " *Is the line a forgery ?*" Make what use of it you please ;
print it, or send it to your correspondent. Does it look like an
interpolation ?† Has your correspondent no friend or friend's
friend at Geneva, who will take the trouble of casting a search-

---

* Brit. Mag., vol. xix., p. 192 [see p. 162, *supra*].

† The Editor [of Brit. Mag.], thus appealed to, is bound to say, that he
does not see anything in the fac-simile that looks like interpolation or forgery.
Whether the poem is of anything like the antiquity which that line is supposed
to indicate is a question on which he is so unfortunate as to differ from both
Dr. Gilly and his opponent. He takes, however, a lively interest in the discussion of the subject between such parties, because he believes that it will tend
to elicit great and important truths, and will be glad to assist by any means
in his power. He has sent the fac-simile to the author of the papers on the

ing eye over the book, and ascertain whether there may have been any erasement, substitution, interpolation, or interlineation? Is not the librarian at Geneva, M. Diodati, to be trusted? I am sure, to judge from the trouble he has given himself to reply to my letters, he would do as much for your correspondent. He would tell him truly everything that may be said of the MS., of Girard's memoranda, and of those *"renseignements"* of M. Favre Bertrand, communicated to M. Raynouard,* which excited the suspicions expressed in vol. xix., pp. 19, 20. Mr. Favre Bertrand is still living at Geneva. Let him be questioned. I am confident that both Mr. F. Bertrand and M. Diodati would report frankly and correctly on all the points of your correspondent's doubts and misgivings. It is certainly much easier and more tempting to indulge in critical conjectures, in smart witticisms, and in all that running fire by which controversialists can distinguish themselves, than to pursue the slow process of scrutinizing existing records in their place of deposit, and of collating documents in manuscript with copies of them in print. Let us go to the original sources, and let us get together all the facts we can, or we shall remain where we are; and we shall continue to express ourselves as if we were more suspicious and uncharitable than we really are.

For my own part, I would rather state one fact, or produce one document, than hazard a hundred clever but somewhat ungenerous conjectures; and in this work of collecting authentic materials I have been toiling for years, and continue to labour, and I have not been unrewarded. Your correspondent in a note has given me credit† for bringing forward one piece of documentary evidence which has never before, to his know-

---

" Poems of the Poor of Lyons ;" and, if it is thought that it will throw any light on the matter, he will be very happy to have it engraved.

* [See pp. 147, 148, *supra.*]

† Brit. Mag., vol. xix., p. 261 [p. 179, *supra*].

ledge or to mine, appeared in any controversy relating to Waldo, or the Subalpine Waldenses—viz., the "Chronicon Laudunense," and yet this is the only full contemporary record of Waldo's first steps towards separation from the Church of Rome. I have been equally fortunate in other attempts to throw light upon the Waldensian question.

Through the kindness of Dr. Bandinel, the highly respected librarian of the Bodleian Library, and a friend at Oxford, I have been enabled to put *the whole* of Walter Mapes' treatise concerning the "Poor Men of Lyons" in print, Ussher having given a short extract only. My appeals to the assistance of the librarians of the public libraries of Grenoble and Zurich have also been successful in rescuing from their obscurity two ancient codices—vernacular translations of Scripture in the language of the Subalpine Waldenses. One of these I described in my last letter to the British Magazine* (though your correspondent took no notice of it), and it has led to the announcement of a MS. copy of the Grenoble Codex of the year 1522, preserved in the library of Trinity College, Dublin, an account of which, and of some of the Ussher MSS., will shortly appear, I trust, in your Magazine, from the pen of Dr. Todd. Le Long, in his "Bibliotheca Sacra," describes this as an *Italian* version, and my letter of inquiry on the subject was answered by a very courteous communication from Dr. Todd.

These are proofs sufficient of the kind and ready attention which the conservators of public libraries pay to requests made to them, such as I recommend your correspondent to make for the removal of some of his suspicions.

I care not what transpires, so as we do but get hold of the truth. In proof, Mr. Editor, of my readiness to produce what makes in favour of the hypothesis of others, as well as my own, I now furnish you with an account of the Zurich Codex,

* [See p. 164, *supra.*]

which confirms in part one of Mr. Maitland's doubts, expressed in his "Facts and Documents," p. 130 [*n.*, in these words]:—

" *Le Long refers to a duodecimo of which he only says*, 'N. Testamentum lingua Pedemontano-Vallensi per Barbetum quemdam seu ministrum Vallensem translatum. Codex in 12 scriptus post annum MC. Bibl. Civica Tigurina: Ottius.' *That this MS. was written after the year* 1100, *I fully believe ; and if the writer styles himself a Barbe and a Vallesian minister, I should imagine, a good while after. It does not appear that Le Long knew any more about it than I have extracted from chap. viii. p.* 162."

Dr. Orelli's* opinion, in his account of the Zurich Codex, corresponds with Mr. Maitland's conjecture :—

" Codex MS. Novi Testamenti 𝟭𝟴𝟴 Chartaceus, Sæculi XIV., formæ 12°, nunc constans foliis DIII. Index Latinus a manu recentiore circiter annum 1700 scriptus, idem prorsus atque ille, quem cum Le Longio olim communicavit Io. Baptista Ottius, omissis tamen verbis: ' Scriptus post annum M. C.' quæ quidem per se verissima, sed nimis infinita, et propterea pæne ridicula, sunt. Etenim ego, qui prope omnes Helvetiæ Codices, nonnullos etiam Germaniæ satis accurate inspexi, hunc scriptum censeo inter annos M.CCC.L. et M.CCCC.

" Initio desunt folia aliquot, ita ut codex nunc incipiat a dimidia parte ultimi (XVII) Vers. Cap. III. Evangelii S. Mathæi : *diezent. Aqst* (Aquest) *es lo meo filhama* al ǵl xxxxx. (legi nunc nequit :) *placami.* Excepto vero initio codex est integer atque optime conservatus. Specimen (*fac-simile*), quod optas omni qua par est, observantia tibi mittimus, vides, vers. 2 omissa esse verba: 'Επὶ αρχιερέως 'Ανννα ϛαὶ Καϊάφα, sive in Vulgata Latina, ex qua Valdenses N. T. suam in dialectum converterunt : *sub principibus sacerdotum, Anna et Caipha.*"

It will be worth while to collate the Zurich Codex with that at Grenoble. At present I can only assist your readers in taking a comparative view of the two by presenting them with the following extracts, which I have received, with fac-similes, from the beginning of the third chapter of St. Luke :—

* Communicated to me in a letter received from Dr. Orelli, the present librarian of Zurich, at the beginning of the current month (March) [1841].

ZURICH Codex,* 12mo, said to be of the fourteenth century.

"Al quinzen an de lenperi de Tiberi Cesar quant pilat segnoriiava en iudea, e herode era Segnor de Galilea, e lo seo frayre Phelip segnor de la region de Iturea e de Traconita, e Lisania segnor de la region de Abelina, la parolla fo fayta sobre hiohan filh de Zacaria al desert sot li princi de li preyre Anna et Cayphas."

GRENOBLE CODEX,† 4mo, said to be of the thirteenth century.

"Mas la parolla del segnor fo faita sobre Johan filh de Zacharia al desert al 15 an de lemperi de Thiberi cesar, ponc pilath procurant Judea, e herode quart princi de Galilea, e felip lo fraire de lui quart princi de Yturea e de la region de trachonitient, e lisania quart princi de Abelina sot li princi de li prever Anna e Caypha."

I have not yet been able, at this distance from public libraries, to ascertain whether the very peculiar reading in the Grenoble Codex (which begins with mention of the Word of the Lord coming upon John before it gives the date of the year, or states the names of the emperor and the tetrarchs), agrees with any other ancient version; and I shall be much obliged by information on this subject.

In the Grenoble MS. the year is denoted by Arabic characters, a mode of notation which was not commonly used in the twelfth and thirteenth centuries; but it had been introduced by the Moors and Saracens into the Sub-Alpine and Pyrenean regions long before.

The dialect of each is called, very properly, Pedemontano-Provençal, and was understood on each side of the Alps. Partaking, therefore, of the vernacular language of Italy, the Grenoble MS. furnishes us with an early version, which is a curiosity in literature, it having been unknown, according to the author of "Facts and Documents," p. 130, to Le Long, Muratori, and Magliabecchi; for, though the former refers to a codex in

* The Zurich Codex seems to contain a translation of the New Testament only.

† The Grenoble MS. has not only the whole of the New Testament, but also the five books of Solomon, as they are called—viz., Proverbs, Ecclesiastes, Wisdom, Ecclesiasticus, and the Song of Solomon.

the same language, on the authority of Thomassin de Mazangue, and Remerville de St. Quintin, he had never seen it
himself.   I hope I may therefore take some credit to myself
for bringing this litigated point to a close, as far as the existence of such a version goes, and for making this accession to
our stock of biblical information.

The description of the codex by Thomassin de Mazangue
corresponds with that of the MS. now at Grenoble in so many
particulars that it must be of the same family, to say the least.
He recognised traces in his copy of the antiquity of 400 years,
" *canitiem* 400 *annorum*," and contended that it was from a
version much more ancient, "*versionem vero esse antiquiorem.*"*
There is no difficulty, therefore, in believing that the Grenoble Codex is a MS. of the thirteenth century, and that the
version it contains may have been of a still older date.   Many
vernacular translations were then in use, and why may not
the Sub-Alpine Waldenses have had theirs ?   James I., King
of Arragon, and Count of Provence, in the year 1213 prohi-
bited the circulation of Books of the Old and New Testament,
translated into the *Romaunt dialect.*†

Pope Innocent III., in 1199 or 1200, wrote to the clergy of
Metz to make inquiries about a vernacular translation of the
Gospels, the Epistles of St. Paul, the Psalms, the Book of Job,
and other passages of holy writ.‡   And about 1180, Peter
Waldo circulated his vernacular translations, some of which I
still believe were made in the Romaunt dialect, for the use of

---

* Le Long, " Bibl. Sacr.," i., 368 ; and Suppl. Nat. Alex. 19, p. 75.

† The book which Robert Playce, Rector of Brompton, left in his will in
1345, as stated in my last letter, may have been a transcript of the Grenoble
Codex, because it is called " *Bibula* (Biblia?) in Romanam linguam translatam," and therefore contained more than the New Testament.

‡ The translators of this version were unknown, for Innocent asks a great
many questions about them :—Who were they ?   What was their object in
translating the Scriptures ?   For whom was the version intended ?   What
was their faith, &c.

O

the Sub-Alpine Waldenses, by whatever territorial name they may have been called; for it is certain that, when Waldo fled from Lyons, he and his "Poor Men of Lyons" took refuge among the mountaineers of Provence and Lombardy, whom *he found* to be, and not whom *he caused to be*, impugners of Romish errors.—(See Stephen de Borbone, who derived his account from one whom Waldo had employed to make his translations.) Vernacular Scripture was abroad at a still earlier period, even in the retired spot from which I write this letter. The Book of the Monk Reginald, written about the year 1172, relates an anecdote of a "*layman*" employed in the repairs of Norham Castle by Bishop Pudsey (who presided over the diocese from 1153 to 1194). This layman carried a book with him, out of which he recited passages from the Scripture, especially from the Gospels, very much to the surprise of his hearers. They were amazed, says Reginald, that he should have built his faith on those texts, especially as they were "non autentica, non tamen fidei canonem excedentia."—(See vol. i. of the publications of the Surtees Society, 1835, pp. 94–98.)

I venture to make a digression to a kindred subject. In your Notice to Correspondents at the end of the last Number [Brit. Mag., vol. xix., p. 368], there is the following query:— "It is known that there are editions of the French New Testament which translate Acts, xiii. 2, by ' *Or comme ils offroient au Seigneur le Sacrifice de la Messe*,' &c. Will any reader, who is able, say how many, and which?"

Mr. Hartwell Horne, in his "Introduction to the Study of Scripture," vol. ii., part 1, sec. vi. § 3, p. 99, in a note, gives the information your querist asks for:—"Le Nouveau Testament de notre Seigneur J. C. traduit de Latin en François par les Théologiens de Louvain; imprimé à Bordeaux, chez Jacques Mongiron-Millanges, Imprimeur du Roi et du College, 1686. Avec approbation et permission." "Two copies are at Oxford, one in the Bodleian Library, and another in that of Christ Church College; two others are in Dublin, in the University

Library, and in the library founded by Archbishop Marsh; and a fifth is in the possession of His Royal Highness the Duke of Sussex."

To this list given by Mr. Horne I am able to add one more. The library of the Dean and Chapter of Durham has a copy of this notorious *mis*translation of the Theologians of Louvain. The reason given by one of the translators for the falsification was, " because he had often been asked by Calvinists what Scripture affirmed the apostles said mass." Horne, *ibid.**

I remain, my dear Sir, yours truly,

W. S. GILLY.

NORHAM VICARAGE, *March* 9, 1841.

---

* The Editor [of Brit. Mag.] is much obliged to Dr. Gilly; and his thanks are also due to Mr. Milliken for a letter on the subject. His inquiry, however, was rather to elicit information respecting *other* editions containing the same mistranslation as that of Bordeaux. He thinks he has heard of one at Mons. At any rate, Leslie, in the 16th section of his "Case stated between the Church of England and the Church of Rome," makes the Romish lord say, " Have you any objection against the Louvain translation now printed and sold at Paris, with the approbation of the doctors and divines there?" and the English gentleman replies, " Yes, my lord, here is one in my hand, bought in the Rue St. Jacques, in *Paris*, where they are printed, with the approbations before them, in the year 1701. And in this translation there are many mistranslations; I will show your lordship one; it is said, Acts, xiii. 2," &c. It may be presumed that he referred to the edition of 1699, of which the Editor has now before him the only copy which he remembers to have seen, and which he met with lately at a shop in Holborn. The title page is, " Le Nouveau Testament de Notre Seigneur Jesus Christ de la traduction des Docteurs de Louvain. Reveuë et corrigée de nouveau, si exactement qu'elle est au vray une nouvelle Traduction, sur l'ancienne Edition Latine, reconnuë par le Commandement du Pape Sixte V. et publiée par l'autorité de Clement VIII. Avec deux Tables, l'une des Epistres et des Evangiles, et l'autre des choses principales. Nouvelle Edition. A Paris. Chez Nicolas le Gras au troisième Pilier de la grand' Salle du Palais, à l'L couronnée. M.DC.XCIX. Avec approbation." It has not been collated with the Bourdeaux edition; but the translation of Acts, xiii. 2, is as it stands above; and in the "Table des choses Principales contenuës au Nouveau Testament" (which is not in the Bourdeaux edition) we find, " *Messe* celebrée par les Apostres, Act. 13, 2." Iu-

deed, this Table is very explicit, and worthy of the work. For instance, *"L'adoration* faite aux bois, aux hommes et aux Anges. Heb. xi. 21; Act. x. 25 ; Apoc. xix. 10 et xii. 9."—*"Les Apostres* étoient sans femmes, et si quelqu'un d'eux en a eu une, il l'a quittée quand il a été fait Apôtre. Matt. xix. 27." &c.—*" La Confession* des pechez se doit faire au Pasteur. Marc, i. 5," &c.—" Les Apostres ont donné aux fideles la *Communion,* sous une espece. Acts, xx. 42," &c.—*" Indulgence.* Dieu use *d'indulgence,* Matt. xi. 22, 24, 29. Il veut aussi que son Eglise en use, Matt. xviii. 18, 22," &c.—*" Marie* . . . elle avoit fait vœu de Virginité, Luc. i. 34."—*"Pelerins* et *Pelerinage* approuvez de Dieu, et authorisez dans l'Ecriture, ceux qui leur font du bien, seront sauvez ; et ceux qui ne leur en font point seront damnez, Marc [*read Matt.*] xxv. 35, &c."—*"Purgatoire,* Matt. v. 25, et xii. 33."—*" Reliques* des Saints sont à avoir et reserver, puisque Dieu fait beaucoup de miracles par elles, Matt. ix. 20, et xiv. 36, &c."—" Il ne faut pas converser avec ceux qui rejettent les *Traditions,* 2 Thess. iii. 6, 14." One circumstance about this particular copy may be worth mentioning. Whether the binder made a mistake, or whether the owner was ashamed to be known to have the book on his shelf, and wished it to pass for one which few would wish to take down, cannot now be determined, but certain it is (from the legible impression on the back, though the lettering piece is gone), that the volume has been lettered COKE ON LITTLETON. With regard to the *Bordeaux* edition, the Editor apprehends that several copies might be added to the five mentioned above; and that, like many other *libri rarissimi,* this Testament is not so *very* scarce as has been imagined. Perhaps one of the five may be a copy from Cæsar de Missy's collection, which was sold by auction, by Mr. Evans, in 1821, and which fetched, the writer believes, £22 ; but the catalogue of that sale mentions three other copies (one in the Duke of Devonshire's library, a second in the Archiepiscopal Library, at Lambeth, and a third the writer does not remember where), and it is certain that all of these three copies cannot be included in those mentioned by Mr. Horne. Can any one give information as to the identity or difference between the editions of Bourdeaux and Paris, or point out any other editions ?

DR. GILLY'S THIRD LETTER ON THE WALDEN-
SIAN MANUSCRIPTS.

[In this letter* Dr. Gilly pointed out that the Morland MSS. G. and H. were safe in Cambridge. Finding copies, or perhaps the originals, of some of the documents they contain in the Dublin MS. C. 1. 6. and believing at the time that *all* the Morland MSS. had disappeared, I had too hastily thrown out the suggestion (see p. 21, *supra*), that portions at least of the vols. G. and H. may have found their way to Dublin. I may add here that, although the volume C. 1. 6. is in the same press with the Ussher MSS., there is no absolute proof that it ever formed a part of the Archbishop's Collection. See above, p. 74.—J. H. T.]

My dear Sir,—The discussion of the Waldensian question in the British Magazine has at length led to the production of documents which will extricate it from many of its difficul-ties. I beg, therefore, to offer you my very sincere thanks for the space which you have allowed me to occupy in your pages; and to acknowledge, at the same time, the service which Dr. Todd has rendered to the cause, by his description, in your two last Numbers, of the Waldensian manuscripts preserved in the library of the University of Dublin.

It is indeed refreshing to find, in the rough and rugged path of controversy, a few green spots, on which we may rest with confidence, and interchange some of those kindnesses which generate mutual esteem.

I have lately been to Ireland to inspect the Waldensian do-cuments; and Dr. Todd not only granted me that unrestricted access to the MSS. in the University Library at Dublin which his office of librarian enabled him to give, but he also favoured

* [This letter appeared in the Brit. Mag., vol. xix., p. 637. The letter is, of course, addressed to the Editor of the Magazine.]

me with much of his valuable time, and assisted me in decy-
phering them. And, more than this, I am indebted to him
for permission, from the Provost and Fellows of the University to bring away with me (to have them transcribed)
" The Waldensian New Testament," and " The Collection
of Letters and other Documents relating to the Mission
of George Maurel and Pierre Masson to Bucer and Œcolampadius, in 1530 ;" of which Dr. Todd has given so impartial
an account in the British Magazine, vol. xix., p. 396. [See
above, p. 8, *sq.*]

I find the Ussher Collection of MSS. in Dublin contains the
substance, if not the counterparts, of almost all the ancient
treatises which Morland deposited in the library at Cambridge,
in volumes, marked A, B, C, D, E, and F, and which have
been since removed, nobody knows how or when. But I have
no reason to think that any of those missing books or parchments have found their way to Dublin. The portions which
Dr. Todd believed he had discovered in the Dublin library are
transcripts, in a more modern handwriting, of part of volumes
G and *H*, which are still remaining in the Morland Collection
at Cambridge. The Ussher Collection of Waldensian MSS. was
made many years before Morland's.

A letter from Ussher to Lydyat, in 1611, speaks of his search
after documents to throw light on the history of the Waldenses;
and in July, 1634, one of the Egerton family wrote thus of an
interview which he had with Archbishop Ussher :—" *I had
much private conference with him ; and, after dinner, hee tooke mee
into his closett, where, although there bee not verye many bookes,
yet those that are, are much used and imployed. Herein he shewed
mee the whole workes of the Waldenses, which are verye rare ;
they cost him 22l. sterling. They are in folio and octavo, about
ten or twelve volumes. The language wherein they are printed
is a miscellaneous language, mixt French and Spanish ; these
were sent him from a councellor in Fraunce, as alsoe a copie*

*of the plotts, and designes, and proceedings of the Inquisiteors in Fraunce."**

As far as I can judge, most of the parchments and papers in the Ussher Collection of Waldensian MSS. contain copies from more ancient documents. Some few may be originals; but the New Testament, for example, completed in 1522, is unquestionably transcribed from the Grenoble Codex of the thirteenth century, or from the same archetype.

The collection of letters relating to the mission of Maurel and Masson to the Swiss and German Reformers is a translation, in the Waldensian dialect, of the correspondence, which was originally conducted in Latin.   In fact, Gilles, the Waldensian historian, relates that Perrin was supplied with translations, and other materials for his history, by the Piedmontese pastors, especially by a pastor of Angrogna; and this confirms Dr. Todd's opinion, that the little book containing the substance of the Maurel correspondence is the identical "*Livre de George Morel*" described by Perrin, and out of which he cited several passages.† The discrepancies between Maurel's account of Waldensian doctrine and discipline and the representations which are given in other relations, in that of Archbishop Claude Seyssel, for example, admit of explanation. Maurel and Masson were pastors of two of the scattered congregations of French Waldenses, and described the condition of the French Waldensians.   Claude Seyssel's statements, on the other hand,

* This statement is taken from the " Christian Examiner," vol. ii., p. 219. [where extracts are published " from an old MS.," entitled " Travels in Ireland in 1635;" but it is not said in whose possession the MS. then was. The owner proposed to publish the work (iii., p. 34), but subscribers, it would seem, were not to be had.   The statement quoted by Dr. Gilly favours the supposition that the documents in the vol. C. 1. G. were in Ussher's Collection.—J. H. T.]

† In page 106, Perrin refers to " George Morel en ses Mémoires, p. 54;" and in the MS. Book of the Correspondence which passed between the two pastors and the reformers we find, in p. 54, so altered from fol. 27, the very passage to which Perrin directs attention.

relate to the Waldenses of the valleys of Piedmont only, whose locality and franchises enabled them to abide by a more settled and consistent form of church government than their brethren on the western side of the Alps.

With respect to other MSS., also, in the Ussher Collection, I observed that many different treatises were written out on pages of a uniform size, to make up into a volume, such as that which contains the " Liber Virtutum," or Book of Virtues, and other tracts on a variety of subjects. Perrin makes reference to this volume under three different titles, " Livre des Vertus," pp. 16, 17, 24, 57, 182 ; " Almanach Spirituel," pp. 18, 20, 79, 211, 217 ; " Lumiere et thresor de la foy," pp. 24, 25, 201. I agree with Dr. Todd in thinking that " *a careful comparison of these MSS. will certainly throw much light on the manner in which the documents published by Perrin, Morland, and Leger, were compiled.*" I have now seen enough to believe that these writers made an unskilful and unfaithful use of the materials which fell into their hands, and that they unfairly endeavoured to show therefrom that the ancient Waldenses held tenets nearer to the doctrine and discipline of the German and Swiss Reformers than was really the fact.

The inspection of the Ussher MSS. satisfies me, at the same time, that a case will be made out, favourable alike to the antiquity and religious character of the community of sub-Alpine Christians, in the Cottian Alps, especially in the valleys of Piedmont.

Dr. Todd thinks that some of these treatises may be "identified with something which already exists in Latin." I think so too ; but I am of opinion that they have come down from a purer and earlier period than the middle ages ; and that the very tracts of the middle ages which they resemble, Wickliffe's " Trialogus"* among the rest, contain the substance of passages

* In the third book of Wicliffe's "Trialogus," the seven mortal sins, and their remedies, are placed in the same order as they appear in the treatise in the

in some of the ancient Fathers. I believe the originals of most of the oldest of these Waldensian documents to have been the celebrated translations from Scripture, and from the ancient Fathers, made by Waldo between the years 1173 and 1189— that is before Waldo was excommunicated from the Latin Church, and whilst he was a reformer and a protestor against her errors, being yet within her bosom.

At that time the Christian communities also of the Cottian Alps, since called *territorially* and *ecclesiastically* the Waldenses, had not separated from the provincial churches under the jurisdiction of the Bishops of Turin and Embrun. They may be compared with the Wesleyan Methodists of the last century. There was then no occasion for them to separate or " to come out," because, under the security of chartered franchises* peculiar to themselves, they might protest in safety against the errors of Romanism, and be witnesses of the truth on the great principles which afterwards became the basis of the Reformation.

For the use of these people, therefore, Waldo was likely to have translations of holy writ, and of sacred treatises, made in the vernacular tongue of their country—one of the dialects of the *Romaunt*. The *Romaunt* was the universal language of the Sub-Alpine and Pyrenean regions, and of the south of France, and the language in which some of Waldo's translations were made. *Walter Mapes* says that Waldo translated into the *Gallic* ; *Stephen of Bourbon*, into the *Romaunt*. Each meant probably the same. That Waldo did make such translations of Scripture, and of treatises of the ancient Fathers, which bear witness against Romish corruptions, is clear, on the authority of writers who were contemporary, or nearly so,

MS. closet of the library of the dean and chapter of Durham, which seems to have been collected from the Latin Fathers.

* See " Historiæ Patriæ Monumenta," Chartarum tomus i. passim. This volume was published at Turin by the Royal Historical Commission, 1836.

with Waldo, and who show that he proceeded in his work of reformation without losing sight of order and concurrent antiquity.

Walter Mapes relates that he was present at the Lateran Council, held under Alexander III., in 1189, and there saw the *Valdesians,* who were so called from their primate Valdo, a citizen of Lyons; and who presented a volume to the pope, written in the Gallic tongue, which contained *the text* and *glosses* of the Book of Psalms, and several other Books of the Old and New Testaments.* The author of the Chronicle of Laon confirms this by stating that Waldo was present at that council, and that the pope embraced him.†

Reiner represents Waldo as having conduced to the teaching of Scripture in the vulgar tongue.‡

Moneta states that Waldo went to the pope, and promised to conform his teaching to that of the four doctors, Ambrose, Augustin, Gregory, and Jerome.§

* " Vidimus in Concilio Romano sub Alexandro Papâ tertio celebrato Valdesios homines ydiotas illiteratos a primate ipsorum Valde dictos, qui fuerat civis Lugduni super Rodanum, qui librum Domino Papæ præsentaverunt linguâ conscriptum Gallicâ, in quo textus et gloss Psalterii plurimorumque legis utriusque librorum continebantur."—MS. Bodl. 851.

† " Anno Domini 1178, Concilium Lateranense a Papa Alexandro hujus nominis tertio celebratur. Damnavit hoc Concilium hæreses et omnes hæreticorum fautores, necnon et defensores. Valdesium amplexatus est Papa approbans votum quod fecerat voluntariæ paupertatis, inhibens eidem ne vel ipse aut socii sui predicationis officium præsumerent, nisi rogantibus sacerdotibus."—Bouquet, " Recueil des Hist.," vol. xiii., p. 682.

‡ " Cum autem esset aliquantulum literatus, Novi Testamenti textum docuit eos vulgariter; pro qua temeritate cum fuisset reprehensus, contempsit, et cœpit insistere doctrinæ suæ dicens discipulis suis ; quod Clerus, quando malæ vitæ esset, invideret sanctæ vitæ ipsorum, et doctrinæ."—"Bib. Patr.," tom. iv., p. ii. 749 : Paris, 1624.

§ " Vos venistis a Valdesio, dicatis unde ipse venit ; constat quod non nisi a Papa Romanæ Ecclesiæ ; ergo Papa est solus hæres Ecclesiæ primitivæ. Si autem dicant quod non sit a Papa ; *ad quid ergo venit ad Papam ?* et promisit servare quatuor Doctores, scilicet Ambrosium, Augustinum, Gregorium,

Stephen of Bourbon's evidence is still more express; he affirms, on the authority of one of the translators employed by Waldo, who was then alive, and communicated the information to him, that Waldo had translations made of Scripture (in Romaunt, " *in Romano*," and the Vulgar tongue, " *in vulgari*"), and of passages out of the ancient Fathers, which he collected together in volumes under their several heads, and called them " Sentences."* Stephen adds, that when Waldo and his followers were banished from Lyons, they went into Lombardy and Provence, and joined themselves to heretics, among whom they sowed error and *imbibed* error.†

The mention of Lombardy and Provence connectively identifies the Waldensian region, which formed part of Lombardy‡ on one side of the Alps, and of Provence on the other side of the Alps. And that this region was infected with what was called heresy before Waldo went thither, appears first on the evidence of Peter of Clugny,§ who, distinctly speaking of this locality, wrote in the year 1127 and 1143 against the heretics

et Hieronymum, et sic accepit a Papa prædicationis officium, cujus rei testimonium facile potest inveniri."—Moneta, " Contra Valdenses," lib. 5, c. i., p. 402. Editio Ricchini: Romæ, 1743.

* " Quidam dives rebus in dicta urbe dictus Waldensis audiens evangelia, cum non esset multum literatus, curiosus intelligere quid dicerent, fecit pactum cum dictis sacerdotibus, alteri ut transferret ei in vulgari, alteri ut scriberet quæ ille dictaret, quod fecerunt: similiter multos libros Bibliæ, et auctoritates sanctorum multas per titulos congregatas, quas sententias appellabant."—Step. de Borbone, apud Echart "Script. Ord. Præd.," vol. i., p. 192. It was a very common practice in the twelfth and thirteenth centuries to select miscellaneous passages from the Fathers, and to transcribe them in scrolls, which formed one volume or bundle. Many of these are preserved in the MS. library at Durham.

† " Postea in Provinciæ terra et Lombardiæ cum aliis hæreticis se admiscentes, et errorem eorum bibentes et serentes hæretici sunt judicati ecclesiæ infestissimi."—Ibid.

‡ In those days the whole of the country of Piedmont, up to the summit of the Cottian Alps, was included under the name of Lombardy.

§ See " Bib. Patr.," vol. xii., pars. 2, p. 208, ed. Col. 1618.

of the diocese of Embrun; and, secondly, of a passage in vol. 3 of " Historiæ Patriæ Monumenta," which states that the whole of that mountain territory was infected with heresy in 1164.*

Many of the books and treatises in the Dublin collection of Waldensian MSS. offer internal evidence of having been translated into the Waldensian dialect at a time previous to the separation from Rome. The New Testament, for example, is evidently a translation from a version in use in the Latin Church,† for it contains the following readings :—" *Lo filh de la vergena,*" Matt. viii. 20, and wherever the words *the Son of man* occur in our version. "*Ma Yeshu regardant en li seo deciple dis a Simont Peyre Si lo tes frayre,*" &c. An interpolation between the 14th and 15th verses of Matt. xviii.

There are also many treatises in the collection which, when more closely examined, will, I am convinced, be identified with passages in the ancient Fathers, especially Ambrose, Augustine, Jerome, and Gregory. I earnestly beg, therefore, with Dr. Todd, that some learned reader will turn his attention to this subject, and assist us in tracing them to their rightful sources.

At this moment, not having the MSS. before me, and being too far from public libraries to make an accurate investigation, I can only state that I have found myself closely on the track of some of them. Take the following as samples :—

The paper volume of the Dublin Waldensian MSS., C. 5. 22.

---

* See " Storia delle Alpi Marittime." *Hist. Pat. Mon.* 1839, p. 844.

† Waldo's assistants were ecclesiastics, according to Stephen of Bourbon :—" Incepit autem illa secta per hunc modum, secundùm quod ego a pluribus qui priores eorum viderunt, et a sacerdote illo qui satis honoratus erat et dives in civitate Lugdunensi et amicus Fratrum nostrorum, qui dictus fuit Bernardus Ydros, qui cum esset juvenis et scriptor, scripsit dicto Waldensi priores libros pro pecunia in Romano quos ipsi habuerunt, transferente, et dictante ei Stephano de Ansa, qui postea beneficiatus in Ecclesia majore Lugdunensi."

described by Dr. Todd, Brit. Mag., vol. xix. [see above, p. 22, *sq.*] pp. 502-511, and called by Perrin, "*Almanach Spirituel*," "*Liber Vertutum*,"* and "*Lumière et Thresor de la Foi*," is a fasciculus of treatises.   After fol. 94 follows a chapter on the remedies of sins of the tongue, "*Lo remedi contra lo pecca de la lenga*."   With fol. 119 begins the first of several chapters on the seven deadly sins, in the following order—"*Superbia*" (or Vana Gloria), "*Envidia*," "*Ira*," "*Tristicia*," "*Avaricia*," "*Golicia*," "*Luxuria*."

In the MSS. Library at Durham, there is a volume containing fourteen tracts. B. II. 4, principally taken from the works of Chrysostom, Augustin, Jerome, and Gregory.   They are all written by the same hand; and Rudd, in his catalogue, made between the years 1707 and 1725, calls them MSS. about 400 years old, i. e., written between 1307 and 1325, or thereabouts. No. II. is thus described:—"*De veneno (peccati) et remedio ejus, sic incipit.   Ratio veneni potissime convenit peccato.   Auctoris nomen non apponitur.   Agitur hic de 7 Capitalibus Peccatis, quibus singulis Remedium proponitur.   Scilicet, Superbiæ, Humilitas.   Invidiæ, Charitas.   Iræ, Patientia.   Accidiæ*†

---

* In the Appendix of the sixth volume of the Benedictin edition of Augustin a work is inserted, with the title, "Liber de Conflicta Vitiorum et Virtutum."

† It is singular, that in "Wicliffe's Trialogus," liber 3, the same word *accidia* occurs, for *tristitia*.   But was not Wicliffe more likely to borrow from a MS. at Durham, or its archetype, than Rudd to be ignorant that the Durham MS., which is tied up with treatises of orthodox Fathers, should be the work of the heterodox Wicliffe?   Besides, all of the same fasciculus were written, says Rudd, "ab eadem manu—ante annos circiter 400 ;" and at the beginning of it, "*e coi libraria Monachor. Dunelm*."   The copies of the "Trialogus" are very rare.   Could it have escaped all the editors and collectors of Wicliffe's works [Wickliffe's works have never yet been edited or collected—J. H. T.], and all the deans, prebendaries, and librarians of Durham, that at Durham there was part of the "Trialogus" to be seen in manuscript?   But a collation of the MS. with the "Trialogus" will show.

(τῇ Ακηδιᾳ), *Prudentia. Avariciæ, Restitutio. Gulæ, Absti-nentia. Luxuriæ, Continentia.*" It is a remarkable coinci-dence, that the order of the seven deadly sins should be the same in the Waldensian and in the Durham manuscript.

In another Durham volume of MSS., containing five tracts, B. IV. 42, No. 2, is thus described—"*Excerpta Patribus La-tinis de Septem Vitiis Mortalibus. Sic incipiunt. Intentio nostra in isto opere est colligere, de libris originalium 4 Doc-torum (Augustini, scilicet Hieronymi, Ambrosii, Gregorii), et copulare sub compendio dicta eorum, et primo de mortalibus 7 peccatis.*"

These are curious facts to help us to identify the age and character of the MSS. in circulation among the Waldenses. Mo-neta and Stephen de Bourbon both attest that Waldo sent forth his translations of Scripture with passages from the ancient fathers. Moneta names those fathers—Ambrose, Augustin, Gregory, and Jerome. But it was not an unusual practice in the middle ages to select passages from these fathers for tran-scription. There are proofs of it, as I have shown, still ex-isting in the MS. Library at Durham.

To follow this clue in our labyrinth :—

In the Dublin volume of Waldensian MSS., C. 5. 22, "On the back of fol: 120," says Dr. Todd, "there is a chapter en-titled in rubric *la Cubiticia*, beginning, '*Autre pecca eys de Superbia loqual non es de li sept pecca mortal. Enayma dis Ambroys, Cubiticia non se po partir de superbia.*'" Waldo se-lected sentences from Ambrose. The Durham MSS. contain extracts from Ambrose, in treatises, some of which, Rudd says, were as old as the time of William of Careleph, who died Bishop of Durham, 1096.

Fol. 133 of the Dublin vol. C. 5. 22, has a chapter entitled *Meczonia.* Augustin wrote treatises " *De Mendacio,*" " *Contra Mendacium ;*" one of which begins, " *Magna questio est de Mendacio, quæ nos in ipsis quotidianis actibus sepe disturbat.*"

Fol. 172. A tract on the punishment of hell; beginning, "*A lenfern es mancament de tot ben, e habundancia de tot mal.*" Augustin has a treatise, " *De Pena Inferni.*"

Fol. 173. On Paradise. "*De li ben del paradis ;*" beginning, "*Tota humana eloquencia non es sufficient a recointar de la lausor.*" Fol. 330, "*Goy de Paradis.*" Augustin wrote treatises on this subject, " *De Gaudiis Paradisi,*" " *Quæstio de Paradiso.*" " *De Gaudio Electorum et damnatorum supplicio.*" Ambrose also wrote an epistle, " *De Paradiso.*"

Fol. 242–254, " *De la Penitencia.*" Fol. 247, " *Falsa Penitentia.*" Fol. 254, " *Penitencia vera.*" Augustin wrote " *De vera et falsa penitentia Liber.*"

Ambrose also wrote an epistle, " *De Penitentia.*"

Fol. 301. " *Di li 8 Pensier.*" Can this be part of Augustin's epistle, or treatise, " *De octo questionibus*" ?

Fol. 385. Sermon; beginning, " *O frayres sabent a quest temp, car hora es ia a nos levar del sopu.*"

There is a sermon in the Durham collection of MSS., attributed to Augustin, from the text Rom. xiii. 12.

Fol. 150. " *Sermon d'Erodiana ;*" beginning, "*Enaquel temp herode fey pilhar e ligar e encarcerrar Joh. baptista.*"

St. Chrysostom has a sermon on the beheading of John the Baptist.

Fol. 353. Sermon on the Nativity ; beginning, " *E cū Yeshu fossa na em bellem d'iuda en li dia de herede lo rey.*" St. Gregory has a sermon on this text, Matt. ii. 1.

Fol. 158. " *Li parlar del phillesophe.*"

Fol. 171. " *De li parlar d alcun Doctors.*"

" The doctors quoted are Seneca, Jerome, Augustin, Basil, and the Decretum."

The Durham volume of MSS,, B. II., 20, said to be written about the year 1307–1325, contains No. 17, " *Sententiæ quorundam Philosophorum.*" No. 17, *Proverbia Senecæ.* " Eas sequuntur sententiæ aliæ a Christiano aliquo conscriptæ."

I think I have now pointed out marks enough to direct to further inquiry, and to give weight to my conjectures that many of the Waldensian MSS. in the Dublin Collection were translations made by Waldo between 1173 and 1179, for the Sub-Alpine community protesting against the errors of the Latin Church; and that Waldo made the same use of the four Latin Fathers, Ambrose, Augustin, Jerome, and Gregory, which was the usual practice in the middle ages before and after his time—viz., to transcribe passages from ancient authorities, and make them up in a miscellaneous fasciculus.

More might have been done, if I had been writing in the MS. closet at Durham, with the Dublin volume C. 5. 22. in my hands, and with the folios of the Fathers within reach; but these remarks have been hazarded, to put the learned upon a critical investigation of the subject.

In a second letter, written last month to the British Magazine, my friend, Dr. Todd, at the same time that he allows that the line of the "Noble Lesson" which contains its supposed date, 1100, is not an interpolation, alluding, I suppose, to the particular copy, and not to the original, speaks of the absurdity of calling the Genevan Codex of the "Noble Lesson" a MS. of the twelfth century. He assigns it to 1450, or thereabouts. Who shall decide when doctors disagree? Mr. Senebier and Mr. Raynouard have pronounced it to be their opinion that the Genevan MS. is a document of the twelfth century; and the author of the papers " On the Poems of the Poor of Lyons" concludes that the original of the " Noble Lesson" " was composed in, or shortly after, the year 1200."—(See Brit. Mag. vol. xix., p. 264 [p. 184, *supra*]).

We are advancing towards the truth, notwithstanding our present disagreement.

I remain, my dear Sir, yours faithfully,

W. S. GILLY.

NORHAM VICARAGE, *May* 15, 1841.

ON THE AGE OF THE GENEVAN MS. OF THE NOBLE LESSON.

[THE letter alluded to by Dr. Gilly at the close of the foregoing communication is as follows. It was addressed to the Editor of the British Magazine*]:—

ON THE AGE OF A MS. OF THE " NOBLE LESSON."

DEAR SIR,—The fac-simile of the Genevan MS. of the " Noble Lesson," alluded to by Dr. Gilly [see p. 188, *supra ;* and cf. p. 185], was sent to me with a request that I would give my opinion of its age.

I should be disposed to pronounce it, from the character of the writing, a MS. of the latter end of the fifteenth, or beginning of the sixteenth century, and to have been written by a German rather than an Italian scribe.   It appears to me quite absurd to speak of it as a MS. of the twelfth century, and I shall be much surprised if it should turn out to have been written before the year 1450.

There is nothing in the fac-simile sent me to lead to the supposition that the line by which the date of the " Noble Lesson" has generally been determined is an interpolation. It was evidently written at the same time, and by the same hand as the rest of the manuscript.

Your faithful servant,

J. H. TODD.

TRINITY COLLEGE, DUBLIN,
Easter Tuesday, 1841.

[I am tempted to add here that my opinion of the date of the Genevan MS. has since been fully confirmed, notwithstanding the authority of Senebier and Raynouard, which may be quoted against me.

Dr. Gilly was quite correct in supposing that I spoke in the above letter of the age of the Genevan *manuscript* only, for that was the question proposed to me, and not of the date of the " Noble Lesson" itself.—J. H. T.]

* See Brit. Mag., vol. xix., p. 512.

DISCOVERY OF THE LONG LOST MORLAND MANU-
SCRIPTS. By Henry Bradshaw, M.A., F.S.A., Fellow
of King's College, Cambridge.

[The following remarkable paper, here reprinted with the permission of the
Author, forms a fitting conclusion to the documents collected in the present
volume. It was read before the Cambridge Antiquarian Society, March 10,
1862, and is published in the twelfth number of the "Communications,"
made to that body, p. 203, *sq.* The Author has added to this reprint one or
two additional notes, which are marked with his initials. In addition to the
important discovery of the Morland MSS., about whose supposed loss so
much has been said, a most important inquiry is opened up in this Paper,
as to the original and true reading of the celebrated line— " Ben ha mil e
cent an compli entierement." Mr. Bradshaw proves beyond all question that
the date implied in these words has been tampered with ; and having had an
opportunity myself, since his paper was published, of examining the MSS.
at Cambridge, I can add my testimony to his, that the reading of the Morland MS. B. was originally " Ben ha mil e 4 an," &c., the Arabic number
" 4 " being still visible, notwithstanding the attempt to erase it, and that the
MS. C reads distinctly, " Ben ha mil e cccc. an," &c.

The Dublin MS., which is on paper, and written in the early part of
the sixteenth century (see p. 43, *supra*) has the verse thus :—

" Ben ha mil ^cₐ cent an," &c.

The *e* having been interlined as a correction, apparently in the handwriting
of the original scribe.—J. H. T.]

It will be known to all who have interested themselves in the
history of the Vaudois, that Morland, the envoy from the Protector Cromwell to the Duke of Savoy on their behalf in 1655,
wrote, on his return in 1658, what he calls a History of the
Evangelical Churches in Piedmont, based not only upon previous writers, but upon authentic documents which he brought
home and deposited in the Public Library of this University.

He tells us that it was Archbishop Ussher who stirred him

up to lose no opportunity of securing any old books or papers which could throw light upon the early history and religious opinions of the Vaudois; and the results of his efforts may be appreciated by any one who will read the detailed catalogue of his books and papers which is prefixed to his History.

At the close of the last century, Mr. Nasmith, who was employed to make a fresh Catalogue of the Manuscripts in the Library, and under whose eye every single volume must have passed, stated that the papers were almost all safe, but that the six books or volumes mentioned by Morland had unacountably disappeared. During the last forty years much has been written on the subject, and infinite trouble has been taken by Dr. Maitland, Dr. Todd, Dr. Gilly, and other writers at home and abroad after them, both to search out any existing remains of the early Vaudois literature, and to account for the mysterious disappearance of these treasures from Cambridge. Their loss, it was justly alleged, was the more provoking, because they contained copies of portions of the Bible, of religious treatises, and specimens of poetry, all written in the old Vaudois dialect, and to which Morland assigned very early dates, ranging from the 10th to the 13th century. The copies were so old, says Morland, and the writings probably much older.

It was a point of considerable importance that the Cambridge manuscripts should be examined; for not only Morland and his Vaudois friends, but also their advocates in our own time, agreed in maintaining the claim of this community to have held the pure Genevan doctrines long before the time of Calvin. The historians of the 17th century, knowing that in the 13th the followers of Peter Waldo had been separated from the Roman communion, and knowing that their descendants in the 17th held the doctrines of Geneva, were illogical enough to conclude that therefore their ancestors in the 13th had anticipated Calvin's views by three centuries.

A long controversy was carried on in the "British Magazine" about twenty years since. Amongst the good results of this, it elicited from Dr. Todd a most minute and careful description of the whole of the Ussher Collection of Waldensian MSS. in the Dublin University Library; and from this it appears that all the books there were written from 1520 to 1530, or at any rate in the 16th century. A volume at Geneva was also described, which was attributed by the librarian there to the 12th century, but which, from the writing, Dr. Todd and other judges assigned without hesitation to the middle or latter half of the 15th.

One poem in particular, the "Noble Lesson," was the subject of much discussion. Near the beginning occur the two lines which Morland prints and translates thus :—

> Ben ha mil e cent an compli entierament,
> Que fo scripta lora, Car son al derier temp.

> There are already a thousand and one hundred years fully accomplished,
> Since it was written thus, For we are in the last time.

The Geneva and Dublin copies both appear to agree with Morland's representation of the Cambridge copy, as far as the date goes, and all parties were accordingly at a loss for an explanation of the appearance of a clearly Waldensian poem before the days of Peter Waldo. It even afforded to the followers of Leger and Morland an additional argument for the derivation of the name from Vallenses, or Churches of the Valleys, rather than from the name of the founder of the sect.

It will be readily believed, therefore, that it was with much pleasure and some surprise that I laid my hand upon the whole of these volumes a few weeks ago. In the same binding as the rest of the documents,—three of them with Morland's and the donors' names and the date on the first page,—all six with the reference-letters A, B, C, D, E, F, clearly written inside the cover,—and all standing on the shelves as near to the " documents" as the difference of size would allow,—the only wonder is how they could ever have been lost sight of.

The insinuation in the "British Magazine" that the collection was placed here but a few weeks before Cromwell's death, and that, on that event, these books were removed to some safer stronghold of the Genevan views with the connivance of the Puritan librarian of the day, I had long since felt to be groundless. Not only was the place then held by the model librarian and devoted loyalist William Moore,* of Caius College, but I some time since found a cancelled receipt (dated 1689) for four of these very volumes, in the handwriting of Peter Allix, who seems to have examined them for his " Remarks on the Ecclesiastical History of the Ancient Churches of Piedmont," published in 1690.

* It must be borne in mind that ever since the death of William Moore (in 1659), under whom every part of the library seems to have been thoroughly explored, all the librarians and their assistants have uniformly, though unaccountably, declined to make themselves in any way acquainted with the manuscripts under their charge. So, when fresh catalogues were required, both Mr. Nasmith and, more recently, the laborious compilers of the printed catalogue, were employed, at a large cost to the University, as being supposed to know a good deal of the *subjects* of the works existing in MS., but a knowledge of the *history* of the individual volumes was not to be expected from them. These facts afford the only possible explanation of the reputed loss of the Waldensian MSS. as well as others from our library. Their history was lost sight of, and they had come to be regarded as miscellaneous pieces, apparently in Spanish, of no particular importance.

[It is curious that the same mistake was also made in Dublin. The volume, No. V., described above, p. 47, *sq.*, has been lettered by the binder, "Tractatus in Hispanica lingua ;" and in the unpublished Catalogue of the MSS., compiled by Dr. John Lyon, about 1780, this volume, together with some others (viz., No. II., p. 8, No. III., p. 22, No. IV., p. 43, and No. VI., p. 54), is spoken of as " Hispanice scripta." Dr. Lyon had described the Waldensian New Testament (No. I., p. 1) as being in *Italian ;* but the word " Italice" has been erased, and " Hispanice" written over it in the handwriting of the late Dr. Nasb, formerly Fellow of Trinity College.—J. H. T.]

It will be sufficient for the present purpose to give but a brief description of these six diminutive volumes; for, though undoubtedly the oldest extant relics of Vaudois literature, even when brought down from the 10th, 12th and 13th centuries (to which Morland ascribes them) to the 15th, yet it cannot be doubted that, when they are once brought into due notice, which it is the object of this paper to procure, they will engage the attention of some scholar who is able to use them. To take them in the probable order of age :—

F is a parchment volume measuring 5⅓ by 4¼ inches, and written, I should say, at the close of the 14th century. It contains the greater part of the New Testament, and certain chapters of Proverbs and Wisdom, in the following order: St. Matthew (beginning gone), *no St. Mark*, of St. Luke only i. 1—iii. 6, followed at once by St. John, *no Romans*, 1st (*no 2nd*) Corinthians, Galatians, Ephesians, Philippians, *no Colossians*, *of 1st Thessalonians only the first few words, and that clearly by mistake, and without heading, no 2nd Thessalonians*, 1st and 2nd Timothy, Titus, *no Philemon*, of Hebrews only ch. xi. followed at once by Proverbs, ch. vi., and Wisdom, ch. v. and vi., Acts, James, 1st and 2nd Peter, followed possibly by the Epistles and Revelation of St. John, but all after f. 158, 2 Pet. ii. 5, is wanting. There are leaves missing in several places, but in no case (except at the end) so as to prevent our knowing what the contents originally were.

B is a parchment volume measuring 4¼ by 3¼ inches, and written probably in the first half of the 15th century. It consists of three portions, but the handwriting is uniform. The first portion (ff. 1–124) contains (1) the Seven Penitential Psalms, and (2) the *In principio* from St. John, in Latin; (3) *Glosa Pater noster*, partly printed from this by Morland (*History*, p. 133), (4) *Treçenas*, (5) *Doctor*, (6) *Penas*, (7) *Li goy de paradis*, (8) *La pistola de li amie*, and the poems, (9) *Novel*

confort, (10) *Lo novel sermon,* (11) *La nobla leyçon,* printed
from this by Morland (*History,* p. 99), (12) *Payre eternal,* and
(13) *La barca.* The second portion (ff. 125–241) consists of a
long treatise on the (1) ten commandments, (2) twelve articles
of the faith, (3) seven deadly sins, (4) seven gifts of the Holy
Ghost, (5) theological virtues, (6) cardinal virtues, (7) *De li
ben de fortuna e de natura e de gratia,* (8) *De seys cosas que son
mot honorivol en aquest mont;* and the remaining nine pages are
occupied by two sermons* and a paragraph *De las abusions.*
The third portion (ff. 242–271) is imperfect at both ends, but
now contains seven sermons.

C is on paper, measuring 3⅜ by 2⅓ inches, and written about
the middle of the 15th century. It consists of three portions,
all in one handwriting. The first (ff. 1–24) contains two sermons (1) *De la confession,* and (2) *De la temor del segnor,* the
latter printed from this by Morland (*History,* p. 119). The
second (ff. 25–32) contains one sermon; and the third portion
(ff. 33–112, &c.) consists of (1) a sermon headed *Tribulacions,*
(2) 7 folios, that is, a translation of 2 Macc. vii. from the Vulgate, (3) *Job,* a translation of Job i. ii. iii. and xlii. from the Vulgate, (4) *Tobia,* a translation of the whole book of Tobit from

---

* [These two sermons are on the following texts :—

Mat. 12.—*Mas yo dic a vos que de tota parola auciosa.*

Eph. 4.—*Sia renovellu perlesperit de la vestra pensa.*

The others are these :—

1. Beginning gone; headed *Bernart.*

2. *Lo fantin yhesus remas* . . .

3. *Yhesus fo amena del esperit eldesert.* Beginning :—*En aquest present
avangeli lesperit es demostra en 4. manieras.* . . . . .

4. *O segnor salva nos peren.*

5. Luc. 14.—*Un home era ric lo cal vestia polpra e bis.*

6. Jo. 6.—*Cum sera fossa fayta la nao era almeç.*

7. Mat. 13.—*Lo regne de li cel es fayt semblant a lome lo cal semenc bon
semeny al sio camp.* Imperfect at the end.—H. B.]

the Vulgate, (5) *La nobla leyçon*, which breaks off abruptly at the beginning of the fourteenth verse, the rest of the volume being lost.

A is on paper and parchment, measuring $3\frac{7}{8}$ by $2\frac{7}{8}$ inches, and written in the latter half of the 15th century. It consists of six different portions, all in one handwriting, except, perhaps, the last.* Part I. (ff. 2–99) contains (1) *Genesis*, a translation of Gen. i.–x. from the Vulgate; (2) a Treatise on the nature of different animals; (3) *Lo tracta de li pecca;* (4) a sermon *De la parolla di dio*. Part II. (f. 100) is in Latin, and contains instructions to the clergy, headed *Sequitur de imposicione penitencie*. Part III. (f. 136) is a discourse beginning *Alcuns volon ligar la parolla de dio segont la lor volunta*, on the *quatre manieras de trametament*, that is, of God, of God and man, of man alone, and of usurping preachers. Part IV. (f. 172) is a treatise entitled *Herman*. Part V. (f. 180) is a collection of Latin pieces. Part VI. (f. 232) contains, after three short paragraphs, a small historical passage on the voluntary poverty of the Church, unfortunately imperfect at the end, but of peculiar interest.

D is on parchment, measuring $3\frac{1}{2}$ by $2\frac{1}{2}$ inches, and written also in the latter half of the 15th century. It is imperfect at both ends, but now contains (1) a collection of medical recipes (beginning gone); (2) a discourse on tribulations, headed *Ayci comença sant ysidori;* (3) a sermon on the seven deadly sins and their remedies, on the text *Donca vos mesquins perque*

---

* [On a more careful examination, I should say that the last sheet of Part I., and Parts II., III., and V. of volume A are by a different scribe, and they are certainly *rubricated* by a different hand from the rest. It is this hand which has written the sermon on the word of God, with the date 1530; and it is the same hand which refers in one place (fol. 159, verso) to the 11th *verse* of the Epistle of St. Jude, which throws the date later still. The treatise headed *Herman* is, I find, a translation of a small portion of the *Pastor* of Hermas.—H. B.]

tarçen de ben far, &c. ; (4) a sermon on almsgiving, on the text *O vos tuit li qual lavora*, &c. ; (5) three short pieces beginning *Dio bat li ome en .5. modo . . . Nota che la son quatre cosas que nos apellan . . . Nos vesen esser na .3. perilh en aquisti temp.* . . . ; (6) several short moral paragraphs ; (7) a short Discourse on the twelve joys of paradise, on the text *Voç dalegreça e de salu es en li tabernacle de li iust ;* (8) a general but brief exposition of Christian doctrine, commencing *A tuit li fidel karissimes christians sia salu en yh" xp' lo nostre redemptor Amen . .,* and arranged under eight heads, but unfortunately breaking off in the middle of the third.

E is on paper, measuring $4\frac{1}{4}$ by $3\frac{5}{8}$ inches, and consists of four parts, the handwriting not uniform throughout, but agreeing well with the dates 1519, 1521, which are found in the book. Parts I. and II. are parts of a Latin grammar. (1) *De interrogationibus, De participiis, De casu genitivo locali, De comparativis, De gerundivis*, with some *Flores legum* on one of the blank leaves at the end; (2) *De verbis*, with the translation of the verbs in the Vaudois dialect. In rubric at the beginning is: *Anno domini millesimo q :*1521: *dies :*9: *mensis Januarii*. Part III. contains Latin abstracts of (1) Proverbs, (2) Ecclesiastes, (3) Ecclesiasticus, followed by (4) some sentences from St. Gregory ; (5) a poem of 24 lines, beginning :

Tout ce que la terre nourist ;

(6) a poem of 282 lines, headed : *Sequuntur mettra ceneche* (or *ceueche*) and beginning :

Commensament de tout ben es
Temer diou soubre tout quant es ;

(7) a piece contained on one leaf, headed : *Sequitur liber Arithmetti[cus] extractus a Johannono Albi filio mgri Johannis Albi notarii de Fenestrellis sub Anno domini ·*1519. *et die .*22. *mensis Augusty*, and beginning, *Per ben entendre lart . . . .* Part IV.

contains (1) *Albertani* moralissimi opus de loquendi ac tacendi modo*, an abridgment only; (2) *liber primus de amore et dilectione dei et proximi et de forma vite, ejusdem domini Albertani*, also an abridgment; (3) *versus morales*, beginning:

> Est caro nostra cinis,
> modo principium modo finis;

(4) *Exortation de bien vivre et bien mourir*, in 100 lines, beginning:

> Qui a bien vivre veult entendre;

(5) *Optima consilia;* (6) Sentences headed *Philosophus*, with translations in verse; (7) 42 *versus morales*, beginning:

> Au jorn duy qui se auausse trop,

with which the volume concludes.

Judging from Dr. Gilly's edition of St. John, the text and dialect of our New Testament closely resemble the Grenoble, Zurich, and Dublin copies; and, but for the alleged antiquity of the Grenoble and Zurich copies, the incompleteness of this one might suggest the inference† that at this date the entire

---

* [This was Albertinus of Brescia, " Brixiensis Causidicus," flor. circ. 1240. His works here mentioned have been printed, but are of extreme rarity. For some account of him see Oudin, De Scriptt. Eccl. iii. 189.— J. H. T.]

† An examination of Dr. Gilly's facsimiles rather confirms than weakens the suggestions made in the text. To judge from these, the Grenoble MS. must bear a very strong resemblance to our F, and the Zurich MS. to our C, the former of which I should assign to the close of the 14th, and the latter to the early part of the 15th century. The truth is that so very few volumes bear an actual date, that persons who are familiar with MSS. may gain a fairly correct notion of the *relative* age of different volumes, and yet differ from other critics as to the *actual* age. I have very little doubt that most judges, if the four copies were placed open before them, would range them (1) Cambridge, (2) Grenoble, (3) Zurich, (4) Dublin. Of the Lyons copy I can say nothing, as no facsimile is given.

New Testament was not as yet in circulation among the Vaudois. Those parts which were read as Epistles and Gospels in Church would naturally be the first translated, and we find these in MS. B; and were this suggestion confirmed, we should have no proof of the existence of a regular translation of the New Testament earlier than the period which produced the Wycliffite versions in our own country.

In B the most noticeable pieces are the *Treçenas* and the *Nobla Leyçon*. The four *treçenas* are the four quarters of the year, each containing *thirteen* Sundays, and the Epistles and Gospels are headed 1st, 2nd, 3rd . . Sunday of the 1st, 2nd . . *treçena*, without any further distinctive name derived from the season. On a minute comparison, however, with the unreformed Roman, as well as other missals, they appear to be precisely the same, with only such small variations as are found to exist between the uses of different churches at the same time; and this is particularly interesting, as so very few relics of the early Vaudois ritual are still in existence. The copy of the *Nobla Leyçon* in this volume is the one which has created all the discussion, by the expression which I have quoted before, " *Ben ha mil e cent an*," &c. It is, therefore, highly satisfactory to notice that the line runs in this copy:

Ben ha mil e * cent an compli entierament,

with an erasure before *cent*, where, by the aid of a glass, the Arabic numeral 4 is visible, of the same shape as those frequently used in this volume. The only thing which could be needed to prove the certainty of this reading, is that in MS. C there is the commencement of another copy of this same poem, which, as it is but a short fragment, and has escaped the attention of Leger and Morland altogether, I shall give entire. It is written continuously, the divisions being marked by points and coloured initial letters.   It runs as follows* :

AYCI COMENÇA | LA NOBLA LEYÇON. |

O frayres entende u|na nobla leyçon. |
Sovent deven velhar e|istar ennauracion.
Car nos | ven aquest mont esser pres | del chauon.
Mot curios | deoran esser de bonas obras | far.
Car nos ven aquest mont || a la fin apropiar.
Beu ha | mil e .cccc. anz compli en|tiernment.
Que fo scrita lo|ra ara sen al derier temps. |
Pauc daurian cubitar | car sen al romanent. |
Tot | iorn ven las ensegnas | venir a compliment.
Acre|ysament de mal e amerma|ment de bens.
Ayço son | li perilh que lescritura di. |
Li auangelin o recoytan | e saint paul atresy.
Car | neun home que viva non | po saber sa fin.
Perço|| . . . [The leaves which should follow are wanting.]

There can be no doubt that the Geneva and Dublin copies are both later than our two; and, however we may explain the omission from them, it is at least the evidence of two earlier against two later copies, and this added to the great difficulty of giving a reasonable explanation of the lines, seems enough to satisfy the most strenuous advocates of the antiquity of the poem.

A is the volume which, at the end of the sermon *De la parolla de dio*, contains the supposed date of transcription, 1230. The conclusion of the sermon is as follows :—

Da 4ª. endurczis enayci fay alio me la
parolla dedio, &c.

1530.

I can see nothing in the second figure but a badly made 5, though I confess it is difficult to explain the meaning of it.   It

* The divisions mark the ends of the lines on the page in the MS.; the *italics* denote the abbreviations of the original.

seems to be in the original ink, and beyond any suspicion of tampering, but the handwriting and figures are clearly not those of the year 1530, nor indeed of 1430; while 1230, as the date of transcription, even apart from palæographical considerations, is out of the question. In Part V. the collection of Latin pieces, the *Doctor Evangelicus* (Wyclif) is cited. And further, in the historical passage at the close of the volume, after speaking of *Piero de Vaudia* and his excommunication, mention is made of the success of his followers until, two hundred years (*dui cent an*) after his time, a persecution arose, which continued even to the times of the writer. This brings the date of the composition to the beginning of the 15th century at the earliest. It is true that *dui* has been partly erased, but even *cent an* would bring the piece down much later than 1230; while it must be allowed that it is somewhat suspicious, that Morland has taken no notice in his catalogue either of this piece or of the fragment of the *Nobla Leyçon* containing the true date, even though his list in many cases deals with the most insignificant details.*

* * * * * * *

D contains no indication of a date, as far as I have examined, but the headings of the eight divisions of the *Exposition of Christian Doctrine* are worth noticing, though, from the mutilation of the volume, only three chapters remain. The prologue enumerates these divisions thus :—

" Donca prumierament nos diren breoment coma la ley del veray Dio e veray home Yh[u] X[l] per si sola es suficient a la salu de tota la generacion humana, E es plus breo e plus comuna e

---

* [Here Mr. Bradshaw has inserted the passage On the voluntary poverty of the Church, which is contained in part VI. of vol. A. I have omitted it, as not being necessary to the immediate purpose of the present work. The reader who wishes to refer to it can see it in the " Communications made to the Cambridge Antiquarian Society," No. XII. (No. 3 of vol. ii.), p. 212, *sq.*—J. H. T.]

plus legiera a complir, e es ley de perfeita liberta, a la qual non besogna aiogner ni mermar alcuna cosa, E non es alcuna cosa de ben la qual non sia suficientment enclusa en aquella meseyma soa ley.   Segondariament diren de la sancta fe catholica, la qual se conten en li article e en li sacrament e en li comandament de Dio. 3ᵃment diren de la vera e de la falsa penitencia e de la vera confession e de la satisfacion.   La 4ᵃ diren alcuna cosa del vero purgatori e segur e de la falseta e meçonia se meᵃ sobre lui.   La 5ᵃ diren de la envocacion de li sant e de li herror sobre semeᵃ.   La 6ᵃ diren de la auctorita pastoral dona de Dio a li sacerdot de Xⁱ.   La 7ᵃ diren de las clavs apostolicas donas de Yhᵘ Xⁱ a sant Peyre e a li autre seo veray successor.   La 8ᵃ diren de las veras endulgencias."   fol. 81.

In Ch. 2, the sacraments are enumerated thus :

" Sept son li sacrament de la sancta gleysa.   Lo prumier es lo batisme lo qual es dona a nos en remesion de pecca.   Lo .2. es la penitencia.   Lo .3. es la cumunion del cors e del sanc de Xpⁱ.   Lo .4. es lo matrimoni ordena de Dio.   Lo .5. es loli sant. Lo .6. es lenpusament de las mans.   Lo .7. es ordenament de preyres e de diaques.   fol. 88ᵇ."

To sum up then, briefly; after the most important fact—the determination of the true date of the *Nobla Leyçon*—the primary results gained from the recovery of these manuscripts, and a comparison of them with what we already know of others of the kind, is, that besides the Dublin collection, all of which seem to have been written in the 16th century, we have two miscellaneous volumes at Geneva (MSS. 207 and 209) and four at Cambridge (A, B, C, D), as well as more than one copy of the New Testament, all assignable to the 15th century; and in addition to these, at Cambridge and at Grenoble, one incomplete and one complete copy of the New Testament, which may be ascribed to the close of the 14th century.   It is a small collection, doubtless; but it is a very precious one, even though not carrying us back to the 10th and 12th centuries, as we were led to expect; and it is much to be hoped that the authorities at our University Press will soon offer some encouragement towards bringing out a careful edition of at least the most important treatises in the collection. Whatever Cromwell and his friends were politically, it is at least certain that, as a literary body, we owe them a debt which it would take us a long time to repay, and which at present we refuse to acknowledge even in our annual commemoration of benefactors. We have for two hundred years ignored both the gift and the giver, and it is time that we should begin to make some reparation.

INDEXES.

Q

INDEX

OF

WALDENSIAN TREATISES.

———◆———

INDEX OF MATTERS.

THE END.